AEPS

Assessment, Evaluation,
and Programming System
for Infants and Children
SECOND EDITION

VOLUME 4 — *Curriculum* for
Three to Six Years

Other volumes in the AEPS series
edited by Diane Bricker, Ph.D.

AEPS Administration Guide
by Diane Bricker, Ph.D., Kristi Pretti-Frontczak, Ph.D.,
JoAnn (JJ) Johnson, Ph.D., and Elizabeth Straka, Ph.D., CCC-SLP,
with Betty Capt, Ph.D., OTR, Kristine Slentz, Ph.D.,
and Misti Waddell, M.S.

AEPS Test
Birth to Three Years and
Three to Six Years
by Diane Bricker, Ph.D., Betty Capt, Ph.D., OTR,
and Kristie Pretti-Frontczak, Ph.D.,
with JoAnn (JJ) Johnson, Ph.D., Kristine Slentz, Ph.D.,
Elizabeth Straka, Ph.D., CCC-SLP, and Misti Waddell, M.S.

AEPS Curriculum for
Birth to Three Years
by Diane Bricker, Ph.D. and Misti Waddell, M.S.,
with Betty Capt, Ph.D., OTR, JoAnn (JJ) Johnson, Ph.D.,
Kristie Pretti-Frontczak, Ph.D., Kristine Slentz, Ph.D.,
and Elizabeth Straka, Ph.D., CCC-SLP

AEPS

Assessment, Evaluation,
and Programming System
for Infants and Children

SECOND EDITION

VOLUME 4 *Curriculum* for
Three to Six Years

by

Diane Bricker, Ph.D.
University of Oregon, Eugene

and

Misti Waddell, M.S.
University of Oregon, Eugene

with

Betty Capt, Ph.D., OTR, JoAnn (JJ) Johnson, Ph.D.,
Kristie Pretti-Frontczak, Ph.D., Kristine Slentz, Ph.D.,
and Elizabeth Straka, Ph.D., CCC-SLP

·P·A·U·L·H·
BROOKES
PUBLISHING Co ®

Baltimore • London • Sydney

Paul H. Brookes Publishing Co.
Post Office Box 10624
Baltimore, Maryland 21285-0624

www.brookespublishing.com

"Paul H. Brookes Publishing Co." is a registered trademark of
Paul H. Brookes Publishing Co., Inc.
"AEPS®" is a registered trademark and AEPS™ is a trademark of Paul H. Brookes Publishing Co., Inc.

Typeset by Barton Matheson Willse & Worthington, Baltimore, Maryland.
Manufactured in the United States of America by
Versa Press, East Peoria, Illinois.

The following AEPS forms can be purchased separately in packs:
Child Observation Data Recording Form I: Birth to Three Years, and II: Three to Six Years
Family Report I: Birth to Three Years, and II: Three to Six Years
Child Progress Record I: Birth to Three Years, and II: Three to Six Years

A CD-ROM of printable masters of the AEPS forms is also available, and also includes a Child Observation Data Recording Form with Criteria for Birth to Three Years and Three to Six Years not found in any of the volumes. To order, contact Paul H. Brookes Publishing Co.

Please see page ii for a listing of the other volumes in the AEPS series. All AEPS materials are available from Paul H. Brookes Publishing Co., Post Office Box 10624, Baltimore, Maryland 21285-0624 (800-638-3775 or 410-337-9580). Find out more about AEPS on www.brookespublishing.com/aeps.

Fifth printing, October 2014.

Library of Congress Cataloging-in-Publication Data

Assessment, evaluation, and programming system for infants and children
    edited by Diane Bricker . . . (et al.)—2nd ed.
      p.   cm.
    Includes bibliographical references and index.
     ISBN 1-55766-562-1 (v. 1) — ISBN 1-55766-563-X (v. 2) — ISBN 1-55766-564-8 (v. 3) —
ISBN-13: 978-1-55766-565-2
ISBN-10: 1-55766-565-6 (v. 4)
     1. Assessment, Evaluation, and Programming System.   2. Child development—Testing.
   3. Child development deviations—Diagnosis.
    RJ51.D48 A87 2002
    618.92'0075—dc21

                                                      2002071124

British Library Cataloguing in Publication data are available from the British Library.

CONTENTS

ABOUT THE AUTHORS

Diane Bricker, Ph.D., Professor, College of Education, and Director, Early Intervention Program, University of Oregon, 5253 University of Oregon, Eugene, Oregon 97403

Diane Bricker is Professor and Associate Dean for Academic Programs, College of Education, at the University of Oregon and a highly respected, well-known authority in the field of early intervention. She has directed a number of national demonstration projects and research efforts focused on examining the efficacy of early intervention; the development of a linked assessment, intervention, and evaluation system; and the study of a comprehensive, parent-focused screening tool. Dr. Bricker directs the Early Intervention Program, Center on Human Development, at the University of Oregon.

Misti Waddell, M.S., Senior Research Assistant/Project Coordinator, Early Intervention Program, University of Oregon, 5253 University of Oregon, Eugene, Oregon 97403

Misti Waddell is a Senior Research Assistant/Project Coordinator at the Early Intervention Program at the University of Oregon. She also has contributed to the development, research, and training of the *Assessment, Evaluation, and Programming System for Infants and Children* (AEPS) since the early 1980s. She has used the AEPS in classroom settings and has coordinated several federally funded, field-initiated research projects and outreach training projects. Ms. Waddell is Project Coordinator for the outreach training project titled "Creating and Sustaining Change Across Diverse Early Intervention Systems (CASCADES)."

Betty Capt, Ph.D., OTR, Research Associate, Early Intervention Program, University of Oregon, 5253 University of Oregon, Eugene, Oregon 97403

JoAnn (JJ) Johnson, Ph.D., Director, Research and Educational Planning Center and Nevada University Center for Excellence in Developmental Disabilities, University of Nevada–Reno, Reno, Nevada 89557

Kristie Pretti-Frontczak, Ph.D., Assistant Professor, Department of Educational Foundations and Special Services, Kent State University, 405 White Hall, Kent, Ohio 44242

Kristine Slentz, Ph.D., Professor and Chair, Special Education Department, Western Washington University, Miller Hall 318b, Mail Stop 9090, Bellingham, Washington 98226

Elizabeth Straka, Ph.D., CCC-SLP, Consultant, New England Early Intervention Consulting, 58 Turtle Cove Lane, Wells, Maine 04090

ACKNOWLEDGMENTS

We are most grateful to the many caregivers, children, and interventionists who have used the curriculum items and provided feedback on their usefulness and effectiveness. It is our hope that this second edition reflects the input from users and enhances the intervention efforts of those working with young children who are at risk for or have disabilities and their families.

Many individuals collaborated to make the first edition of the *AEPS Curriculum for Three to Six Years* possible and their contributions are reflected in this second edition. The content contained in this second edition was initially developed by Liz Twombly, Val Oldham, and Younghee Kim. Other early contributors included Juliann Cripe, who provided the initiative and motivation to begin work on the development of the curriculum. Sheryl Norstad edited early versions of curriculum items, and the format reflects some of her ideas. Kimberly Megrath contributed substantially to the initial development of the Fine Motor and Gross Motor Areas. Kimberly's extensive knowledge of motor development and her practical experience working with young children provided useful ideas and suggestions for integrating children with a wide range of motor abilities into a variety of group activities. Elizabeth LaCroix contributed to reorganizing the content and added to the sections on working with children with motor disabilities. Debra Hamilton provided valuable suggestions for working with children with visual impairments. Lorraine Duke provided the concurrent goals listed for each curriculum item as well as many examples included in the goals section. Sue Taylor and Susan Petterson contributed to the development of group and individual activity plans and schedules based on their classroom experience.

The planned intervention activities contained in Appendix B of this second edition were provided by Naomi Rahn, who is currently a course instructor, field experience coordinator, and student supervisor, and Barbara Schneider, Barbara Sommerville, and Amy Johnson, who are all teachers currently working in the field.

A project of this magnitude requires multiple reviews, proof readings, and edits. Contributors to this process include Dave Allen, Karen Lawrence, Kate Ray, and Renata Smith. Kate and Renata completed the many hours spent word processing. A special thanks to Karen for overseeing all the many pieces of this project and ensuring continuity between volumes and to Dave for his willingness to step in and take responsibility for completing a variety of important tasks.

AEPS
Assessment, Evaluation,
and Programming System
for Infants and Children
SECOND EDITION

VOLUME 4 *Curriculum* for
Three to Six Years

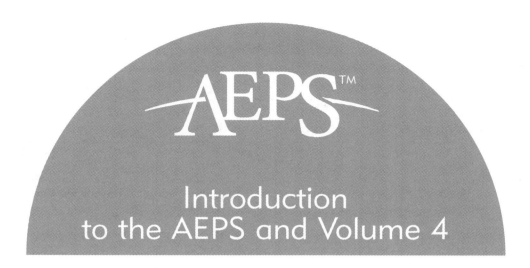

Introduction
to the AEPS and Volume 4

The importance of early experience for young children has long been recognized and has been the foundation for early intervention programs designed for young children who have or who are at risk for disabilities. Early intervention programs have evolved into comprehensive approaches that produce positive change in the lives of participating children and their families. In large measure, the increasingly positive outcomes engendered by early intervention programs have occurred because of the growing sophistication of personnel, curricular materials, and assessment/evaluation tools. Previous approaches that treat program components as isolated and unrelated units are being replaced by approaches that systematically link the major components of assessment, goal development, intervention, and evaluation. The *Assessment, Evaluation, and Programming System for Infants and Children (AEPS®)* is one such linked approach.

This is the fourth volume of the AEPS series. Figure 1 shows the four volumes and presents an overview of each volume's content. The focus of Volume 4 is the curricular materials designed to accompany the *AEPS Test for Three to Six Years* contained in Volume 2.

WHAT IS THE AEPS?

The AEPS offers a variety of related materials that enhance the link between assessment outcomes, targeted goals, intervention activities, and evaluation strategies. The AEPS is referred to as a system because its components work together to assist interventionists and caregivers in developing functional and coordinated assessment, goal, intervention, and evaluation activities for young children who have or who are at risk for disabilities. The AEPS is a comprehensive and linked system that includes assessment/evaluation, curricular, and family participation components for the developmental range from birth to 6 years. The AEPS is divided into two developmental levels—Birth to Three Years and Three to Six Years. Also, as shown in Figure 1, each level is com-

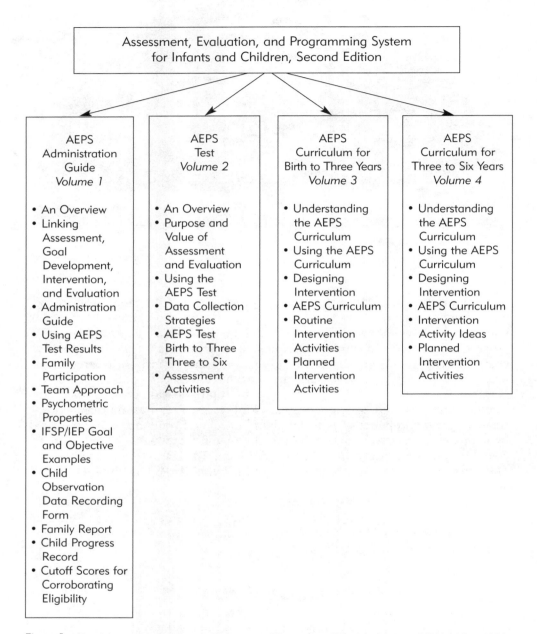

Figure 1.   Four volumes of the *Assessment, Evaluation, and Programming System for Infants and Children, Second Edition.*

posed of a test contained in Volume 2 and an associated curriculum contained in Volume 3 (Birth to Three Years) or Volume 4 (Three to Six Years).

Volume 1 presents information on the conceptual and organizational structure of the AEPS, how to get started using the system, components of a linked system, interpretation of test outcomes, family involvement strategies in the assessment/evaluation process, and team collaboration suggestions when using the system. Also in Volume 1, a new strategy for using AEPS test results to corroborate standardized, norm-referenced test findings for eligibility determination is described.

Volume 2 contains the test items for the birth to three year level and the three to six year level divided into six developmental areas: Fine Motor, Gross Motor, Adaptive, Cognitive, Social-Communication, and Social. Volume 2 also contains Assessment Activities that are simple scripts to guide the assessment of a range of AEPS test items during specific activities (see Volume 2, Appendix A).

Volumes 3 and 4 contain the curricular material for the developmental range birth to 3 and 3 to 6 years, respectively. In addition, these volumes contain a variety of intervention activities appropriate for a range of children.

OVERVIEW OF VOLUME 4

Volume 4, AEPS Curriculum for Three to Six Years, is the curricular component of the *AEPS Test for Three to Six Years* and was developed for two purposes. First, the AEPS Curriculum provides interventionists (e.g., teachers, child development specialists, occupational therapists, physical therapists, psychologists, communication specialists) and caregivers with a range of activities that can be used to facilitate children's acquisition of functional and generalizable skills. Second, the AEPS Curriculum provides a direct link among assessment, goal development, intervention, and evaluation. The AEPS Test and AEPS Curriculum were developed to provide a direct and ongoing correspondence between initial assessment, individualized family service plan (IFSP)/individualized education program (IEP) development, intervention planning, intervention activities, and subsequent evaluation.

Target Population

The AEPS Test and Curriculum for Three to Six Years are appropriate for children who present a broad range of intervention needs. Some will be young children with identified developmental disabilities such as Down syndrome, spina bifida, or cerebral palsy. Others will exhibit delays attributed to chronic health conditions or unknown causes. The AEPS is appropriate for children who live with high-risk conditions such as poverty and parents with addiction problems. Whatever the cause, the resultant impairments in early skill development require systematic intervention. The content of the *AEPS Test for Three to Six Years* includes functional skills for children whose development is in the 3- to 6-year range. This test is appropriate for children who have or are at risk for a wide range of disabilities. Use of the AEPS Test and Curriculum with children whose chronological age exceeds 6 years may require modification of content.

Children with severe disabilities will likely have a team (e.g., occupational therapist, physical therapist, communication specialist, physician, special educator, service coordinator) who will be involved in developing strategies for intervention. The *AEPS Curriculum for Three to Six Years* lends itself well to a team approach because it permits input from a variety of specialists for embedding individualized objectives, cues, prompts, and correction procedures within activities that are fun and interesting to children.

AEPS Curriculum Content

Volume 4, AEPS Curriculum for Three to Six Years, is divided into two sections. Section I provides an introductory overview of the AEPS and contains three chapters. Chapter 1 describes activity-based intervention and the linked system approach to assessment, goal development, intervention, and evaluation using the AEPS systems. Chapter 2 explains how to use the AEPS Curriculum in conjunction with the AEPS Test. The direct link between the AEPS Curriculum and Test permits efficient movement between the two. Chapter 2 also includes information about working with children with severe disabilities. Chapter 3 describes how to use child initiations, daily routines, environmental arrangements, and planned intervention activities to work on children's goals/ objectives. Section II presents specific curricular content and strategies for goals/objectives in the Fine Motor, Gross Motor, Adaptive, Cognitive, Social-Communication, and Social areas of the AEPS Test. Appendix A provides a variety of ideas for intervention activities, and Appendix B contains a series of planned intervention activities.

The content of the *AEPS Test for Three to Six Years* is developmentally sequenced beginning with simple skills and moving successively to more advanced skills. This curriculum includes a general and flexible set of considerations, strategies, and activities to address each of the skills. The *AEPS Curriculum for Three to Six Years* relies on the interventionist to individualize each child's program.

The *AEPS Curriculum for Three to Six Years* emphasizes an activity-based approach to enhance the behavioral repertoires of young children. Child-initiated activities, daily routines, environmental arrangements, and planned intervention activities are adopted as the contexts for intervention. Focusing on functional skills and on motivating activities is ideal for inclusive program settings that integrate children with developmental delays and disabilities. Because the AEPS Curriculum capitalizes on child-initiated activities, daily routines, environmental arrangements, and planned intervention activities rather than direct instruction of specific skills, it is well suited for use in the home, community-based preschools, or child care settings. The *AEPS Curriculum for Three to Six Years* has been designed to accommodate a wide range of service delivery locations and models.

Overview of the AEPS™ Curriculum
Three to Six Years

1

Understanding the AEPS Curriculum

The AEPS Curriculum was designed to accommodate an approach known as *activity-based intervention (ABI)*. The AEPS Curriculum provides information to the interventionist that encourages integration of goals/objectives into a child's daily activities and life experiences. The format of the AEPS Curriculum emphasizes child-initiated, routine, and planned intervention activities as vehicles for embedding a child's selected goals/objectives.

ACTIVITY-BASED INTERVENTION APPROACH

The ABI approach was designed to take advantage, in an objective and measurable way, of everyday instruction that parents and other caregivers use with their young children:

> Activity-based intervention is a child-directed, transactional approach that embeds children's individual goals and objectives in routine, planned, or child-initiated activities, and uses logically occurring antecedents and consequences to develop functional and generative skills. (Bricker, Pretti-Frontczak, & McComas, 1998, p. 11)

Two features of the ABI approach and the AEPS Curriculum should be emphasized. First, multiple skills (e.g., motor, communication, social, cognitive, adaptive) can be addressed in single activities; for example, an art activity in which children are assembling materials can be used to promote communication (e.g., "Where is the paper?"), social skills (e.g., sharing materials with other children), adaptive skills (e.g., distributing the materials), motor skills (e.g., grasping and using materials), and cognitive skills (e.g., deciding what materials are missing). For each goal and associated objectives, the AEPS Curriculum has a section titled "Concurrent Goals" that helps identify the goals that can be targeted during a single activity. Incorporating multiple goals into one activity is preferable to developing a separate activity for each goal.

A second feature of ABI and the AEPS Curriculum is the inherent reward for children when they participate in fun and interesting activities. When activities are child selected, they usually provide ample motivation for the child, and artificial contingencies may not be necessary. The AEPS Curriculum provides a description of activities that preschool-age children will likely find fun.

There are many advantages to using an activity-based format with infants and young children. First, the notion of providing relevant antecedents and consequences within an activity is incorporated into teaching functional skills in the child's usual environment. When antecedents and consequences are a meaningful part of an activity, motivation and attention tend to increase. Second, the ABI approach and the AEPS Curriculum address the issues of generalization and maintenance. Teaching a particular skill is not limited to just one activity; rather, the skill can be taught by a variety of interventionists and family members across different materials and settings. Third, an activity-based approach helps keep targeted skills functional for the child because the skills selected for intervention are embedded in daily activities. They are likely to be useful to the child in coping with environmental demands. A fourth advantage is that embedding skill training in daily activities allows other people, such as caregivers and peers, to become change agents and teaching resources. Fifth, the ABI approach and the AEPS Curriculum can be used with heterogeneous groups of young children. Children can act as peer models for one another and can be involved in presenting antecedents and consequences; for example, in a store activity, children can play different roles (e.g., clerk, customer). Suni can select a variety of objects from the shelves, and José can ask her to pay for them. Other children can model Suni's and José's behavior or engage in other activities such as placing cans on the shelves, counting pennies, or naming foods to be purchased. Such activities promote children's participation and independence.

AEPS Curriculum users who would like more information on how to employ ABI are referred to *An Activity-Based Approach to Early Intervention* (2nd ed., Bricker, Pretti-Frontczak, & McComas, 1998).

LINKING ASSESSMENT, GOAL DEVELOPMENT, INTERVENTION, AND EVALUATION

The AEPS Curriculum provides a direct link between assessment, goal development, intervention, and evaluation. *Assessment* refers to the process of establishing a baseline or entry-level measurement of the child's skills and desired family outcomes. The assessment process should produce the necessary information to select appropriate and relevant intervention goals/objectives and desired family outcomes. Figure 2 provides an illustration of the linked assessment, goal development, intervention, and evaluation approach. The major components are represented by boxes linked by vertical arrows to indicate the sequence in which they should occur. In addition, the diagonal arrows reflect the need for professional collaboration and family participation in each of these components.

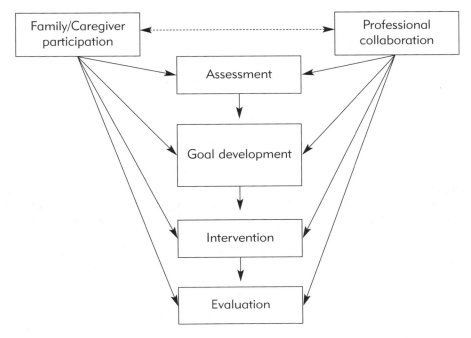

Figure 2.   Schematic of a linked assessment, goal development, intervention, and evaluation approach to early intervention with collaborative professional and family participation.

Phase 1: Program Assessment

The link among assessment, goal development, intervention, and evaluation begins when children enter an intervention program. The major purpose of the initial assessment is to formulate useful and appropriate IFSP/IEP goals/ objectives.

In the initial assessment, a curriculum-based measure is administered to determine the content of IFSP/IEP goals/objectives. This content provides the road map for moving children from their beginning skill repertoires to the acquisition of skills specified as annual goals in their IFSP/IEP. For the family, this initial assessment should help determine priority interests to be developed into family outcomes. An accurate assessment of a child's beginning skill level is crucial to the formulation of a useful IFSP/IEP so that an intervention plan can be developed to improve areas in which a child may be lacking. An assessment that measures functional skills and is sensitive to the conditions in which a child is most likely to perform a skill will facilitate the development of appropriate and useful IFSPs/IEPs. For this reason, the *AEPS Test for Three to Six Years* was developed.

An IFSP allows opportunities to target family outcomes as well as child goals. Family assessment should yield program-relevant information that will aid in developing functional outcome statements, but the process and tools should not be intrusive to family members. Completing the Family Report

(Volume 1, Appendix D) is recommended to assist families in developing outcomes they consider relevant and important to their child and family.

Phase 2: Formulation of IFSPs/IEPs

The initial IFSP/IEP will be based primarily on information accumulated during Phase 1. (Results from this initial assessment should be validated at the first quarterly evaluation.) Relevant information is obtained from caregivers' knowledge of their children as well as from professional observation and testing. This initial information is used to develop a plan of action for the interventionists and caregivers to identify specific content areas that the IFSP/IEP will address. The IFSP/IEP should be straightforward so that it can be used as a guide for interventionists and caregivers. It can also be used as a criterion against which success of the intervention is evaluated.

The child's portion of the IFSP/IEP itemizes goals/objectives and a time frame for meeting the selected goals. The family's portion of the IFSP contains a statement of family resources, concerns, and priorities related to enhancing the child's development, based on the family's identification of their interests and needs. Collaborative discussion with appropriate family members establishes priorities. A set of outcome statements evolves from these priorities, and activities, resources, and a timeline for reaching outcomes are all specified. Further information on the development of IFSPs/IEPs can be found in Chapter 4 of Volume 1.

Phase 3: Intervention

Once the IFSP/IEP has been formulated by caregivers and interventionists, the actual intervention activities can be initiated. The child's performance on the program assessment indicates where intervention should begin. Having an assessment tool that directly links to a curriculum, such as the AEPS, assists interventionists in efficiently identifying activities developed to facilitate acquisition of specific goals/objectives. The AEPS provides a direct correspondence between the assessment items (skills) identified as goals/objectives and the intervention content and strategies specified in the associated curriculum. Chapter 4 of Volume 1 provides an example of how to link assessment outcomes from the AEPS Test to intervention activities in the AEPS Curriculum.

Phase 4: Ongoing Monitoring

A useful IFSP/IEP specifies both the tasks to be conducted and the manner in which success is to be evaluated. A variety of strategies may be used for daily or weekly monitoring of child progress (e.g., trial by trial, brief probes during or after intervention activities). Targeted goals/objectives, program resources, and the need for daily or weekly monitoring to keep intervention efforts on track, will all help determine the strategies selected.

Phase 5: Quarterly and Annual Evaluation

Quarterly evaluations should focus on determining the effect of intervention efforts on goals specified in the IFSP/IEP. This can be done by using the initial assessment measures (e.g., re-administration of the AEPS Test) in conjunction with the weekly data collection. Quarterly evaluations should be used to compare the child's progress with some standard or expectation for progress. Without assigning expected completion dates for goals/objectives, it is difficult to determine if the child's progress is acceptable.

Annual or semi-annual evaluations are used to evaluate the progress of individual children and families as well as the overall effectiveness of the program (i.e., group or subgroup analysis). Without subgroup comparisons, it is difficult to know how to improve intervention strategies for subpopulations of children and families. Methodological design and measurement problems that face the field of early intervention make subgroup evaluations difficult; however, analyses of subgroups may yield important findings on generalization of outcomes for selected groups of children and families.

SUMMARY

The AEPS Curriculum is designed to be used with an ABI approach and emphasizes the use of routine and planned activities to develop children's targeted IFSP/IEP goals/objectives. An understanding of ABI serves as an excellent foundation for curriculum users.

The five phases of the linked system emphasize the importance of directly relating the processes of assessment, goal development, intervention, and evaluation. Employing this system allows efficient use of resources, accountability of program impact over time, and individualization through the design of programs specific to the needs of children and their families. Fundamental to such a system is an appropriate assessment/evaluation tool and an associated curriculum, such as the AEPS Test and AEPS Curriculum.

Chapter 2 relates how teams can use the *AEPS Curriculum for Three to Six Years,* whereas Chapter 3 discusses designing and implementing interventions. Section II contains the curricular suggestions linked to AEPS goals/objectives.

2

Using the AEPS Curriculum

The AEPS Curriculum contains intervention activities and strategies for addressing AEPS Test goals/objectives. The numbering system used in the AEPS Test and Curriculum permits the user to move directly from assessment or evaluation outcomes to appropriate and relevant intervention activities. For AEPS Test goals/objectives, the AEPS Curriculum describes relevant intervention content and a variety of intervention strategies from child initiated to adult guided. Prior to using the AEPS Curriculum, it is essential to read the administrative procedures in this chapter that describe the curriculum's format and procedures for use.

The AEPS Curriculum has important features that make it compatible with the AEPS Test. First, the AEPS Curriculum provides intervention content that is directly tied to the IFSP/IEP goals developed from the AEPS Test results. Program information tied directly to assessment outcomes enhances efficiency of program staff. Second, the curricular content is focused on assisting program staff and caregivers to target functional and useful skills. Finally, information provided in the AEPS Curriculum assists interventionists in implementing an activity-based intervention (ABI) approach, which encourages generalization of learned skills through the integration of targeted goals into daily activities.

AEPS CURRICULUM FORMAT

The AEPS Curriculum is designed to be used in conjunction with the AEPS Test. The content of this test covers the areas of behavior and specific skills considered essential to independent functioning and coping with environmental demands for young children who function in the developmental range of 3 to 6 years. Six broad areas of development are used in the AEPS Test and Curriculum: Fine Motor, Gross Motor, Adaptive, Cognitive, Social-Communication, and Social. Each area encompasses a set of skills or behaviors traditionally seen as related developmental phenomena called *strands*. Strands, which organize related groups of behaviors under a common category, contain a series of items referred to as *goals*. Associated with each goal is an accompanying set of *objectives* that represents more discrete skills. These objectives enable the examiner to accurately pinpoint a child's level within a specific skill sequence.

The AEPS Curriculum follows the same identification system for strands, goals, and objectives as the AEPS Test, providing a direct correspondence between the assessment and the curriculum. The consistent numbering system ensures that users can move efficiently between the AEPS Test and Curriculum. The identification system associated with the strands (e.g., A, B), goals (e.g., 1, 2), and objectives (e.g., 1.1, 1.2) reflects the sequential arrangement of the test items on the AEPS Test.

The cross-referencing system in the AEPS Curriculum utilizes an abbreviated term for the name of the area (e.g., SC for Social-Communication) and then the strand, goal, and objective are listed; for example, Soc A:1.3 refers to the Social Area, Strand A, Objective 1.3; GM B:2 refers to the Gross Motor Area, Strand B, Goal 2. Goals are identified by a single digit, and objectives are identified by the number of the goal, a period, and then the number of the objective. The names of each area are abbreviated as follows:

Fine Motor Area: FM

Gross Motor Area: GM

Adaptive Area: Adap

Cognitive Area: Cog

Social-Communication Area: SC

Social Area: Soc

Section II in this volume contains the curricular activities associated with each goal and the accompanying objectives. Each of the six areas begins with an introduction that provides a list of the AEPS test items and a brief developmental overview of the area. Following the introduction are four main sections: Intervention Considerations, Suggested Activities, Using Activity-Based Intervention, and Area Goals. The Intervention Considerations section provides a description of strategies to be adopted to help children reach their IFSP/IEP goals/objectives. The Suggested Activities section provides general information on resources and activities that will be helpful in addressing area goals/objectives. The section titled Using Activity-Based Intervention provides suggestions of how interventionists and caregivers can incorporate activity-based strategies to enhance the development of a child's targeted goals/objectives within daily occurring activities. The final section, Area Goals, contains information appropriate to teaching each goal contained on the AEPS Test. The Area Goals section begins with a brief overview and is followed by individual descriptions of the curriculum for each goal in the strand. The curriculum content is outlined with the letter and title of the strand, the goal, and its associated objectives, as well as the following information:

- *Concurrent Goals* lists other AEPS Test items that can be targeted while the child works on the current goal or associated objectives. This section identifies targets that can be combined into activities, rather than developing a specific activity for each targeted goal. This section is particularly helpful when developing planned intervention activities for groups.

- *Daily Routines* provides a list of routine home and classroom events that may be useful teaching times. These routines are likely to provide opportunities for the child to practice targeted goals. Because home and classroom routines vary between settings and families, it is important that this section is adapted to meet individual child and family needs.

- *Environmental Arrangements* lists examples of environmental arrangements that may offer opportunities to embed targeted goals and associated objectives during child-initiated, routine, and planned intervention activities. Some strategies are specific to a targeted goal (e.g., providing button-up shirts in the dramatic play area to increase opportunities for children to practice buttoning), whereas other strategies are more general (e.g., providing fewer materials than children need to increase opportunities for children to request additional items).

- *Intervention Activities* offers strategies and suggestions for embedding targeted goals and associated objectives in intervention activities that are fun and interesting for young children. A comprehensive list of intervention activities, with brief descriptions for each, typically found to be motivating for children whose development ranges from 3 to 6 years can be found in Appendix A. Intervention activities should have an accompanying explicit plan of instruction for individual children. Interventionists should assemble materials and plan prompts, cues, and consequences necessary to provide frequent opportunities for targeted goals to be practiced within each activity. A planned intervention activity form containing nine components is recommended to assist interventionists in planning for materials, prompts, cues, and consequences to address intervention for individual or whole groups of children. Appendix B contains completed examples of planned intervention activities.

LINKING THE AEPS TEST WITH THE AEPS CURRICULUM

The strength of the AEPS and similar systems that foster a direct link between assessment, goal development, intervention, and evaluation activities is the assistance that they provide to caregivers and professionals in moving from assessment results, to IFSP/IEP goal development, to intervention planning and implementation, and, finally, to evaluation. The steps to link child/family outcomes from the AEPS Test to the selection of intervention activities in the AEPS Curriculum are described next.

Step 1: The professional team completes the AEPS Test on the child by using the Child Observation Data Recording Form while the parent or other caregiver completes the Family Report. Completion of the Family Report is dependent on the family's interest in doing so.

Step 2:   Team members and family members review results from the AEPS Test and Family Report. IFSP/IEP goals/objectives are selected and prioritized.

Step 3:   Using the AEPS Curriculum, team members locate the appropriate section for each priority goal/objective. They read the introduction and review suggestions given for concurrent goals, daily routines, environmental arrangements, and planned intervention activities.

Step 4:   Using the information provided by the AEPS Curriculum, team members develop an intervention plan to address each priority goal/objective.

Step 5:   Team members develop an individual or group activity schedule to guide the embedding of selected goals into routine and planned activities.

Step 6:   Team members develop intervention activities for embedding selected child goals/objectives into specific activities that can be routine, planned, or child initiated.

Step 7:   Team members evaluate the child's progress using the Child Progress Record and make curricular adjustments as necessary.

An example is provided to illustrate this stepwise progression. Tanya is a 4-year-old child with a developmental delay of unknown origin, making her eligible for early intervention services in her community. Step 1 suggests that, upon entry into the program, the intervention team members observe Tanya over a 2-week period using the AEPS Test to guide their observations. During the same period, Tanya's foster parents agree to complete the Family Report.

At the scheduled IFSP/IEP meeting, the professional team and Tanya's foster parents share and compare their findings (Step 2). Figure 3 shows a portion of the Adaptive Area from the Child Observation Data Recording Form completed by professionals, and Figure 4 shows a portion of the parent-completed Family Report. An examination of Tanya's performance on Strand A: Mealtime indicates that both foster parents and professionals agree that she reached criteria for Goal 1 (Eats and drinks a variety of foods using appropriate utensils with little or no spilling) but has not reached criteria for Goal 2 (Prepares and serves food). After discussing these outcomes, the foster parents and other intervention team members select Goal 2 as the IEP goal for the Adaptive Area. In addition, they choose Objectives 2.1, 2.2, and 2.3 as short-term objectives.

Step 3 requires reviewing the AEPS Curriculum section that relates directly to the Adaptive Area, Strand A, Goal 2. The information provided by the AEPS Curriculum will assist the team in developing an appropriate intervention plan for Tanya's Goal 2 (Step 4), an activity schedule (Step 5), and intervention activities (Step 6). Finally, the team will monitor Tanya's progress toward the targeted goals (Step 7).

ADAPTIVE AREA

S = Scoring key	N = Notes
2 = Consistently meets criterion	A = Assistance provided
1 = Inconsistently meets criterion	B = Behavior interfered
0 = Does not meet criterion	D = Direct test
	M = Modification/adaptation
	Q = Quality of performance
	R = Report

Name: Tanya

Test period: 1
Test date: 6-02
Examiner: NB

	IFSP/IEP	S	N	S	N	S	N	S	N
A. Mealtime									
1 Eats and drinks a variety of foods using appropriate utensils with little or no spilling (p. 142)		2							
1.1 Puts proper amount of food in mouth, chews with mouth closed, and swallows before taking another bite		2							
1.2 Takes in proper amount of liquid and returns cup to surface		2							
1.3 Eats a variety of food textures		2							
1.4 Selects and eats a variety of food types		2							
1.5 Eats with utensils		2							
2 Prepares and serves food (p. 143)		1							
2.1 Prepares food for eating		0							
2.2 Uses knife to spread food		1							
2.3 Pours liquid into a variety of containers		1							
2.4 Serves food with utensil		2							

Figure 3. Portion of a professionally completed AEPS Child Observation Data Recording Form II for the Adaptive Area, Strand A for Tanya.

AEPS CURRICULUM AND CHILDREN WITH SEVERE DISABILITIES

Learning and development can be enhanced in young children with severe disabilities if teams individualize assessment and intervention, accurately target areas of need, and use developmentally- and age-appropriate activities. Intervention activities should be tailored to accommodate the individual child's physical or cognitive limitations or both, as well as the environmental de-

Adaptive Area

Adaptive skills are those that involve being able to care for oneself. These skills include eating, drinking, preparing and serving food, using the toilet independently, taking care of personal care needs, dressing, and undressing.

1. Does your child eat and drink appropriately? (A1)
   NOTE: Place a "Y," "S," or "N" by items a through e:

   date 6/02   **Y**

   __Y__ a. Does your child put a proper amount of food in his or her mouth, chew with mouth closed, and swallow the food before taking another bite? (A1.1)

   __Y__ b. Does your child drink from a cup and return the cup to the table without spilling? (A1.2)

   __Y__ c. Does your child eat and drink foods of different textures? For example, does your child eat soft foods such as bananas, drink liquids such as milk, and eat hard foods such as raw vegetables? (A1.3)

   __Y__ d. Does your child choose to eat different kinds of food, such as dairy, meats, and fruit? (A1.4)

   __Y__ e. Does your child eat and drink many kinds of foods using forks, spoons, and other utensils with little or no spilling? (A1.5)

2. Does your child help prepare and serve food? (A2)   **S**
   NOTE: Place a "Y," "S," or "N" by items a through d:

   __N__ a. Does your child remove peels and wrappers before eating food? For example, your child peels a banana and removes a candy wrapper. (A2.1)

   __S__ b. Does your child use a knife to spread soft foods such as cream cheese or peanut butter onto bread or crackers? (A2.2)

   __S__ c. Does your child pour liquid from one container into another, such as juice into a cup? (A2.3)

   __Y__ d. Does your child serve food from one container to another with a fork or spoon? For example, your child spoons applesauce from a jar into a bowl. (A2.4)

Figure 4.   Portion of a parent-completed Adaptive Area section of the Family Report II for Tanya.

mands. Teams should not have a set of intervention activities to be used with all children regardless of their needs or goals but should have a range of intervention activities available that can be individualized to meet specific needs of children. An activity-based approach offers a structure to accommodate a wide variety of intervention activities that can be tailored to meet the needs of individual children.

Although children with severe disabilities may be 3–6 years old, it might be necessary to use the *AEPS Test for Birth to Three Years* to obtain an accurate assessment and the corresponding Birth to Three Curriculum for intervention activities. It is important to note that these activities may need to be modified to make them appropriate for older children. Some children with severe disabilities may fall between the two assessments, requiring the use of the *AEPS Test for Birth to Three Years* for some areas and the *AEPS Test for Three to Six Years* for other areas.

Teams may find that for some children with severe disabilities, even the *AEPS Test for Birth to Three Years* is too complex or advanced, requiring that objectives in this assessment be further refined through task analysis. In general, conducting a task analysis requires three steps: 1) identifying the objective, 2) dividing the objective skill into smaller steps, and 3) sequencing the steps for teaching.

An important consideration when working with children with severe disabilities, regardless of the severity of disability, is to embed targeted goals/objectives in activities appropriate to a child's chronological age; for example, a 5-year-old child may have the goal of orienting to (i.e., turn, look, reach, move toward) auditory, visual, and tactile events (a goal taken from the *AEPS Test for Birth to Three Years*). It may be appropriate to shake a rattle for a child younger than age 2 to provide an opportunity to turn toward the sound, but for a 5-year-old child a rattle is not appropriate. Shaking a tambourine near the child during a music activity may be more appropriate.

Considerations When Working with Children with Severe Disabilities

1. If a special assistant is assigned to a child in a center-based setting, then he or she should only provide assistance as needed and should fade involvement in a child's play whenever possible. One-to-one assistants should consider themselves part of the whole classroom, teachers to all children, but of special assistance to one particular child when necessary.

2. Children learn how to interact with others in part from adult models, so it is vital to be conscious of the subtle messages that are communicated to children (e.g., do not use "baby talk" with children). Interventionists should try to include all children in all activities, at whatever level they are able to participate.

3. Attention should be drawn to children's strengths, and all children should be allowed to take on responsibilities that affect the group (e.g., preparing snack, being line leader). Activities should be designed to capitalize on a child's strengths and abilities; for example, during a painting activity, a child with profound hearing and visual impairments may enjoy using the sense of smell or touch to explore materials. Materials can be added or

adapted to an activity to provide opportunities for all children to participate to the greatest extent possible.

4.   The interventionist should translate a child's behavior whenever neces-
     sary. Children with more pronounced disabilities or severe communica-
     tive impairments often have difficulties joining play activities with other
     children. Their peers may have difficulty "reading" behaviors and com-
     municative attempts different from those they know. Adults play a cru-
     cial role in translating the child's behavior for peers; for example, during
     a song at circle time, Denzel, who has cerebral palsy, starts to "sing," but
     his voice sounds almost like a cry. The children appear alarmed, and the
     interventionist reassures the children, "I can hear Denzel singing to the
     music."

5.   Adults may need to provide assistance to help children gain access to and
     participate in different play activities. The child care worker can suggest
     play ideas (e.g., "I wonder if you all could build a house together?") and
     provide suggestions for how a child with more severe impairments might
     participate in an activity (e.g., "I bet Eric could hold onto the sheet while
     you get some chairs to make a tent"). Peers often have ideas for how to
     include other children in activities. Simple solutions such as altering the
     location of activities may provide opportunities for children with dis-
     abilities to be included.

6.   Children may need additional structure and guidance to practice and en-
     hance their social skills. Activities such as rocking a boat, playing seesaw,
     and playing catch encourage children to play in pairs. Modeling questions
     such as "Can I play, too?" or "Do you want to play house with me?" or
     using sign language with nonverbal children are effective strategies.

7.   The child should be allowed to be as independent as possible with peers;
     for example, the interventionist can let peers know that they can ap-
     proach a child with a visual impairment and say, "Hi, Eric, it's Joey." A
     child with cerebral palsy who uses a wheelchair might participate in an
     art project by sitting in a modified chair at a table with other children
     rather than in the wheelchair.

8.   Straightforward, honest answers to questions posed by children will help
     facilitate understanding of disabling conditions. Specialized equipment
     may isolate a child if the equipment remains a mystery. The interven-
     tionist should be open and honest when answering questions from the
     child's peers and allow them to explore adaptive equipment (with the
     permission of the child), with the understanding that the equipment is a
     tool and not a toy.

9.   The interventionist should assist children without disabilities in learning
     how to interact and play with peers with disabilities; for example, one
     can tell the peer that, when he or she colors with a child with a visual im-
     pairment, it is helpful to put markers back in the original place; when a
     peer talks to a child with a hearing impairment, it helps to face the child
     and speak clearly. Peers should be encouraged to address children with
     disabilities directly (e.g., "Can I push your wheelchair outside?").

10. It is helpful to enhance the social image of children with disabilities by selecting clothing and toys that are age appropriate and currently popular.

SUMMARY

This introductory material is included to set the stage for efficient and effective use of the AEPS Curriculum in conjunction with the AEPS Test. The user is urged to carefully read this material prior to employing the curriculum. In addition, the authors recommend that the AEPS Curriculum be used in association with the AEPS Test. Without accurate, in-depth knowledge of children's behavioral repertoires, selecting appropriate intervention activities is guesswork, as is monitoring progress. The field of early intervention has become, through legal, professional, and parental interest, a legitimate enterprise that should not tolerate less-than-quality outcomes. Producing outcomes for children and families is dependent on careful and comprehensive assessments that lead to appropriate intervention accompanied by ongoing evaluation. Use of the AEPS Test and AEPS Curriculum may help interventionists attain this quality.

3

Designing and Implementing Intervention

This chapter is designed to assist teams in using the AEPS Curriculum by employing an activity-based approach that emphasizes children's involvement in child-initiated, routine, and planned intervention activities, as well as strategies on how to effectively arrange the learning environment. The primary purpose of this chapter is to address a variety of topics that will assist the user in the understanding and application of the AEPS Curriculum and will help interventionists establish a coordinated and cohesive approach to curricular programming.

The content and strategies offered in this curriculum are designed to be used in conjunction with developmentally appropriate practices to encourage child-initiated activities, encourage self-exploration and self-control, promote communication, support problem solving, enhance social interactions and play, and move toward independence. The age and range of disabilities and delays exhibited by the children in a program should be considered when selecting the curricular content, intervention strategies, and environmental arrangements. Promoting effective learning in children who are at risk or who have disabilities requires flexibility in approach, attention to the individual's needs, and engagement in meaningful activities. Adopting such an approach requires that developmentally appropriate practice is used and opportunities are available that address children's targeted goals/objectives.

Developmentally appropriate practice is predicated on three essential features. First, children are offered a variety of activities, events, and environmental arrangements appropriate to their developmental capacities. Second, these activities, events, and environmental arrangements should be meaningful to children. A final essential element is that the activities, events, and environmental arrangements provide a balance between children learning to follow the directions of others and learning to initiate activities to meet their own desires and interests.

For children who have or are at risk for disabilities, it is particularly important that activities be guided into productive endeavors. It is essential to offer children developmentally appropriate activities with multiple opportunities to work on the acquisition and maintenance of targeted goals/objectives. Creating developmentally appropriate activities is not sufficient; activities should offer many opportunities for children to practice behaviors that enhance communication and problem-solving skills and build toward independence. Ongoing observation and evaluation are necessary to ensure that the environment offers adequate opportunity for children to practice their targeted goals. Without careful monitoring of progress, children may engage in fun and meaningful self-initiated activities but fail to improve in targeted areas.

The following sections describe a range of strategies that promote a developmentally appropriate approach and provide multiple opportunities for targeting children's goals. These strategies include using 1) child initiations, 2) daily routines, 3) environmental arrangements, and 4) planned intervention activities. Supplemental information can be found in *An Activity-Based Approach to Early Intervention* (2nd ed., Bricker, Pretti-Frontczak, & McComas, 1998).

CHILD INITIATIONS

When employing an approach such as activity-based intervention (ABI), the preferred strategy is to follow children's leads and to guide their behavior in desired directions. It is important to note that interventionists and caregivers cannot rely exclusively on child initiations to provide the necessary opportunities to practice goals/objectives and, therefore, the use of daily routines, environmental arrangements, and planned intervention activities need to be considered as well. To the extent possible, however, adults should become careful observers of children's behavior and introduce intervention content into activities that children initiate and choose.

In an ABI approach, the caregiver or interventionist is a facilitator and guide rather than a director of the child's learning. Through observation and interactions with the child, the adult provides the least level of assistance necessary for the child to practice targeted goals or solve problems; for example, Jamal's mother may observe his attempts to build a tall block tower. Jamal uses a small block for the base, the tower continues to topple over, and the child cries. His mother provides support, but rather than hand Jamal a large block to use as the base, she moves a block nearby to encourage him to try a new strategy to solve the problem.

Interventionists and caregivers who are sensitive to children's needs in an activity-based program do not stay involved in the children's play longer than necessary. Interventionists and caregivers can use a variety of techniques to facilitate rather than direct learning in children.

Techniques for Encouraging Child Initiations

Follow the Child's Lead

When participating in an activity with a child, the caregiver or interventionist should follow the child's lead whenever possible and appropriate. Although children can be enticed into activities of the adult's choosing, it is often easier and more effective to subtly change or redirect an activity chosen by the child into a vehicle for practicing a targeted goal/objective; for example, if a child is playing in the sandbox, then the interventionist follows the child's lead and joins in the play. If the child picks up a stick and pokes it in the sand, then the interventionist imitates the play. To become effective at following a child's lead, it is critical that interventionists and caregivers be good observers of children, watching them to learn about their interests and motivations and their actual capabilities.

Model Desired Behaviors or Draw Attention to Peer Models

Adults and peers with more sophisticated skills can provide excellent models of desired behaviors and targeted goals/objectives throughout child-initiated, routine, and planned intervention activities. This strategy can be used to expand on the child's initiations by taking the activity one step further. In the sandbox activity described previously, the interventionist, knowing that the child has an objective to copy simple shapes, might draw a circle in the sand or draw the child's attention to peers who are drawing shapes in the sand.

Provide the Least Level of Assistance

Prompts provide additional information or support to help a child perform a behavior correctly; however, adults should offer the least assistance necessary for the child to perform the target response. Providing too much support or direction may result in the child becoming overly dependent on the adult for assistance and delay the development of independent skills and problem-solving behavior. Examples of prompts follow, generally from the least intrusive to the most intrusive.

- *Verbal prompts:* Adults make statements that help the child perform the behavior; for example, if the objective is to tie shoes, then a verbal prompt might be, "First you make a bow."

- *Gestural prompts:* Adults make hand, arm, or other movements that communicate information to the child about what to do; for example, if the objective is to remain seated during a large group activity, then a gestural prompt is to pat the floor with your hand indicating to the child to come and sit with the group.

- *Model prompts:* Adults or peers demonstrate the desired behavior.

- *Partial physical prompts:* Adults partially physically guide a child's movements.

- *Full physical prompts:* Adults physically guide a child's movements.

Group Children Heterogeneously

Children of varied ages or developmental levels should be grouped together. Heterogeneous groupings provide opportunities for children to learn new skills by observing peer models or enhance skills by assisting children who are less able.

Plan Time for Children to Complete Tasks

During busy schedules at home and school, adults often find themselves rushing children through activities to stay within a schedule. When possible, adequate time should be allowed for children to complete tasks independently or with as little assistance as possible.

Adjust Speech Complexity

When addressing young children, it is important to adjust the complexity of one's speech to reflect the child's level of understanding (this, of course, does not mean using "baby talk"). It is important to remember that too much adult talk may interfere with the development of the child's communication or with child-to-child communication. Adults should monitor their talk and actions to permit children adequate time to respond or initiate conversations and to communicate with each other.

Use Different Types of Talk

When possible, use a variety of ways to talk to the child including

- *Self-talk:* Talking aloud to oneself; verbalizing what one sees, hears, does, and feels; describing actions, objects, and events throughout the day for children (e.g., "I'm going to go wash up for dinner.")

- *Parallel talk:* Using talk that focuses on what the child is seeing, hearing, doing, and feeling (e.g., "Juan is sharing with Maria.")

- *Expansion:* Expanding on what the child says; for example, if the child says "outside" after getting his or her coat, then an expansion might be, "Do you want to go outside?"

- *Elaboration:* Using the previous example, the interventionist might say, "Do you want to go outside? Ruby and J.T. are outside playing."

Provide Choices

Offering choices can prompt a verbal response from children; for example, instead of asking a child, "Do you want to go outside?" offer a choice such as "Do you want to go outside and play, or would you like to have a snack?" Choices also provide an excellent strategy to less intrusively direct a child; for example, if a child consistently avoids manipulative activities and needs to practice fine motor goals, it may be appropriate to offer a limited choice such as, "The activities to choose from this morning are cutting out pictures for your book or drawing your own pictures."

Use Open versus Closed Questions

Questions should be used sparingly when working with children because questions can put children "on the spot" to respond and may inhibit communication. Using open questions, however, may require children to use more complex language in response. Open questions cannot be answered in one word and typically begin with "what," "why," "how," or "could" (e.g., "What do you want to do now?" "How did you make that picture?"). Closed questions can be answered in one word and often begin with "is," "are," or "do" (e.g., "Do you want to go outside?").

Use the Mand/Model Procedure

In the mand/model procedure, the interventionist may initiate an interaction by making a statement or asking a question (the "mand") that requires a response about the activity in which the child is engaged. If the child does not respond or only partially responds, then the interventionist provides a "model" of the verbal response with an emphasis on a targeted word or phrase; for example, while playing with bubbles, the interventionist holds up the bubble wand and says, "What should I do?" If the child does not respond, then the interventionist might model, "Say, 'Blow bubbles.'"

Try Forgetfulness

The interventionist fails to provide the necessary equipment or materials or omits a familiar component of a routine or activity; for example, a food is not immediately available for snack time, providing an opportunity for the children to recognize the missing element (e.g., "Where are the crackers?") and providing practice in asking questions, searching for materials, and engaging in other problem-solving behavior.

Use Visible but Unreachable

Objects that are desirable or necessary for the completion of activities are placed within sight of children but out of their reach. Children will need to use language and problem-solving skills to retrieve the items; for example, placing the playground balls on a shelf just over the child's head forces the child to find a step stool to reach the balls or to go to an adult for help.

Violate Expectations

Omitting or changing a familiar step or element in a well-practiced or routine activity violates children's expectations. Children's recognition of change will provide information about their discrimination and memory abilities and provide ideal situations for problem solving; for example, the interventionist tries to draw or write with a pencil by using the eraser. The child recognizes the problem and suggests a solution (e.g., turning the pencil so the pointed end is down).

Use Interruption

Interruption requires that the interventionist or caregiver stop the child from continuing a chain of behaviors that has become routine; for example, during hand washing, the interventionist or caregiver interrupts the child who is reaching for the soap and asks, "What do you want?" The child must then indicate what is needed to complete the task.

Require Assistance

This strategy involves using materials in activities that require assistance from an adult or peer to access and use; for example, placing a snack in a clear container with a lid that the child cannot remove independently prompts the child to communicate a need for assistance.

Practice Negotiation

If inadequate amounts of materials are provided for a given activity, then the child must "negotiate" with his or her peers to get more materials; for example, during an art activity, several colors may be provided, each in a separate container. The children must share and communicate with each other if they want to use different colors.

DAILY ROUTINES

Daily routines at home and in community-based preschool and child care programs give children choices about activities, although adults should not give children complete freedom to decide what they will do. Adults create a framework by designing the environment, choosing materials and activities, and taking a facilitative role in the learning process. As children explore their environment and expand on play activities, adults capitalize on child initiations and create additional learning experiences and opportunities.

Daily routines that occur at home or at child care or school settings can be used to provide multiple opportunities for children to practice targeted goals/objectives across important developmental areas. The use of daily routines (e.g., meals, clean-up, travel, bedtime) should be encouraged for two important reasons. First, daily routines are likely to be important and meaningful to children; therefore, the interventionists or caregivers do not have to create artificial or special activities, nor do they have to find ways to make the activities relevant. Second, daily routines help people get through activities that need to be accomplished on a regular basis (e.g., dressing, eating). Because these activities occur routinely, they can be used effectively and efficiently as teaching times.

An analysis of the home or other child care setting will reveal a variety of activities or events that occur regularly and predictably; for example, upon waking, most families follow bathing, dressing, and eating routines that prepare them for the day. With thought, these routines may be used to assist children in learning and practicing targeted goals/objectives; for example, dressing provides preschoolers the opportunity to work on adaptive skills (e.g., pulling on pants, buttoning, zipping), social-communication skills (e.g., "Where are my shoes?"), or cognitive skills (e.g., finding clothes, matching socks or shoes). Breakfast, lunch, and dinner provide numerous opportunities to practice cognitive skills (e.g., help set the table with appropriate number of utensils; find salt, napkins; locate what is missing) and social-communication skills (e.g., indicate food choices). Without analysis of events and consideration of the child's goals, caregivers may overlook opportunities to use daily routines to target skills. Not all daily routines, of course, will be appropriate teaching times for all families (e.g., families who have tight timelines for getting to work may find it difficult to use breakfast as a teaching time).

A similar analysis of daily routines in center-based programs will yield a variety of routines that can be used to target children's goals; for example, arrival at school offers opportunities to practice motor skills (e.g., walking up stairs) and social skills (e.g., greeting other children). Washing up for a snack gives children the opportunity to practice social skills (e.g., taking turns), adaptive skills (e.g., washing hands), and social-communication skills (e.g., asking what's for snack, asking a peer to sit nearby). By observing program activities, interventionists can identify numerous opportunities for children to practice targeted goals/objectives as they engage in daily routines.

To assist caregivers and interventionists in the use of routine activities to target specific goals/objectives from across many developmental areas, a routine activity planning format has been developed. Figure 5 presents an example of one daily routine activity (e.g., bedtime) that targets goals from multiple developmental areas. The AEPS goal/objective for each developmental area is listed, and, for each goal/objective, specific actions and possible materials necessary for the routine activity are suggested. For additional examples of this routine activity format and a variation of a routine activity format, see Chapter 3 and Appendixes A and B of Volume 3.

ENVIRONMENTAL ARRANGEMENTS

Children's environments can be arranged in a variety of ways to provide multiple opportunities to practice targeted goals/objectives. A useful strategy for young children in center-based programs is to arrange the environment into activity centers, equipping each area of the classroom with specific materials. Classroom space can be creatively organized to afford multiple opportunities for children to engage in activities that enhance learning. The goal is to design the environment so that multiple skills across areas can be elicited in the activity centers and that multiple opportunities to practice skills are provided.

The use of activity centers is an excellent strategy for encouraging child-initiated activities. When a child initiates an activity—begins to play with a toy, asks a question, or creates a game—the activity is likely to be of considerable interest to the child. Encouraging child initiations capitalizes on children's involvement in activities that they find motivating and fun. Self-selected activities often do not need artificial reinforcers or other external supports to maintain the child's interest and involvement. Section II of this volume provides additional suggestions for specific environmental arrangements for each goal in the AEPS Test for Three to Six Years.

Well-designed activity centers concentrate a child's interest and effort in multiple skill areas. An activity center with puzzles, blocks, and other manipulatives can be used to promote fine motor and cognitive skills. An obstacle course encourages the use of gross motor and social skills. A book or listening area promotes early literacy skills and may encourage labeling feelings, identifying colors, or solving problems. A sample illustration of an activity center is shown in Figure 6.

Routine Activity: Bedtime

FINE MOTOR AREA

Goal/Objective	What to Do	Materials
Uses two hands to manipulate objects, each hand performing different movements (A:1)	Encourage the child to brush teeth before bedtime. If needed, remind the child to squeeze the toothpaste on the toothbrush.	Toothbrush, toothpaste

ADAPTIVE AREA

Goal/Objective	What to Do	Materials
Puts on pullover garment (C:2.3)	Encourage the child to get ready for bed by putting on her or his pajamas.	Pajamas with pullover top

SOCIAL-COMMUNICATION AREA

Goal/Objective	What to Do	Materials
Uses words, phrases, or sentences to describe past events (A:1.4)	While settling into bed or right before bedtime, talk to your child about the events that occurred during the day (e.g., "I want to hear about your trip to the park today," or " What did you do at Grandma's house today?").	

GROSS MOTOR AREA

Goal/Objective	What to Do	Materials
Jumps from platform (B:1.2)	Have the child jump down from a low platform or step stool after brushing teeth at the bathroom sink.	Low platform or step stool

COGNITIVE AREA

Goal/Objective	What to Do	Materials
Reads words by sight (H:3)	Ask the child what books he or she would like to read before bedtime. Have the child read familiar titles or words from the titles of the selected books.	Familiar bedtime story books

SOCIAL AREA

Goal/Objective	What to Do	Materials
Selects activities and/or objects (D:1.2)	Allow the child to make choices during bedtime preparations (e.g., "Do you want to brush teeth first or put on your pajamas?" "Which stuffed animal are you going to sleep with?" "Which pajamas do you want to wear to bed?")	A variety of books, different sets of pajamas, variety of cuddly stuffed animals to take to bed

Figure 5. A sample of a routine activity format using one activity—bedtime—to target multiple goals across developmental areas.

Figure 6. A sample activity center.

Designing a variety of activity centers allows interventionists to target developing skills across areas. Children can make choices among activity centers, and appropriate assistance from an interventionist facilitates opportunities to learn and practice targeted skills. Activity centers can be a permanent foundation for a center-based program, and a rotation of materials is necessary to capitalize on children's ideas, to expand activities, and to maintain children's interest throughout the year. Development of activity centers involves the following:

1. Planning five to seven "centers" and designing space accordingly.

2. Identifying materials, rules of access, and adult roles for each activity center.

3. Determining targeted IFSP/IEP goals/objectives to be addressed in each center.

The number and type of activity centers designed will depend on space, daily schedules, the age and developmental level of children, and available resources (e.g., materials, equipment); for example, programs that have an outdoor play space may not need to develop a gross motor activity center. It is important to provide definition to activity centers and to separate noisy and quiet centers as much as space allows. Shelves or commercial dividers help separate and define spaces.

Arrangement of space to promote multiple uses is preferable. Many classrooms have a "messy" area with tables that are easily cleaned after sand or water play, snacks, or art activities. Another favorite is a "quiet" area of books, CDs and tapes, comfortable chairs, and pillows. This space might be used for group storytime, independent use of books, CDs, and tapes, or even naps. A

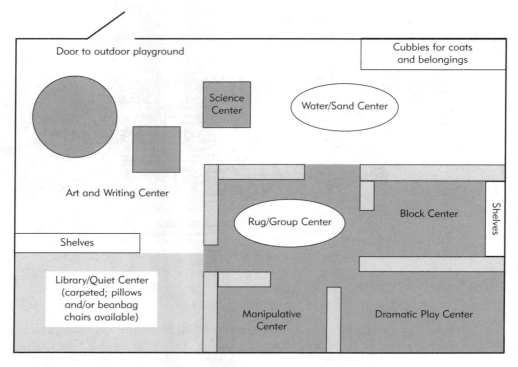

Figure 7.   Schematic of a classroom with a variety of activity centers.

dramatic play center provides an area for children to dress up, role play, and act out story sequences while supported by a changing array of furniture, props, decorations, and clothing. Figure 7 shows a schematic of a classroom with a variety of activity centers.

Once the desired activity centers have been established, each one should be outfitted with materials designed to promote overall skill development (e.g., motor, communication) and with materials that will facilitate practice on children's targeted IFSP/IEP goals/objectives; for example, addition of a coat, cups, a stuffed cat, and a plastic corn cob to the dramatic play center will provide multiple opportunities for a child to practice the "k" sound. Selection of appropriate materials should be keyed to ability levels of children, expertise and interests of interventionists, and available resources. An important consideration is that the children can safely use all materials. Regular introduction of novel materials into an ongoing center maintains interest and expands the practice of new skills. Figure 8 shows an example of a block center outfitted with materials, as well as a list of targeted IFSP/IEP objectives, intervention strategies, and prompts for two children who will be using the center.

As children engage in the activities of a center, interventionists should evaluate the usefulness of the activities in moving children toward their IFSP/IEP goals/objectives. Activity centers that do not consistently engage children are likely to be ineffective, whereas those that address both target areas and

- Block building can help children learn sizes, shapes, numbers, order, area, length, and weight as they select, build with, and clean up blocks.

- Block building can help children use large muscles to carry blocks from place to place. As they carefully place blocks together to form a bridge or an intricate design, they refine small muscles in their hands, which is important for writing skills.

- Block play can help social development. One child's idea of how to build a zoo may differ from another's, but children learn to respect different viewpoints and learn from one another. As children build together, they solve problems and learn the benefits of cooperation.

Illustration by Jennifer Barrett O'Connell. (Illustration used and text adapted with permission from Teaching Strategies, Inc., "The Creative Curriculum® for Preschool, 4th Edition." Copyright © 2002 by Teaching Strategies, Inc., P.O. Box 42243, Washington, DC, 20015, www.TeachingStrategies.com. All rights reserved.)

Name	Objective	What the adult can do	Current prompting level
Tama	SC B:1.6 (Uses present progressive "ing")	Comment, using "ing" (building, driving, stacking, sharing)	Model
Tama	Cog G:1.2 (Counts three objects)	Ask Tama, "How many blocks are in your zoo?"	Partial physical assistance to point to objects one at a time
Joey	Soc A:2.1 (Joins others in cooperative activity)	"Look, Tama's building a bridge." "It looks like she needs more blocks."	Partial physical assistance to carry blocks over to Tama
Joey	Cog A:1.2 (Demonstrates understanding of five different shapes)	Ask Joey to sort the square, rectangular, and triangular blocks into piles.	Verbal cue or partial physical assistance

Figure 8. Example of a block center.

elicit child engagement will be more effective. In addition, centers should be changed from time to time to maintain children's interest and help generalize learned skills to new activities.

The roles of adults may vary from center to center. A science center may require more adult interaction than a block center. Children with severe delays and disabilities may need additional assistance from adults in using activity center materials. Posting a brief description of each center and a summary of the skills targeted in that center helps adults, including assistants, volunteers, and specialists, provide consistent guidance to children.

Access to activity centers is an important consideration. Children need specific rules about when they may use activity centers, how many children may be in a center, and how to move from one center to another. Most classrooms have specified times when activity centers are used (e.g., free play, choice activity groups) and other times (e.g., circle time, snack time) when centers are not available. The size of the center and the nature of the activity will determine the number of children allowed in the center. Five or six children may work well at an art table, whereas three or four children may be more appropriate for a gross motor center.

Use of a child-initiated approach will require flexibility in activity centers. If rules for materials and the center are too rigid, then interventionists risk losing valuable learning opportunities; for example, if a child is building a house in the block center and has an idea to bring dolls from the dramatic play center to live in the house, then this can be encouraged by the interventionist, facilitating independence of thought and creativity in the child. The interventionist might expand the activity to provide opportunities to practice targeted goals/objectives. If a child's idea is safe and will not cause undue disruption to the classroom, then flexibility in the use of materials should be allowed. Effective learning in activity centers may be enhanced by the following factors:

- Equipment, materials, and activities are safe for all children.

- Guidelines for the activity center are posted.

- Potential goals/objectives are listed for each child.

- Reminders are provided to encourage child initiations.

A hallmark of effective early intervention is systematic and consistent environmental arrangements that promote learning in children. In center-based programs, thoughtfully designed activity centers provide children with a set of materials and events that are developmentally appropriate and promote opportunities for practice of targeted goals/objectives.

PLANNED INTERVENTION ACTIVITIES

Planning is necessary to successful intervention because it helps ensure that opportunities to practice targeted IFSP/IEP goals/objectives are arranged. This planning is essential at many different levels and should include all team members (e.g., caregivers, specialists) when possible. Large-scale planning may include the themes to be addressed during the year, the general arrangement of the environment to promote skill development across developmental areas, the roles and responsibilities of adults in the classroom, and adaptations necessary for children with special needs. Strategies to assist interventionists in planning include intervention plans, activity schedules, and intervention activities, as described next.

Intervention Plans

Intervention plans can be used to delineate the intervention content, outline teaching guidelines, and determine criteria for monitoring progress on priority goals/objectives. Intervention plans should be developed cooperatively by the team. Input from team members can be shared and then synthesized into an intervention plan to guide intervention activities and ensure a cohesive, coordinated approach to addressing the child/family goals/objectives.

Intervention plans can specify the goal and its associated objectives for individual children as shown in Figure 9. These plans can include intervention strategies, teaching considerations, curriculum modifications, procedures for monitoring child progress, and decision rules for change. In addition, potentially effective antecedents/prompts/cues and consequences can be listed under teaching strategies and considerations. Intervention plans are much like an architect's blueprint in that they provide the specifications necessary to reach a goal. Intervention plans should be followed and modified as necessary so that interventionists and caregivers always have a specific plan to guide their activities.

Activity Schedules

Most children are sensitive to changes in their environment and may become upset if continually unable to anticipate or predict future events. Providing a level of consistency and predictability to home- and center-based environments can greatly enhance a child's independent functioning and increase a sense of security. Developing weekly and daily activity schedules is one way to provide some consistency and predictability. Quality preschool programs offer a balance of child-initiated and planned intervention activities, large- and small-group activities, active and quiet activities, and indoor and outdoor activities. Figure 10 displays a weekly schedule for a center-based program; Figure 11 displays a daily schedule. Schedules help staff balance activities and plan opportunities to address children's targeted goals.

Center/Group Activity Schedules

Activity schedules help an interventionist or caregiver determine the best times for children to practice targeted IFSP/IEP goals/objectives. Center-based programs have a variety of daily routines that have potential as excellent training vehicles; for example, arrival can be used to practice social skills (e.g., initiate greetings) and foster independence (e.g., select an activity prior to group time). Snack time can be used to practice and improve cognitive skills (e.g., counting number of chairs needed for all children eating snack), social-communication skills (e.g., request items, discuss the day's events), and adaptive skills (e.g., use fork to eat food). Clean-up is often an opportune time to promote social interactions and cooperation (e.g., children help each other pick up toys), improve fine and gross motor skills (e.g., put toys on shelves or in boxes), and practice social-communication skills (e.g., follow directions, ask questions).

Activity schedules can be developed for an individual child or groups of children. The development of activity schedules for young children with disabilities may be vital to providing adequate opportunities to practice targeted goals/objectives. Figure 12 illustrates an activity schedule developed for three children in a center-based program. The children's names are placed across the top of the matrix, and their specific goals/objectives are listed below their names. On the left side of the matrix are the daily classroom activities and times. An "X" is placed in the box of each goal/objective to indicate that a

INTERVENTION PLAN

Child: _____Jesse_____ Team members/Interventionist: _____Ms. Husesta_____
Date initiated: _9/02_ Expected date of completion: _12/02_
Type of setting: __x__ Group _____ Individual _____ Home

SOCIAL AREA
Target Goal and Objectives

AEPS Test: Social Area Strand A, Goal 2

Initiates cooperative activity using verbal or nonverbal strategies once a day for 2 weeks. For example, Jesse may say, "It's time to clean up" to a group of friends, assign jobs to be done, and encourage peers to carry them out.

AEPS Test: Objective 2.1

Joins others in cooperative activity using verbal or nonverbal strategies such as requesting items, sitting and watching, and giving objects to peers twice a day for 2 weeks. For example, Jesse approaches group of friends building a sand castle, sits next to them for a while, then begins to help friend who is digging a tunnel to the castle.

AEPS Test: Objective 2.2

Maintains cooperative participation with others (i.e., maintains job, role, or identity that supplements another's job, role, or identity during a cooperative activity) six times a week for 2 weeks. For example, Jesse's friend may say "You hold these," and Jesse holds two blocks together while his friend puts a third block on top to build a house.

Intervention Strategies and Teaching Considerations

List of strategies that will be used to provide an opportunity for Jesse to practice the targeted goals and objectives	List of possible child behaviors: targeted and expected (+) or nontargeted and unexpected (−)	Consequences or what will be done following Jesse's targeted behaviors (+) or nontargeted behaviors (−)
· Set up activities that require more than one child and the sharing of materials · Model cooperative play by drawing attention to when other children join or initiate · Read stories about children playing together and sharing toys · Encourage Jesse to join or stay in cooperative activities · Ask Jesse to select a friend and an area in which to play · Assign roles or tasks to Jesse and a partner during clean-up	· Initiate (verbally or nonverbally) (+) · Join (verbally or nonverbally) (+) · Maintains (verbally or nonverbally) (+) · Ignore request or model (−) · Grab toys (−) · Walks away when peer extends an invitation to play (−)	· Comment on how well children are working or playing together (+) · Smile or praise Jesse (+) · Continue modeling (−) · Make request again or encourage again (−) · Remind Jesse how to initiate/join/maintain cooperative play (−)

Figure 9. Jesse's intervention plan for Social Area, Strand A, Goal 2.

Figure 9. *(continued)*

Curricular Modifications
1. Start with small group activities (i.e., less than four children) 2. Select activities and materials of high interest to Jesse

Child Progress Procedures			
Who	Where	When	How
· Ms. Husesta · Family	· Snack · Circle · Free Play · Home	· Once a day at home · Twice a day in three different activities	

Decision Rule
If adequate progress does not occur in ___3 weeks___ (specify time frame), then the team will: _x_ modify intervention strategies ___ modify curricular content (i.e., targeted goals, objectives) ___ other (describe)_____ _____ _____

training opportunity is likely to occur within the activity. A variation is to insert brief descriptions of possible activities in each box; for example, under Chris' goal "Follows three-step directions," the 9:00–9:20 circle time could be noted to have Chris help prepare for circle (i.e., gather books from the library center, pass one out to each child, sit down in the circle). Activity schedules will differ depending on settings and their restrictions and resources, as well as on the individual needs of children. Figure 13 provides an example of a modified activity schedule that can also be used as a progress monitoring (i.e., data collection) system. As shown in Figure 13, dates are written under each objective, and a child's progress is recorded below the date each time the child independently performs the skill (+), does not perform the skill (–), or performs the skill with assistance or prompting (p).

Observing each skill daily may be overwhelming; a monitoring system in which observations are staggered (i.e., by child, day, objective, setting) may make the task more manageable; for example, a schedule that staggers the activity being monitored may be helpful (e.g., observations will be made during arrival and departure on Monday, in activity centers on Tuesday, during outdoor play on Wednesday). Another example of a staggered monitoring system

Activity schedule	Monday	Tuesday	Wednesday	Thursday	Friday
Arrival					
Art center	Decorate flower pots	Paper flowers	Nature collage	Yarn "worm" art	Watercolor painting with flowers
Dress-up center	Every day: Gardening clothes				
Building center	Every day: Transportation toys				
Circle	Every day: Weather chart—sing: Ring around the rosie, pockets full of posies, thunder, thunder, we all fall down.				
Snack	Sunflower seeds	Garden fresh vegetables	Fresh fruit chunks	Spaghetti "worms"	"Ants on a log"—stuffed celery with raisins
Outside play	Outdoor gardening	Painting with water	Nature walk	Digging for worms—sand table	Obstacle course
Activity center/ social activity	Planting seeds	Washing toys—garden	Washing toys—spring cleaning	Cooking for snack—spaghetti worms	Water play—outdoors
Cleanup					
Circle/story	• Discovery box—planting items • Story about seeds	• Garden items/tools • Gardening story	• Items from hike • Nature story	• Worm/dirt items • Worm or fish story	• Child choice • Cleaning story
Departure					

Figure 10. Weekly schedule for a center-based program.

that might appeal to staff is to plan observations during planned intervention activities and transition times one week and during free play and routine activities the next week. Spreading the responsibility for progress monitoring across staff members is also helpful, as team members are continually reminded to promote opportunities for children to practice targeted skills during daily activities. For example, if a staff person is unable to observe Chris following three-step directions during arrival because no three-step directions are given, then the staff member should concentrate on providing that opportunity during arrival the next day.

Activity	Time
Arrival	8:20–8:30
Activity centers	8:30–9:00
Circle	9:00–9:20
Snack	9:20–9:45
Outdoor play	9:45–10:20
Activity center/special activities	10:20–10:50
Cleanup	10:50–11:00
Circle/story	11:00–11:30
Departure	11:30–12:00

Figure 11.   Daily classroom schedule.

Home/Individual Activity Schedules

Activity schedules can also be used effectively in the home. Caregivers are the best source of information to determine which daily routines address certain skills. Each family's schedule, values, and priorities, combined with their knowledge of the child's preferences, interests, and level of involvement in home and community activities make them, as caregivers, critical to the development of an accurate and useful activity schedule in the home environment. Home/individual activity schedules help communicate an activity-based approach to families and provide a structure for working with children in their routine activities, without creating unnecessary "drill" sessions.

Many possibilities are available to families. Bath time can be a time to expand vocabulary, search for missing objects, or improve adaptive skills. Traveling in the car may be an ideal time to expand the child's communication skills by pointing out people and objects. Figure 14 provides examples of how two IEP objectives for Raynell can be practiced within her family's typical daily routine.

The advantages of using daily routines for teaching are many. First, children are more likely to be motivated to learn a new skill if it is naturally required in the course of a routine. Second, when a skill is acquired in the course of daily activities, generalization of the skill is more likely. The skill is mastered in the setting where it is used, which eliminates the need to transfer the learned skill from a formal teaching situation. Third, caregivers and interventionists do not have to adopt "training" or "instructional" behaviors because they are already engaging children.

	Child's name: Chris		Child's name: Toby		Child's name: Leann	
	Goal/Obj.	Goal/Obj.	Goal/Obj.	Goal/Obj.	Goal/Obj.	Goal/Obj.
	Follows three-step directions	Selects activities and/or objects	Suggests acceptable solutions to problems	Alternates between speaker/ listener role	Watches, listens, and participates during small group activities	Joins others in cooperative activity
8:20–8:30 Arrival	X			X		
8:30–9:00 Activity centers	X	X	X	X	X	X
9:00–9:20 Circle time	X		X	X	X	X
9:20–9:45 Snack	X	X	X	X	X	X
9:45–10:20 Outdoor play	X	X	X	X		X
10:20–10:50 Special activities	X	X	X	X	X	X
10:50–11:00 Cleanup	X		X		X	X
11:00–11:30 Circle/story	X		X	X	X	
11:30–12:00 Departure	X			X		

Figure 12.   Group activity schedule completed for three children.

Considerations When Creating Activity Schedules

The development of useful and efficient activity schedules requires consideration of the following factors.

Preparation: A transition time of approximately 5 minutes will be needed for most children to move from one activity to the next. Ten minutes before the end of an activity time, it is helpful to announce that in 5 minutes it will be time to clean up and prepare for the next activity (e.g., "In 5 minutes we will clean up and wash our hands for snack"). This helps children complete their projects and prepare for the next activity. It is useful to communicate with each child, particularly those who find transitions stressful, to ensure understanding of the upcoming transition.

Time constraints: It is important to provide adequate time for children, especially those with mobility impairments, to clean up and move indepen-

Activity schedule	Goal/Objective: Follows three-step directions Date 9/5	Date	Goal/Objective: Selects activities and/or objectives Date 9/6	Date	Goal/Objective: Suggests acceptable solutions to problems Date 9/5	Date	Goal/Objective: Alternates between speaker/listener role Date 9/8	Date	Goal/Objective: Watches, listens, and participates during small group activity Date 9/5	Date 9/9	Date	Goal/Objective: Joins others in cooperative activity Date 9/7	Date 9/9	Date
8:20–8:30 Arrival							+							
8:30–9:00 Activity centers	+ – –		p –				+++		+	++		++	+	
9:00–9:20 Circle time	++						– p +		+	++		+		
9:20–9:45 Snack	++		++		– – p +							– p +	++	
9:45–10:20 Outdoor play					p +		p ++		++	+++		+	–	
10:20–10:50 Special activities	+++		++				++		+	++				
10:50–11:00 Cleanup					+				– p +	+		++	+	
11:00–11:30 Circle/story	++ +++						– p +							
11:30–12:00 Departure	p +						– – p							

Figure 13. An activity schedule modified to create a progress monitoring system (+ = independently performed skills; – = does not perform skills; p = performs skills with assistance or prompting).

Home/Individual Activity Schedule

Child: **RAYNELL**　　　　　　　　　　　　　　　　　　Date: **9/8**

Activity Schedule	Goal/Objective: Follows directions of three or more related steps that are not routinely given.	Goal/Objective: Alternates between speaker/listener role
Wakeup/Dressing	Ask Raynell to select clothing, get dressed, and come to breakfast.	Greet Raynell—ask about last night's dreams and wait for response. Talk about the type of day it is and have Raynell tell you what type of clothing should be worn.
Breakfast	Ask Raynell to get a bowl, get cereal, and sit at the table.	Ask Raynell about food tastes and plans for the day, and listen for response.
Playing/outing	Ask Raynell to get a jacket, put it on, and wait at the door.	
Lunch	Ask Raynell to wash her hands, set the table, and sit down.	While eating lunch, talk about afternoon plans with Raynell. Have Raynell tell you about the plans, and then ask her to listen as you talk about your plans.
Play group	Ask Raynell to choose an activity. Have her get the materials, bring them to a designated area, and begin the activity.	As Raynell plays, make comments and ask questions about the activity or game. Wait for Raynell to respond.
Dinner	Ask Raynell to wash her hands, put cups on the table, and get silverware.	Have each person at the dinner table talk about the day's events while others listen.
Watching television		Have Raynell help select the TV program to watch. Talk about the program. Listen while Raynell talks and have her listen while you talk.
Story/bath	Ask Raynell to select pajamas, select a book for after her bath, and undress for bath.	
Bedtime		Ask about Raynell's day and wait for response. Read a bedtime story. Ask questions about the story and wait for response.

Figure 14.　Home/individual activity schedule for Raynell.

dently between activities to the greatest extent possible. Interventionists need to exhibit flexibility and sensitivity to meet individual needs. Rigid adherence to a schedule will stifle opportunities to capitalize on a child's initiation, on "teachable moments," and on a child's ability to perform a task independently; for example, it may be tempting to quickly put a basket of materials away for a child with a motor delay. If the child is provided extra time and encouragement, however, then an excellent opportunity is available for the child to use motor, problem-solving, communication, or social skills to complete the task. Interventionists should remind themselves that it is not the cleaning up per se that is important but the learning of new skills that is critical for children.

Attention: Whereas some children may require extra time to shift from one activity to another, others may need a quick transition to hold their attention. Interventionists should anticipate these situations and be prepared to offer additional options to these children; for example, children who clean up quickly, wash their hands, and are ready for snack may be given additional responsibility to help set the table.

Communication: Many programs use pictures to communicate daily schedules to children who have difficulty processing auditory information, as well as children who have difficulty moving between activities. Most children appear to enjoy following picture schedules, and using a picture schedule with all of the children in a center avoids singling out a child with a disability. Picture schedules in the home environment have been very successful for children who have trouble making transitions. Figure 15 provides an example of a picture schedule.

Children with Significant Disabilities

For most children, participation in an enriched, developmentally appropriate, and child-directed program will provide adequate practice on targeted IFSP/IEP goals/objectives. Young children with significant delays or disabilities, however, will need frequent opportunities to learn and perform targeted goals/objectives. Ongoing planning is vital to ensure that these children are given adequate learning and practice time. A review of the AEPS Curriculum and the Section titled AEPS Curriculum and Children with Severe Disabilities contained in Chapter 2 of this volume may be useful when developing intervention activities for children with significant disabilities.

How to Use Planned Intervention Activities

Planned intervention activities can be used with individuals or with small or large groups of children and should generally meet two important criteria. First, they should be activities or events that children find meaningful, interesting, and engaging; for example, when offered the activity, children should show genuine enthusiasm rather than being required to participate. Second, activities should offer multiple opportunities to learn or practice targeted goals. Achieving this second criteria will require thought and preplanning.

Figure 15. Example of a picture schedule.

44

Although planned intervention activities can occur—and often do—apart from daily activities, they can also be meaningfully embedded into daily activities. It may be useful to plan activities for specific times of the day, with the understanding that child-initiated activities may supersede the interventionist's planned activity.

Successful intervention requires preplanning and organization. To assist interventionists in preplanning and organizing intervention activities, we recommend developing planned intervention activities that contain a sequence of nine components:

1. Activity name

2. Materials

3. Environmental arrangements

4. Description of activity

   - Introduction (set up)

   - Sequence of events

   - Closing

5. Opportunities to embed children's goals/objectives

6. Planned variations

7. Vocabulary

8. Peer interaction strategies

9. Parent/caregiver input

A completed planned intervention activity form including the nine components is contained in Figure 16. Additional examples of planned intervention activities are contained in Appendix B.

A planned intervention activity designed for one group of children can be modified for other children; for example, the pet store activity described in Figure 16 can, with modification, be used with most preschoolers. Intervention activities should provide young children experience using a variety of materials throughout the week and should offer children many opportunities and experiences to use and manipulate materials. Intervention activities should also offer children practice in a variety of skills across developmental areas. Many activities can be planned and developed that allow for expansion, change of materials, and differing skill levels. Programs may choose to develop a "bank" of generic intervention activities and modify them as necessary.

Ideas for intervention activities designed to offer multiple opportunities to practice targeted goals/objectives and generally found to be motivating for children whose development ranges from 3 to 6 years are contained in Appendix A. Some of the intervention activities target specific skill areas (e.g., Gross Motor Area), whereas others may permit the embedding of children's goals from several areas; for example, a dress-up activity such as Theater involves

(1) Pet Store

(2) MATERIALS
- Cash register
- Play money
- Pet food
- Pet accessories (cages, toys, small pet beds)
- Assortment of plastic and stuffed animals
- Pretend shopping carts and/or shopping baskets
- Paper bags

(3) ENVIRONMENTAL ARRANGEMENTS

Place pets, pet products, and accessories on low shelves in one area of the classroom. Place the cash register, play money, and paper bags on a small child-size table in the same area. Place pretend shopping carts and/or shopping baskets in the pet shop area too. The teacher can set this up independently or with the children's help.

(4) DESCRIPTION OF ACTIVITY

Introduction
- Teacher arranges dramatic play area with props. Teacher reads a story such as *Nicolas' Favorite Pet* by Inger Sandberg, or another story about a pet such as *Franklin Wants a Pet* or *Harry the Dirty Dog*. Teacher asks children to look in dramatic play area and then tells children that they will be able to play in the classroom pet store today during choice time. The teacher asks children if they have pets and then discusses how they care for them. Teacher asks who would like to play in the pet store.

Sequence of Events
- Children choose roles to play in the pet store (customers, shopkeeper, etc.).
- Children shop for pets and pet supplies.
- Children put the items they want to buy in shopping carts and baskets.
- Children purchase pets at cash register.
- Shopkeeper puts pet supplies in a paper bag for the customer to take home.

Closing
- The teacher explains that the pet store can only stay open for 5 more minutes, then it needs to close. The lights go on and off to let children know that the pet store will close. Children put pets and pet supplies away. The teacher talks with children about what animals they bought at the store, how much they cost, what supplies they needed to buy for their pets, how much they cost, and so forth.

(5) OPPORTUNITIES TO EMBED GOALS/OBJECTIVES

Whole Group Goals and Objectives

Areas	Opportunities
Cognitive	• During cleanup, have children help sort the pet store items into appropriate categories (e.g., pets, pet food, pet supplies) • Talk about characteristics of pets (e.g., furry, slimy, rough, smooth, loud, quiet, big, little)

Figure 16. A sample planned intervention activity. *Note:* Numbers refer to elements of the form.

Figure 16. *(continued)*

Areas	Opportunities
Social-Communication	• Forget to provide an important item such as the money for the cash register to encourage children to request items • Children talk about the pets they have purchased
Social	• Tell children that they must pay for their pets before leaving the pet store to encourage interactions with the children playing the shopkeeper • Talk about how pets make us feel (e.g., happy, silly, possibly scared if we don't know them); ask children to tell about a time when their pet or another person's pet made them feel happy

Individual Child Goals and Objectives

Child	Goal/Objective	Opportunities
Daniel	Counts at least 10 objects (Cog G:1.1)	• When Daniel is the cashier, encourage him to count the money he gives to customers. He can also count how many items each customer buys. • When he is a customer, ask him how many items he is buying for his pet.
	Uses regular past tense verbs (SC B:1.5)	• During closing, ask Daniel to tell about a pet that he bought at the pet store and what he bought for his pet.
	Joins others in cooperative activity (Soc A:2.1)	• Encourage Daniel to pay the shopkeeper for his pet and pet supplies. • Provide a small number of some pet supplies to encourage Daniel to ask his peers for items he wants.

6 PLANNED VARIATIONS

• Children bring in their favorite stuffed animal or a stuffed animal you would find in a pet store.
• Children make a mask of their favorite pet and have a pet parade.
• Children help decide if they want a pet for their classroom, what kind, and then take a field trip to the pet store and buy it.

7 VOCABULARY

• Animal names (dog, cat, etc.)
• Bed
• Food
• Water
• Money (penny, dollar, etc.)
• Veterinarian
• Buy
• Store
• Animal sounds (bark, meow, etc.)
• Alive
• Pretend

8 PEER INTERACTION STRATEGIES

• Children buying pets interact with child at cash register.
• Encourage children to tell each other about the pets that they bought at the pet store.

9 PARENT/CAREGIVER INPUT

• Children can bring their own pets to school.
• Children can visit a veterinarian's office.

children developing peer relationships, manipulating objects, talking and listening, and engaging in pretend behaviors.

The ideas for intervention activities described in Appendix A have been organized into the following categories: Art, Dramatic Play, Construction/Manipulation, Exploratory, Games, Literacy/Communication, Make-it-Change, Make-it-Move, and Nature Activities. Although most of the activities listed in this section incorporate skills across areas, some activities may be particularly helpful for eliciting skills within a specific area. In addition, any of the intervention activities contained in Appendix A can be modified to include the nine components of the planned intervention activity form found in Appendix B. For an example, see Pine Cone Bird Feeders in Appendix B, which is also listed in the Nature Activities of Appendix A.

Planned intervention activities often require modification because an activity that seems appropriate may not be effective with a group of children or the children may choose to use the materials in ways not anticipated. Following the child's lead within the activity is advisable, as long as IFSP/IEP objectives continue to be addressed.

Considerations When Developing Planned Intervention Activities

The development of useful and effective planned intervention activities requires consideration of the following factors.

Set up and cleanup: Although many adults consider setup and cleanup their responsibility, these aspects of an activity often provide excellent opportunities to practice targeted IFSP/IEP goals/objectives; for example, a child with the cognitive objective of counting objects could count the number of smocks needed for a painting activity, a child learning to manipulate objects could be physically assisted to pass out brushes to classmates, a child working on problem solving could find a container to hold water, or two children could work together to wash off the table, promoting social interaction.

Introduction and recap: Introduction refers to a brief preview of an activity before it begins. *Recap* refers to a similar review once the activity has been completed. During the introduction, the interventionist familiarizes children with the sequence of the activity (demonstration with actual objects or pictures may be necessary for some children) and covers basic rules or expectations. The recap provides an excellent opportunity to talk to children about the activity. For preverbal children, alternative methods of communication (e.g., pointing, gesturing) are encouraged.

Process versus product: During an activity, the focus should be on the exploration and learning that occur during the process rather than on the product; for example, during an art activity, the interventionist supplies the children with paper, scissors, glue, and crayons and asks if they can create butterflies. During the process of the activity, the interventionist focuses on facilitating general skill development across areas (e.g., sharing materials) and individual children's targeted IFSP/IEP goals/objectives (e.g., use of concepts, categorizing), rather than on children's abilities to create a recognizable "butterfly." It is useful at times to be nondirective or nonspecific. The interventionist might present materials by saying, "What can you do with these things?" Another approach is to introduce a specific problem to the children; for example, the interventionist might provide wood pieces, a stick, and tape and ask, "Can you make a bridge with these materials?"

SUMMARY

The material in this chapter and supplemental material contained in *An Activity-Based Approach to Early Intervention* (2nd ed., Bricker, Pretti-Frontczak, & McComas, 1998) is designed to set the stage for efficient and effective use of the AEPS Curriculum in conjunction with the AEPS Test. In particular, strategies for using child-initiated, routine, and planned intervention activities to embed children's IFSP/IEP goals/objectives are described. In addition, environmental arrangements, planning of interesting activities, and creation of activity centers to provide opportunities to practice targeted goals/objectives are discussed.

Although the content of this curriculum can be used with teacher-directed approaches, we believe that interventionists should begin by using an activity-based approach. The use of routine, child-initiated, and meaningful planned activities capitalizes on children's interests and motivation and, therefore, should produce effective and efficient learning.

SECTION

II

ÆPS™ Curriculum

Three to Six Years

AEPS™

Fine Motor Area
Three to Six Years

LIST OF AEPS TEST ITEMS

G2   Prints pseudo-letters **67**

2.1   Draws using representational figures

2.2   Copies complex shapes

2.3   Copies simple shapes

G3   Prints first name **72**

3.1   Prints three letters

3.2   Copies first name

3.3   Copies three letters

Motor development provides children a means of independence that enhances sensory exploration as well as interactions with people and the physical environment, facilitating all other areas of development. *Fine motor development* refers to the control of arm and hand movements involved in reaching, grasping, releasing, and manipulating objects. The development of fine motor control skills typically involves stability and strength in the neck, trunk, and arms as well as eye–hand coordination, the perception of touch, accurate visual–spatial perception, the ability to organize and sequence fine motor tasks, an awareness of the body in space, and the coordination of the left and right sides of the body. Children's increasing mastery of fine motor skills contributes to enjoyment of manipulating toys with many small pieces, independence in dressing and undressing, and experimentation during creative and pre-academic activities with scissors and writing implements.

Infants initially have little voluntary control of their arms, hands, and fingers. In the first 6 months of life, the infant's uncontrolled prereaching movements progress to voluntary reaching patterns. The integration of the muscles in the shoulder and elbow with the muscles of the wrist and hand contributes to the development of the infant's grasp. The infant's repeated interactions with the environment and the maturation of the central nervous system are responsible for the development of eye–hand coordination. Babies learn to manipulate simple objects by mouthing, waving, shaking, and banging. Newborns will automatically close their hands when an object is placed in the middle of the palm. Typically, by 12 months of age, the infant's grasping patterns have evolved to include more precise movements. The raking finger movement used in picking up a block and the pincer grasp used in picking up a raisin are two more advanced grasping patterns.

The infant's initial gross response for releasing objects is replaced with fine motor skills required for controlled release of objects. The eye–hand coordination necessary to precisely time grasp-and-release patterns in the manipulation of objects is demonstrated in the young child's independence in eating with a spoon. The infant's ability to coordinate sight and touch is refined as the brain matures and arm movements become more controlled, contributing to the infant's sophistication in manipulating objects. Typically, by 18 months of age, the hand grasp and the random, uncontrolled release has been refined to include independent coordination of the fingers and the thumb. Toddlers experiment with the complex manipulation of two or more objects, and their play becomes more meaningful and goal directed. During play, toddlers become interested in aligning and stacking objects, assembling toys with pieces, scribbling spontaneously, and imitating simple written strokes.

During the preschool years, most young children become increasingly successful in using two hands together, enabling them to perform tasks such as stringing beads. The fine motor control required in the manipulation of hand-held objects becomes progressively more refined between the ages of 3 and 5 years. Preschool children develop the dexterity and speed necessary for early writing skills. This is also the time when most children establish hand dominance in fine motor tasks, and they learn to use the preferred hand to perform a number of skills, such as unscrewing a jar, activating a wind-up toy, and buttoning a shirt. The preschool child's fine motor skills, coordination of the left and right sides of the body, and visual skills enable the child, for example, to tie his or her shoes.

The Fine Motor Area of the AEPS Curriculum was designed to create opportunities for young children to practice reaching, grasping, releasing, and manipulating objects for the purpose of mastering the fine motor skills required for independence in activities of daily living and success in future academic settings. The preferred approach is to embed training goals into the activities and routines that typically occur throughout the child's day. The Fine Motor Area is composed of two strands. Strand A (Bilateral Motor Coordination) focuses on a young child's ability to coordinate two-hand activities, beginning with manipulating objects and progressing to the fine motor control required to manipulate hand-held instruments (scissors). Strand B (Emergent Writing) addresses the use of each hand independently from the other. This is represented in the development of hand dominance and the continued refinement of dexterity, speed, and precision necessary for prewriting skills, beginning with using a three-finger grasp on writing implements, copying simple shapes, and moving to printing letters.

The Fine Motor Area curriculum is divided into four sections: 1) Intervention Considerations, 2) Suggested Activities, 3) Using Activity-Based Intervention, and 4) Area Goals. Intervention Considerations addresses important factors that an interventionist may wish to consider prior to and when working with children who are at risk for or who have disabilities. Suggested Activities provides a selected list of activities that may be particularly helpful when working on fine motor skills. This section also provides suggestions for additional materials that will increase opportunities for children to practice targeted fine motor skills. The third section provides an illustration of how to target IFSP/IEP goals in the Fine Motor Area using an activity-based intervention (ABI) approach. The final section, Area Goals, provides suggestions for Concurrent Goals, Daily Routines, Environmental Arrangements, and Intervention Activities in the home and classroom for each goal and associated objectives identified in the Fine Motor Area of the AEPS Test for Three to Six Years.

Fine Motor

INTERVENTION CONSIDERATIONS

General considerations when working on fine motor goals are discussed next.

- Some preschool special education programs emphasize fine motor skills that relate to school (e.g., writing skills) to give children an academic head start and teach skills that allow participation with peers. It is important to remember that nonacademic skills, such as communicating effectively, practicing social skills, following directions, attending to an activity for short periods of time without supervision, and moving easily from one activity to the next, are as important for success in public school environments as are academic skills such as writing.

- An occupational or physical therapist can help assess children with motor impairments to determine if a fine motor goal is functional and realistically attainable for a child. In addition to providing information concerning the modification of motor activities, environmental arrangements, and utilization of adaptive equipment, a therapist may recommend some type of preparation, such as therapy, to enhance a child's participation in fine motor activities.

- Children will benefit from planned activities that provide practice on fine motor goals. In addition to practicing motor skills, children with motor skill impairments may benefit from compensatory strategies during activities, such as modifications to the environment or adaptive equipment to increase their independence. Lap trays on wheelchairs provide excellent surfaces for children to write, draw, and manipulate objects. Assistive technology devices such as hand splints, adapted scissors, built-up grips for writing tools, nonslip surfaces, and computer hardware and software can provide the support necessary for children to participate in a variety of fine motor activities. It is important to consult a qualified specialist to provide information concerning special equipment and adaptations to the environment, activities, or materials.

- Positioning is an important consideration for children with motor impairments. The child should be upright and well supported when participating in fine motor activities such as cutting with scissors or writing. However, adaptive equipment, such as lap trays on wheelchairs, can also create physical barriers between a child and peers. Whenever possible, children should be seated in regular chairs or in adapted chairs (if extra support is required) or positioned on the floor with peers. Be aware of how assistive devices may prevent children from interacting with their peers.

- Preschool children may intentionally avoid participation in tasks that accentuate their limited fine motor control. Sensitivity regarding interaction with peers is important when encouraging children to participate in fine motor activities at their present level of mastery.

- Plan adequate time for children to complete tasks. Providing sufficient time for the child to practice a skill may make the difference in a child with sensory and/or motor impairments achieving independence in dressing, for example.

SUGGESTED ACTIVITIES

It may be helpful to designate an area of the classroom or home environment for fine motor and manipulative activities. Store materials on low, open shelves to make them accessible and to allow children to be active participants in set up and cleanup activities. Keep the area interesting and appealing to children by rotating materials periodically, making sure that the materials are clean, complete, and in good condition. Remember that many adaptive skills such as eating, dressing, and hygiene skills also provide opportunities to practice on functional use of fine motor skills.

Some adaptations may be required to make activities accessible to children with sensory and/or motor impairments. Adaptations may be simple, such as using a pair of adapted "loop" scissors or a nonslip surface for puzzles, or more complicated, such as assistive devices for arms. Decisions concerning environmental arrangements or modifications of materials may make the difference between the child completing the activity independently or requiring assistance. Consult a motor specialist for adaptations.

The following list of activities and materials may be particularly helpful for eliciting skills within the Fine Motor Area. For a complete list of intervention activities, see Appendix A.

Dramatic Play Activities

Children can work on fine motor goals in a naturally occurring context in dramatic play. Housekeeping and Post Office are two activities that are particularly helpful when embedding fine motor goals.

Other Activities

- Books/Book Making
- Collages
- Dinosaur Eggs
- Fall Colors
- Group Fingerpainting
- Manipulatives
- Paper Bag Animals
- Paper Chains
- Stringing Activities
- Washing Babies
- Weaving

USING ACTIVITY-BASED INTERVENTION

An illustration of how an interventionist can incorporate activity-based strategies to enhance the development of a child's fine motor skills is provided next. The child's targeted IFSP/IEP objective is to copy simple shapes (e.g., circles, crosses, Ts).

- The interventionist observes that Timmy chooses to play in the sandbox. She *follows the child's lead* by joining the child in his play and encourages peers to join. The classroom consists of a *heterogeneous* group of children, providing opportunities for the child to learn new skills by observing peer models or to enhance skills by assisting children who are less able. The interventionist *expands on the child's initiation* by picking up a stick and drawing simple shapes in the sand, using self-talk to comment on her own actions ("I'm going to draw with this stick").

- The interventionist *models* how to draw simple shapes in the sand and draws Timmy's attention to peers who are displaying more advanced skills ("Look at Latifa. She's making circles in the sand").

- The interventionist uses additional strategies to encourage Timmy to practice a skill, such as *parallel talk*, to comment on the shapes he has drawn, or the interventionist provides a new "twist" ("Can you make a big circle?") to encourage Timmy to continue practicing the skill.

- Throughout the activity, the interventionist uses the least amount of assistance necessary for Timmy to successfully practice targeted goals.

AREA GOALS

This section provides suggestions for concurrent goals, daily routines, environmental arrangements, and intervention activities for the fine motor goals listed in the *AEPS Test for Three to Six Years*. For an objective that has been targeted, the interventionist can turn to the corresponding goal and determine which suggestions are relevant to address that objective. A standard format is used for each goal: 1) Strand, 2) Goal, 3) Objective(s), 4) Concurrent Goals, 5) Daily Routines, 6) Environmental Arrangements, and 7) Intervention Activities. Concurrent Goals list AEPS goals from other developmental areas that can often be addressed at the same time that the child works on the target goal or associated objectives. Daily Routines present a list of routine activities that may provide opportunities to practice targeted skills. The Environmental Arrangements should be considered when designing children's programs around child-initiated, routine, and planned intervention activities. Finally, the Intervention Activities offer examples of how to embed targeted goals within the context of intervention activities. Additional information on daily routines, environmental arrangements, and planned intervention activities is provided in Chapter 3.

STRAND A

Bilateral Motor Coordination

GOAL 1   Uses two hands to manipulate objects, each hand performing different movements

Objective 1.1   Holds object with one hand while the other hand manipulates

CONCURRENT GOALS

FM A:2   Cuts out shapes with curved lines
Adap A:1   Eats and drinks a variety of foods using appropriate utensils with little or no spilling
Adap A:2   Prepares and serves food
Adap C:1   Unfastens fasteners on garments
Adap C:3   Fastens fasteners on garments
Soc B:2   Watches, listens, and participates during small group activities
Soc B:3   Watches, listens, and participates during large group activities
Soc C:1   Meets physical needs in socially appropriate ways

DAILY ROUTINES

Routine events that provide opportunities for children to practice manipulating objects include the following:

- Cleanup

- Dressing

- Mealtime or snack time

- Unstructured playtimes

Example: When preparing to go to the playground, Timmy fastens fasteners on his coat. (FM A:1.1)
Example: When cleaning up the art center after free play, Alicia replaces the lids on the markers. (FM A:1.1)

ENVIRONMENTAL ARRANGEMENTS

- Present materials that provide opportunities for children to manipulate objects (e.g., blocks, Tinkertoys, Legos, stringing and weaving activities) and arrange the classroom into activity areas that include a dramatic play center. The home and classroom environment should be arranged to allow safe, purposeful exploration of hand-size objects.

Example: The interventionist assists Eric, who has a visual impairment, in choosing building materials from the shelf in the classroom. She asks Eric, "Do you want to build something with the blocks or the Legos?" as she guides his hands first to the open container of blocks and then to the Legos. After Eric selects the blocks, the interventionist sits down to play with him at the table. Eric puts the blocks together to "build a bridge" with verbal cues and physical assistance from the interventionist; for example, the interventionist tells Eric to hold a block with one hand while putting the other one on top. (FM A:1.1)

- A discussion of adaptations necessary to successfully practice this goal and its associated objective should include the specific activity; the environmental arrangement of the activity, including the arrangement of materials and positioning of children; special equipment needs of the children (assistive devices); and the specific size, shape, texture, and weight of the objects to be manipulated.

- Practice manipulating objects is essential to the development of fine motor control with handheld implements (e.g., scissors, crayons, pencils).

INTERVENTION ACTIVITIES

Two examples of how to embed this goal and the associated objective within activities are presented next. For a list of intervention activities that address goals/objectives across areas, see Appendix A.

Fruit Salad

Children cut soft fruits such as bananas, watermelon, pears, and strawberries into chunks with dull table knives. They put the fruit in a bowl and stir in yogurt or sprinkle granola over the mixture and eat their creations for snack. Children have opportunities to manipulate objects as they do the following:

- Get ready for the activity by buttoning or tying their smocks

- Participate in the activity by stabilizing the fruit with one hand while cutting with the other

- Clean up by putting lids back on yogurt or granola containers

Cereal Necklaces

Children make necklaces out of "O" shaped cereal. The interventionist ties a large knot in one end of a piece of heavy yarn or string and wraps a short piece of tape around the other end to make a firm tip. Additional opportunities can be provided to manipulate two objects by placing the cereal in a plastic jar and encouraging children to take off the lid to retrieve cereal for stringing. Children can string cereal, tie the string ends, and paint the cereal to make the necklace.

Example: When the class prepares to make a cereal necklace, Maria independently walks to the table using her walker. Maria sits in her chair, which is adapted with additional trunk support to maximize fine motor control. The interventionist congratulates Maria on successfully stabilizing the string with her right hand and manipulating the cereal with her left. A few minutes later the interventionist provides physical assistance and verbal cues so that Maria can practice stringing the cereal with her right hand while holding the string with her left. (FM A:1)

GOAL 2   Cuts out shapes with curved lines

Objective 2.1   Cuts out shapes with straight lines

Objective 2.2   Cuts paper in two

CONCURRENT GOALS

Cog A:1   Demonstrates understanding of color, shape, and size concepts
Soc B   Participation (all goals)

DAILY ROUTINES

Routine activities that provide opportunities for children to practice cutting skills include indoor playtimes and family projects (e.g., cutting ribbon for wrapping presents). The use of children's scissors in the home or classroom requires close supervision to ensure a safe, enjoyable play experience.

Example: During indoor play activities at home, Joey's mother draws different sizes of circles on colored pieces of paper. Joey, his mother, brother, and sister follow the lines to cut out the circles. Together they create a funny "circle" animal by pasting the shapes on a large piece of paper. (FM A:2)

ENVIRONMENTAL ARRANGEMENTS

* Materials that provide opportunities for children to use scissors (e.g., paper, card strips, string) should be available for the children to play with during indoor play. Arrange the classroom into activity areas, including an art and dramatic play center. Many children enjoy cutting playdough, which provides a stable material to practice cutting skills.

Example: Timmy is a postal clerk in the classroom "post office." When a classmate arrives to buy "stamps," the interventionist reminds Timmy to first cut out the stamps. Timmy independently cuts straight lines with his adapted (loop) scissors and proudly sells the stamps to his classmate. (FM A:2.1, adapted)

- Art/writing centers in the home or classroom should include an adequate space with tables and chairs, as well as a plan for set up and cleanup with adult and child responsibilities designated.

- The design of activities for children with sensory and/or motor impairments may require consultation with a qualified motor specialist. Adaptations of fine motor activities with scissors for a child with sensory and/or motor impairments will include adequate supervision and safety procedures; the positioning of the child; the height of the surface; the special equipment needs of the child (e.g., assistive devices for the arms and hands); the variety of adapted scissors available; the child's level of participation; and optimal combination of modeling, physical assistance, and verbal cues.

- The fine motor control of handheld implements such as scissors requires strength and stability in the arm and hand, finger dexterity, the coordination of both sides of the body, and the ability to accurately plan and time the necessary fine motor movement pattern for cutting. Hand dominance begins to develop prior to 2 years of age and is followed by a period of apparent ambidexterity between the ages of 2½ and 3½. From 4 to 6 years of age, right- or left-hand dominance gradually increases. In general, 4-year-old children cut with scissors using the preferred hand.

INTERVENTION ACTIVITIES

Two examples of how to embed this goal and the associated objectives within activities are presented next. For a list of intervention activities that address goals/objectives across areas, see Appendix A.

Dinosaur Eggs

The children make dinosaur eggs by cutting out oval shapes from paper and decorating them with crayons, markers, or glitter. Children practice cutting skills as they cut out shapes with straight or curved lines to paste on their eggs for decoration; if necessary, adaptive scissors can be provided. The least level of assistance necessary for each child to complete the activity is provided by the interventionist.

Example: Eric, who has a visual impairment, is responsible for cutting out the various sizes of white dinosaur eggs for the class dinosaur project. His interventionist places the scissors in the regular upper right-hand location on Eric's project tray. After successfully locating the scissors, Eric follows the bold black line on the white paper (high contrast) to cut out his dinosaur eggs. His interventionist's advanced planning allowed Eric to complete his dinosaur project independently. (FM A:2)

My Stegosaurus

In this art activity, children create a stegosaurus. Depending on varying skill levels, the interventionist may provide either an outline for the children to cut out or a precut version for children to decorate with crayons, markers, or glitter. Opportunities can be provided for the children to cut out shapes with straight lines while cutting out triangles to make the plates that line the dinosaur's back. (FM A:2.1)

Emergent Writing

GOAL 1 Writes using three-finger grasp

Objective 1.1 Uses three-finger grasp to hold writing implement

CONCURRENT GOALS

FM A:1 Uses two hands to manipulate objects, each hand performing different movements
FM B:2 Prints pseudo-letters
Cog E:1 Evaluates solutions to problems
Cog H:2 Uses letter–sound associations to sound out and write words
Soc B:1 Initiates and completes age-appropriate activities
Soc B:2 Watches, listens, and participates during small group activities

DAILY ROUTINES

Routine events that provide opportunities for children to practice writing using a three-finger grasp include the following:

- Arrival and departure routines
- Art/creative activities
- Unstructured playtimes
- Writing notes, cards, letters
- Dramatic play
- Shopping

Example: The interventionist provides a sign-in/sign-out sheet on a clipboard that is kept at the door to the classroom. A marker or other writing implement is attached to the clipboard using a string. When Jesse arrives at school, he is assisted by his parent and/or interventionist to grasp the pencil using a three-finger grasp and to practice writing his name or making another mark to symbolize his name. (FM B:1, 1.1, 2, 3)

Example: The interventionist provides a variety of fine motor activities to promote individual finger movements and a variety of grasp patterns. (FM B:1.1)

ENVIRONMENTAL ARRANGEMENTS

- Design the classroom or home environment so that materials are available that provide opportunities for the children to practice using writing implements during indoor play activities. An art center should include a variety of writing implements such as chalk, pens, pencils, markers, and crayons as well as materials to write on, such as lined paper, boards, and construction paper. Work surfaces, such as chalkboards or wipe-off boards, tabletops, and paint easels also should be provided.

- As children approach school age, greater emphasis is placed on table and chair activities specifically designed to refine the adult fine motor grasp. The increased practice of this goal and its associated objectives in a context similar to the requirements of a school environment enhances the probability of a child successfully transferring prewriting skills to the academic setting.

- General adaptations for prewriting skills include using contrasting surfaces such as bold pencil and dark lines on white paper, increasing finger sensitivity for children who use braille, or using raised line paper or a screen board for coloring or writing.

- Consult a qualified motor specialist for adaptations that facilitate a child's ability to print letters. Adaptations include the child's positioning, the height of the writing surface, assistive devices for the arms and hands, and the size and weight of the writing implement.

- Some children with motor impairments will require alternative methods of written communication including computer technology. However, children should also continue practicing writing skills with adaptations as necessary, until it is determined that this will not be a functional method of written communication for the individual child.

INTERVENTION ACTIVITIES

Two examples of how to embed this goal and the associated objectives within activities are presented next. For a list of intervention activities that address goals/objectives across areas, see Appendix A.

Puzzles

Place several puzzles on a child-size table without chairs. Eliminating the chairs allows children to freely choose the puzzles and to trade places with other children once a puzzle is completed. This gives children with physical disabilities an opportunity to also work on standing skills while targeting this fine motor goal. If a child is not able to stand, then provide appropriate supported seating in adapted or therapeutic chairs. To work on a three-finger grasp, provide puzzles that have pegs or handles attached to each puzzle piece to encourage an appropriate thumb, index finger, and middle finger grasp.

Example: Lori is a child with mild cerebral palsy who is able to grasp hand-size objects but has difficulty isolating individual fingers for grasping small objects. As she is assisted with the puzzle activity, her interventionist provides hand-over-hand assistance to keep the ring and little finger tucked into her palm as she grasps the handle on the puzzle pieces.

Where's Chloe the Bunny?

Tape a large piece of newsprint onto a child-size table. Before introducing the activity, draw shapes of various sizes near the outside borders of the paper. Make sure that there is one shape for each child, plus one shape for the interventionist. Draw or tape a replica of a rabbit somewhere on the paper. In the middle of the paper draw a "bunny cage." Draw paths of various widths from the shapes to the bunny. The interventionist can make straight paths and curved paths to the bunny. Provide markers, crayons, and/or pencils. Some children may need special pencil grips applied to pencils or crayons that help encourage proper three-finger grasp (FM B:1.1). Introduce the activity as the children are standing around the table by saying:

> "Jimmy has a rabbit named Chloe. One day Jimmy forgot to feed Chloe. Chloe was very hungry and wanted to find some fresh grass and some pretty flowers to eat. Let's help Chloe find some grass to eat."

Have the children choose a writing implement. The interventionist can demonstrate drawing grass and flowers for children who have difficulty keeping their arm on the writing surface. (FM B:1)

> "Find a special spot to draw some grass and flowers for Chloe to eat. Now draw the grass and flowers going up and down, up and down."

The interventionist demonstrates moving the fingers up and down with his or her arm on the table and moving only the fingers to guide the writing implement. If necessary, the interventionist can gently hold the child's arm steady as the child draws.

> "Now Chloe wants to go home. Let's help Chloe find a way to get back to her cage. Everybody choose a place to start. Find a shape and let's make your shape a special color so that Chloe can find the road to her cage."

The interventionist encourages each child to choose a shape to start. Children are encouraged to negotiate with their peers if more than one child wants a particular shape. During preparation of the activity, the interventionist can draw one less shape than is needed in order to provide an opportunity for children to work on problem-solving skills (Cog E:1, 2). The interventionist then demonstrates coloring a shape using the same pattern of moving the fingers up and down. It is not important that children stay within the outline of the shape as much as working on proper hand movements while coloring.

> "Now let's show Chloe how to get back to her cage."

The interventionist demonstrates coloring in the path using the fingers to draw or color in the path. The interventionist should move the fingers up and down with the arm steady and wrist in place for a few strokes and then move the arm a short distance farther down the drawn path to repeat filling in the path with up and down strokes. Some children may be working on letters and drawing figures (FM B:2). The interventionist can encourage these children to make some "signs" for the bunny to find her way home.

GOAL 2   Prints pseudo-letters

Objective 2.1   Draws using representational figures

Objective 2.2   Copies complex shapes

Objective 2.3   Copies simple shapes

CONCURRENT GOALS

FM A	Bilateral motor coordination (all goals)
FM B:1	Writes using three-finger grasp
FM B:3	Prints first name
Cog A:1	Demonstrates understanding of color, shape, and size concepts
Cog A:2	Demonstrates understanding of qualitative and quantitative concepts
Cog G:2	Demonstrates understanding of printed numerals
SC A	Social-communicative interactions (all goals)
SC B	Production of words, phrases, and sentences (all goals)
Soc B	Participation (all goals)

DAILY ROUTINES

Routine events that provide opportunities for children to write, draw, and copy shapes include the following:

- Arrival and departure

- Art/creative activities

- Dramatic play

- Indoor and outdoor play

- Shopping

- Writing notes, cards, letters

Example: When Shawna's parents are sending letters and cards, they ask Shawna to "Draw a picture for Gramma," "Write Troy's name on the envelope," or "Sign your name on Loury's card." (FM B:2, 2.1, 3)

Example: During a finger painting activity, Pat uses his fingers to scribble. The teacher draws a circle and encourages Pat to copy it. Floureen is already drawing circles, so the teacher draws squares and triangles for her to copy and then suggests that both children "Draw a picture of yourself." (FM B:2.1, 2.2, 2.3)

Example: Tomas has a variety of art supplies at school and at home and is encouraged to draw pictures of people, places, and events that are of particular interest to him. When he asks, "How do I draw my cat?" an adult shows him how to use a circle for the head, triangles for the ears, an oval for the body, a line for the tail, and so forth. Tomas is also asked to "Write your name on the picture before we hang it up," or to "Write a title on your picture to name it." (FM B:2, 2.1, 2.2, 2.3, 3, 3.1)

ENVIRONMENTAL ARRANGEMENTS

• In the classroom, set up a desk at the door or by the cubbies where each child "signs in" at arrival by drawing a circle around his or her name, copying a check or plus by his or her name, or attempting to write his or her name.

Example: Dustin and Lauren arrive at class together and after hanging up their coats they are reminded to "Sign in so we know who is here today." Dustin chooses a marker, finds his name on the list, and quickly puts a checkmark next to his name, saying "Dustin is present. Check!" Lauren takes a metallic pen and carefully makes the letter "L" followed by a series of unrecognizable characters, while carefully sounding out her name (FM B:2).

• Arrange the classroom into activity areas that include a dramatic play center. Integrate a variety of drawing and writing supplies into dramatic play, and provide specific opportunities for children to copy shapes and draw pictures as they participate in dramatic play scenarios.

Example: When the dramatic play area is set up as a grocery store, shoppers can be shown how to use checkmarks, crosses, or lines to keep track of items on shopping lists, marking each off as they put them into shopping carts. If the play area is set up for firefighters and medics, they can copy simple and/or complex shapes to draw houses, roads, and buildings on maps for the drivers. Doctors and restaurant workers can write print characters as prescriptions and when taking orders for meals. (FM B:2, 2.1, 2.2, 2.3)

• During opening circle, have pictures of activity choices across the top of a plastic sheet or chalkboard that can be erased. Ask children to indicate their individual choices by attempting to write their name under the appropriate picture or by copying a shape in which the teacher writes their name.

Example: Meghan indicates her plan to work in the blocks/construction and library centers by writing an "M," a "G," and a few other unrecognizable pseudo-letters under those pictures. Darrell wants to go to the construction center, also, and to houskeeping, so the teacher indicates that he should copy a rectangle under those centers, within which she writes his name. (FM B:2, 2.2)

- Provide pictures, stencils, and models of simple and complex shapes in the classroom art center. Acquire extra supplies for writing and drawing, and make them available for use at home by children who have these goals/ objectives.

Example: Ben has an objective on his IEP to draw using representational figures. In discussing the objective with his mother, the teacher shares a list of art supplies and equipment that are available for loan. Ben's mother is excited about borrowing a small easel and some paints, as well as construction paper and markers. After 3 weeks, the easel and remaining paints are returned along with the markers. In the meantime, Ben has brought pictures into the classroom that he drew at home and identifies them by attempting to label each with a title. (FM B:2, 2.1)

- Give particular attention to positioning of children during fine motor activities such as copying, drawing, and printing. Children need to be seated or standing in stable, supported postures in order to attend to and successfully control hand movements and manipulate writing implements. Consult a qualified motor specialist for individual positioning considerations.

Example: The physical therapist notices that Irene's feet don't reach the floor and watches the child slump in her seat after reaching across the table for different colored markers. The therapist suggests a chair with a tray to contain the markers so that Irene doesn't have to compromise her sitting posture by reaching. The specialist also recommends using something such as a large block to support Irene's feet to increase stability in sitting during art and opening circle.

- Pretend not to know what a child has painted or drawn and purposefully mislabel it, or attempt to hand a prized picture back to the wrong child. Use the "misunderstanding" as an opportunity to have children "write" their names and/or titles on their pictures.

Example: Christopher's father knows that his son is quite proud of the monster truck he has drawn and wants it displayed on the refrigerator. Chris's father prompts his mother to mislabel the picture, and she says "Oh, my goodness! Someone has drawn a huge hay truck here." When Christopher protests, his parents suggest that he write a title for the picture, and they write the letters "M" and "T" for him to copy to begin the words monster truck. (FM B:2)

- Have children make signs for their rooms at home or cubbies in the classroom by drawing pictures of themselves or their favorite things and/or by attempting to write their names.

Example: Shirell's teacher designs an activity center for children to make signs for their cubbies or rooms at home. Shirell draws a picture of herself for her room at home and asks the classroom assistant to write "MY ROOM" on the picture. The assistant writes MY ROOM on another sheet of paper for Shirell to copy. (FM B:2, 2.1, 3.3)

- For children who are having difficulty copying simple or complex shapes, arrange opportunities for them to trace shapes of a variety of sizes and then cut them out for use in constructing representational pictures. Begin with shapes that have straight sides.

Example: Marcus has the idea of copying, and although he readily learned to copy circles and lines, he is having difficulty copying triangles, stars, and rectangles. His teacher asks him to help prepare for an art activity and gives him stencils of ovals, triangles, squares, and rectangles in a variety of sizes. Marcus traces about 15 shapes (FM B:2.1, 2.2) and cuts out a couple of triangles before tiring of the activity and turning the scissors over to a peer.

- General adaptations for prewriting skills may include providing adaptive grips for writing implements, using contrasting surfaces such as dark lines on white paper, increasing finger sensitivity for children who will be using braille, or using raised-line paper or a screen board for coloring or writing.

- Some children with motor impairments will require alternative methods of written communication. However, children should also continue practicing writing skills, with adaptations as necessary, until it is determined that this will not be a functional method of written communication for the child. Alternative modes of writing include computer programs with joy sticks or other adaptive access devices.

- The interventionist should consult with a qualified motor specialist in designing and implementing activities for children with sensory and/or motor impairments. Often, a process of trial and error is important to determine a child's best position; any special adapted equipment needs (e.g., assistive devices for the arms and hands, adapted writing tools); the best writing surface and writing implement; and the ideal combination of physical assistance and verbal cues to promote mastery of prewriting skills.

- Precision in prewriting skills requires not only fine motor control but body awareness; integration of the left and right sides of the body; eye–hand co-ordination; mobility and strength of the neck, trunk, arms, and hands; perception of touch; visual–spatial perception; and correct organization and sequencing of the fine motor pattern. Typically developing children who are 1–2 years old will hold a crayon or pencil with a gross grasp to imitate a scribble or to scribble spontaneously. As the control of handheld implements becomes more refined between the ages of 2 and 4, children will begin to imitate horizontal and vertical strokes, copy a circle, and trace a diamond. Children between the ages of 4 and 6 are able to copy a cross, square, triangle, and diamond using an adult fine motor grasp.

INTERVENTION ACTIVITIES

Two examples of how to embed this goal and the associated objectives within activities are presented next. For a list of intervention activities that address goals/objectives across areas, see Appendix A.

Shaving Cream Fun

Children experiment with the sense of touch while fingerpainting on a surface with shaving cream. The interventionist prompts the children to copy shapes in the shaving cream by providing models of shapes while drawing pictures (a circle for a face, rectangle with two circles at the bottom for a car) and by providing stencils for tracing. Children can also paint shapes on their own faces while standing in front of a mirror or paint one another's faces. Each child is encouraged to draw simple or complex shapes, to try writing their names, and to use similar strokes with the sponge or paper towel when cleaning up.

My Face

Children look at themselves in a mirror, then draw their faces and talk about what the eyes, nose, and ears do. The children can either draw their picture on a piece of paper or, if enough mirror space is available, they can draw their face directly on the mirror with erasable markers. The interventionist can model drawing shapes for faces and provide opportunities for children to copy complex shapes by embellishing pictures. Children practice writing by labeling their pictures with titles and/or their names.

Example: Alice uses a pencil with an adapted grip to draw her face, using both simple and complex shapes. The interventionist models the activity by first drawing a circle for her own face, ovals for eyes, a triangular nose with round nostrils, and lip shapes. She encourages Alice with verbal cues as needed to copy the complex shapes for adding a hat, a body, clothing, and jewelry. Alice titles her picture "Alice at a party," and writes a sideways "A" and other characters using lines and circles. The teacher prints the title next to Alice's characters. (FM B:2, 2.2 adapted)

Note: Creating a perfect picture is not the goal of this activity. Depending on individual goals, children should be given the least level of assistance necessary to practice targeted goals.

GOAL 3   Prints first name

Objective 3.1   Prints three letters

Objective 3.2   Copies first name

Objective 3.3   Copies three letters

CONCURRENT GOALS

Cog H   Phonological awareness and emergent reading (all goals)
SC A:1   Uses words, phrases, or sentences to inform, direct, ask questions, and express anticipation, imagination, affect, and emotions
Soc B:1   Initiates and completes age-appropriate activities
Soc B:2   Watches, listens, and participates during small group activities

DAILY ROUTINES

Routine activities that provide opportunities for children to copy and print letters include indoor and outdoor playtimes.

Example: At school Eric learned to print his name with a screen board, which uses a tactile model so that he can feel the letters that have been written. He is excited about showing his mother how he can write by himself. During playtime at home, Eric uses a name card that allows him to feel his name. His mother encourages his writing by saying, "I can read that. It says Eric." (FM B:3.2, adapted)

Example: Whenever children with this goal complete art projects at school, the interventionist reminds them to write their names on their pictures. By providing the optimal combination of modeling, verbal cues, and physical assistance, the interventionist ensures that the children successfully write their names on their art projects. (FM G:3, 3.2)

ENVIRONMENTAL ARRANGEMENTS

* The classroom environment should have letters and words prominently displayed. Include examples around the classroom of the letters of the alphabet and children's names; for example, children's names can be displayed on helper charts, attendance charts (e.g., the children sign in when they come to school, with assistance if necessary), and individual cubbies. Name cards are made from cardboard to keep in the art center as models. Words for the days of the week, classroom jobs, materials, and snack items can be displayed around the classroom in appropriate locations to provide letter models. Books in the library also provide letter models.

Example: The dramatic play center in the classroom is arranged as a restaurant. Latifa and Joey sit at the table during free play and practice copying letters found in the classroom that represent different menu items. During lunch, Latifa and Joey take several children's food orders by writing the letters on a small pad of paper. (FM B:3.1)

- Design the home and classroom to include materials that provide opportunities for the children to copy shapes during indoor playtimes. Include writing tools such as chalk, pens, pencils, crayons, and markers, as well as materials to write and draw on, such as lined paper, construction paper, and cardboard. Chalkboards, tabletops, sandboxes, and easels offer a selection of work surfaces.

- As children approach school age, greater emphasis is placed on table and chair activities specifically designed to refine the adult fine motor grasp. The increased practice of this goal and its associated objectives in a context similar to the requirements of a school environment enhance the probability of a child successfully transferring prewriting skills to the academic setting.

- General adaptations for prewriting skills include using contrasting surfaces such as dark lines on white paper, increasing finger sensitivity for children who use braille, or using raised-line paper or a screen board for coloring or writing.

- Consult a qualified motor specialist for adaptations that facilitate a child's ability to create letters. Adaptations include the child's positioning, the height and angle of the writing surface, assistive devices for the arms and hands, and the size and weight of the writing implement.

- Some children with motor impairments will require alternative methods of written communication. However, children should also continue practicing writing skills, with adaptations as necessary, until it is determined that this will not be a functional method of written communication for the individual child.

INTERVENTION ACTIVITIES

Two examples of how to embed this goal and the associated objectives within activities are presented next. For a list of intervention activities that address goals/objectives across areas, see Appendix A.

Pudding Painting

The interventionist makes instant pudding (food coloring can be added to vanilla pudding) and puts it on individual paper plates for the children to fingerpaint. Children will be surprised when they realize that they can lick their fingers. Children talk about how the pudding feels, tastes, and smells. The interventionist provides models of different letters and encourages children to copy or print letters in the pudding.

Example: The interventionist writes Joey's name in the pudding, commenting, "I'm writing your name, Joey." Joey writes a "J," an "O," an "E," and a "Y." (FM B:3.2, 3.3)

Sand Print Names

Children write their names on a piece of cardboard, tracing the letters in glue and then sprinkling sand (or cornmeal, glitter, and so forth) over the letters. The glue is allowed to dry and the excess sand is shaken off. The children can then "feel" their names and use their name cards for a model in future activities.

Note: Provide necessary level of assistance for children to produce a good model of their name.

≈AEPS™

Gross Motor Area
Three to Six Years

LIST OF AEPS TEST ITEMS

75

Children's successful negotiation of the physical environment is largely dependent on their gross motor skills. *Gross motor development* refers to movements involving the large muscles of the body including 1) assuming and maintaining postures such as sitting and standing; and 2) performing whole body movements such as crawling, walking, and jumping. The sequence of gross motor development is determined largely by the maturation of the child's central nervous system.

Infants initially have little ability to support their body against gravity and are largely dependent on caregivers to meet their fundamental needs. Involuntary primitive and postural reflexes present at birth are inhibited in the first 12 months of life. Integration of the sensory and motor systems occurs, and infants develop voluntary movement. Gross motor milestones that typically develop in the first 18 months of life include head control, rolling segmentally, sitting alone, crawling, pulling to stand, creeping, and walking independently. Individual differences in the rate of acquisition of gross motor milestones may be a result of the infant's experience with the environment.

Stability, locomotion, and manipulation movements are mastered through practice in the second 12 months of life. The child practices and refines the gross motor skills learned during the first year and becomes more adept at skills requiring balance. The toddler learns to assume a standing position from sitting and begins to take steps backward while pulling a toy. Running and stair climbing are basic motor patterns that emerge during the second year. These gross motor accomplishments enhance children's cognitive and social growth, providing the independence necessary to explore and interact with objects and people in their environment.

During early childhood, increased control of voluntary movement contributes to the child's interest in experimenting with movement through active exploration of the environment. Attaining stability in an upright position against the force of gravity allows children to develop the dynamic and static balance required for standing on one foot or walking on a balance beam. Walking provides the foundation for running, jumping, hopping, and skipping. The combination of stability and movement allows early reach and grasp-and-release responses to evolve into throwing, catching, and kicking activities.

The development and refinement of gross motor movements may be facilitated through play. Encouragement as well as opportunity for practice and instruction promote children's continued learning from experiences with movement. Play in the early childhood period should include activities designed to enhance perceptual motor development. Gross motor movement requires body awareness, the knowledge of body part differentiation, and the ability to organize the body to perform various movements. These skills include spatial awareness, knowledge of the body in relationship to space, directional awareness, temporal awareness, and the coordination of the sensory and motor systems during dynamic movement.

The Gross Motor Area of the AEPS Curriculum was designed to systematically build and enhance children's gross motor movement in daily activities. The preferred approach is to embed training into the activities and routines that typically occur throughout the child's day. The Gross Motor Area is composed of two strands. Strand A (Balance and Mobility) focuses on the refinement of stability. Strand B (Play Skills) encourages a diversity of manipulation and locomotion movements that can be used to facilitate motor development and enhance social interactions with peers. Jumping; skipping; riding and steering a two-wheel bicycle; and bouncing, catching, kicking, and throwing balls are all addressed in this strand.

The Gross Motor Area curriculum is divided into four sections: 1) Intervention Considerations, 2) Suggested Activities, 3) Using Activity-Based Intervention, 4) and Area Goals. Intervention Considerations addresses important factors that an interventionist may wish to consider prior to and when working with children at risk for or who have disabilities. Suggested Activities provides a selected list of activities that may be particularly helpful when working on gross motor skills. This section also provides suggestions for additional materials that will increase the opportunities for children to practice targeted gross motor skills. The third section provides an illustration of how to target IFSP/IEP goals in the Gross Motor Area using an activity-based intervention approach. The final section, Area Goals, provides suggestions for Concurrent Goals, Daily Routines, Environmental Arrangements, and Intervention Activities in the home and classroom for each goal and associated objectives identified in the Gross Motor Area of the AEPS Test for Three to Six Years.

INTERVENTION CONSIDERATIONS

General considerations when working on gross motor goals are discussed next.

- Safety issues are particularly important when working on gross motor goals. Some goals (e.g., jumping forward) may be inappropriate for children with specific disabilities. Children need to be aware of the limits of indoor and outdoor areas and must develop self-protective skills before working on specific goals (e.g., a child with a visual impairment searches for a handrail before climbing stairs or clears a path before running).

- An occupational or physical therapist can help assess children to determine if a gross motor goal is functional or realistically attainable. In addition to providing information about the modification of motor activities, arrangement of the environment, and utilization of adaptive equipment, a therapist might recommend some type of preparation, such as therapy to help normalize a child's muscle tone, to help the child participate in motor activities.

- Children with disabilities may benefit from environmental arrangements and planned intervention activities to attain gross motor goals; for example, a child with a visual impairment may benefit from the adaptation of materials (e.g., audible balls) or from being paired with a seeing peer to encourage gross motor skills. Adaptive equipment such as wheelchairs, standers, or braces can provide the support necessary for children to participate in a variety of activities. A qualified specialist should determine under what circumstances children with motor impairments will need to utilize special equipment.

- Children may intentionally avoid participation in tasks that accentuate their limited gross motor control. Sensitivity regarding interaction with peers is important when encouraging children to participate in gross motor activities at their present level of mastery.

- Plan adequate time for children to complete tasks. Providing sufficient time to practice a skill may make the difference in a child with sensory and/or motor impairment achieving independence in walking, for example.

SUGGESTED ACTIVITIES

The following list of activities and materials may be particularly helpful for eliciting skills within the Gross Motor Area. For a complete list of intervention activities, see Appendix A.

- Animal Moves
- Firefighter Play
- Follow the Leader
- Group Outdoor Games
- Obstacle Course
- Simon Says
- Spaceship

USING ACTIVITY-BASED INTERVENTION

An illustration of how an interventionist can incorporate activity-based strategies to enhance the development of a child's gross motor skills is provided next. The child's targeted IFSP/IEP objective is to bounce a large ball at least twice, using the palm of one hand.

- The interventionist observes Latifa kicking balls during outdoor play. She follows the *child's lead* by joining Latifa in her play and encourages peers to join in as well. The classroom consists of a *heterogeneous* group of children, providing opportunities for children to learn new skills by observing peer models or to enhance skills by assisting children with fewer abilities.

- The interventionist *expands on the child's initiation* with the balls by picking up a ball and bouncing it. The interventionist uses *self-talk* to comment on her own actions (e.g., "I'm going to bounce this ball") and draws attention to peers who are modeling the targeted skill (e.g., "Look at Manuel! He's bouncing the ball with one hand!").

- The interventionist uses additional strategies to *encourage multiple opportunities* for the child to practice bouncing; for example, the interventionist uses parallel talk to comment on Latifa's attempts to bounce or provides a new twist to the activity, such as counting the number of bounces, introducing different types (e.g., sizes, colors) of balls, or trying to bounce the ball on different surfaces to encourage Latifa to practice.

- Throughout the activity, the interventionist uses the *least amount of assistance* necessary for Latifa to successfully practice targeted goals.

AREA GOALS

This section provides suggestions for concurrent goals, daily routines, environmental arrangements, and intervention activities for all of the gross motor goals listed in the AEPS Test for Three to Six Years. If an objective has been targeted, then the interventionist can turn to the corresponding goal and determine which suggestions are relevant to facilitate that objective. A standard format is used for each goal: 1) Strand, 2) Goal, 3) Objective(s), 4) Concurrent Goals, 5) Daily Routines, 6) Environmental Arrangements, and 7) Intervention Activities. Concurrent Goals list the AEPS goals from other developmental areas that can often be worked on at the same time the child works on the target goal or associated objectives. Daily Routines present a list of routine activities that may provide opportunities to practice targeted skills. The Environmental Arrangements should be considered when designing children's programs around child-initiated, routine, and planned intervention activities. Finally, the Intervention Activities offer examples of how to embed targeted goals within the context of intervention activities. Additional information on daily routines, environmental arrangements, and planned intervention activities is provided in Chapter 3.

Gross Motor

Balance and Mobility

GOAL 1   Runs avoiding obstacles

Objective 1.1   Runs

CONCURRENT GOALS

Cog A:2   Demonstrates understanding of qualitative and quantitative concepts
Cog A:3   Demonstrates understanding of spatial and temporal relations concepts
Cog C:1   Follows directions of three or more related steps that are not routinely given
Cog F   Play (all goals)
SC B:1   Uses verbs
SC B:5   Uses descriptive words
Soc B   Participation (all goals)

DAILY ROUTINES

Routine events that provide opportunities for children to run include indoor (if appropriate) and outdoor playtimes. Close supervision of running activities is important to assist children in developing an awareness of their bodies in space and to promote mastery of the gross motor skill.

Example: The doctor informed Timmy's mother that it is important for Timmy to gradually increase his endurance for physical activity. During outdoor playtime in their fenced backyard, his mother chooses the game Hide-and-Seek. She runs a few steps in front of him and hides behind the tree, saying, "Run, Timmy. Come and find me!" (GM A:1.1)

ENVIRONMENTAL ARRANGEMENTS

- Arrange the classroom into activity areas, including a gross motor area. Include an open space (with mats or carpets to protect children if they fall) and an outdoor space (grassy areas are preferred) where children have room to run. Sometimes long hallways free of obstacles provide space to run.

- Create safe running opportunities for children as part of a daily routine by arranging the environment with an appropriate running surface and evaluating the space for obstacles or other safety hazards. Children may begin running with a hurried walk. Not until 2–3 years of age do children truly run with a period of nonsupport (at some point in the running cycle neither leg is on the surface). Running becomes more refined and efficient, with increased speed, by age 5.

- "Running" is in the eyes of the beholder. Children may run on two feet, with a walker, or in a wheelchair. Consult a qualified motor specialist to determine if running is an attainable gross motor goal for a particular child and to discuss adaptations to activities and equipment.

INTERVENTION ACTIVITIES

Two examples of how to embed this goal and its associated objective within activities are presented next. For a list of intervention activities that address goals/objectives across areas, see Appendix A.

Duck, Duck, Goose

This is a favorite for many children. Children sit in a circle, and one child is chosen to be "it." The child who is "it" walks around the outside of the circle, tapping each child's head gently and calling the child either a duck or a goose. Whoever the child chooses as "goose" stands up and chases and tries to tag the first child before he or she sits down at his or her place in the circle. The goose then becomes "it."

Example: Children playing Duck, Duck, Goose in the classroom with Alice begin the game sitting in chairs facing outward from the circle. The group chooses a special style of running (running sideways or backward) before the game begins. If Alice is the "goose," then she runs in her wheelchair. When Alice is "it," the "goose" has a chance to practice an alternative method of running that will also improve coordination and speed and give Alice an opportunity to avoid being tagged by the "goose." (GM A:1.1, adapted)

Chick, Chick, Chickens

Children pretend to be baby chicks following after the mother chicken. The mother chicken leads the chicks in such activities as walking, running, or jumping. A variation can involve setting up cones or chairs as obstacles when a "fox" appears. This provides opportunities for the children to run avoiding obstacles.

Example: The interventionist pairs the children with a buddy, including Eric, who has a visual impairment. The activity is conducted in a large grassy field free of obstacles, and Eric can run confidently. (GM A:1.1)

GOAL 2   Alternates feet walking up and down stairs

Objective 2.1   Walks up and down stairs

CONCURRENT GOALS

Cog C:1   Follows directions of three or more related steps that are not rou-
           tinely given
Cog F:1   Engages in cooperative, imaginary play
Cog F:2   Engages in games with rules
SC B:1   Uses verbs
Soc A   Interaction with others (all goals)
Soc B   Participation (all goals)

DAILY ROUTINES

Routine activities that provide opportunities for children to walk up and down
stairs include the following:

- Indoor and outdoor playtimes

- Transitions (e.g., moving from one activity or place to another)

   Close supervision ensures safety during gross motor activities.
   Example: When Timmy and his father visit the park, Timmy can practice
stair climbing on the slide. His father stands at the bottom of the stairs to offer
the necessary physical support and verbal encouragement. By using his arms
and hands, Timmy can successfully climb the slide with a step-by-step approach. (GM A:2.1)

ENVIRONMENTAL ARRANGEMENTS

- Provide climbing stairs and blocks of varying heights as well as stairs with
  and without handrails. When learning to climb stairs, children may initially use a handrail for support or use a step-by-step approach. Children
  will typically be more successful in climbing stairs lower in height. Eventually, children may no longer require a handrail for support and stairs of
  greater height may be negotiated using a step-over-step approach.

- The outdoor play area can include small climbing structures that do not require arms and hands for support and large slides that necessitate using the
  upper extremities.

- Arrange the classroom into activity areas that include gross motor and
  dramatic play centers. Provide close supervision for all children engaged in
  physical activity, regardless of their present level of gross motor skills.

INTERVENTION ACTIVITIES

Two examples of how to embed this goal and the associated objective within activities are presented next. For a list of intervention activities that address goals/objectives across areas, see Appendix A.

Firefighter Play

A fire station is created in the dramatic play center of the classroom. Children think of props to include in the station, such as fire hats, raincoats, cots, a bell, hoses, chairs, and a steering wheel for a fire truck. A set of portable stairs can be provided to climb up to reach the "burning house." The interventionist should consider the height of the stairs and whether handrails should be present. Encouraging children to hold a hose while climbing stairs provides an opportunity to climb without using the railing for support.

Example: Maria has braces on both legs and uses a walker when playing with her friends in the classroom. When it is Maria's turn to hold the fire hose on the "burning building," the interventionist selects stairs that are smaller in height with the handrails closer together. Maria can climb the stairs independently using the handrails. When she has her balance at the top of the stairs, she can signal her "firefighting assistant" to hand her the fire hose. (GM A:2.1)

Obstacle Course

This activity can be introduced with a discussion about how community helpers (e.g., firefighters, police officers) need to exercise to do their jobs. An obstacle course can be set up with some stair-climbing activities by providing portable steps and a small slide or climbing structure. Include other gross motor activities such as jumping, crawling through tunnels, and weaving in and out of cones. A specific course may be set, and physical assistance, a combination of physical assistance and verbal cues, verbal cues alone, or modeling can be provided as required for the children to successfully practice stair climbing with the goal of achieving functional independence.

Gross Motor

Play Skills

GOAL 1   Jumps forward

Objective 1.1   Jumps in place

Objective 1.2   Jumps from platform

Objective 1.3   Balances on one foot

CONCURRENT GOALS

Cog A: 3   Demonstrates understanding of spatial and temporal relations concepts

Cog C:1   Follows directions of three or more related steps that are not routinely given

Cog F:1   Engages in cooperative, imaginary play

Cog F:2   Engages in games with rules

SC B:1   Uses verbs

SC B:5   Uses descriptive words

Soc A:1   Interacts with others as play partners

Soc B   Participation (all goals)

DAILY ROUTINES

Routine activities that provide opportunities for children to practice gross motor skills involving balance and jumping include the following:

• Dressing

• Indoor and outdoor playtimes

• Transitions (moving from one place or activity to another)

Close supervision ensures safety during gross motor activities.

Example: Joey and his mother are walking in the park. The pathway is lined with small logs. Joey climbs up on a log, walks a few steps, and then jumps off. (GM B:1.2)

Example: When the class moves from one activity to the next, as in going out to play, the interventionist makes the transition from classroom to outdoor play area more exciting by encouraging Latifa and Manuel to hop like bunnies down the hall. (GM B:1, 1.1)

ENVIRONMENTAL ARRANGEMENTS

Environmental arrangements should allow children to successfully participate in balance and jumping activities at their current skill level while promoting higher levels of mastery and independence in gross motor skills.

- Assemble equipment such as minitrampolines, mats, balance beams, short stairs, platforms, small obstacles, or materials such as ropes, sticks, tape, or chalk to mark lines to balance on or jump over. Use gross motor classroom areas for indoor themes or during inclement weather. Closely supervise all children practicing balance and jumping skills.

Example: Joey and Latifa are excited about learning to hop on one foot. First they practice standing on one foot with and without using their arms for support. The interventionist arranges the children in a circle so that all of the children can have fun participating. Alice is seated in her wheelchair in the circle and offers her hand to a peer for support. Maria uses her walker for support when standing on one foot. (GM B:1.3)

INTERVENTION ACTIVITIES

Two examples of how to embed this goal and the associated objectives within activities are presented next. For a list of intervention activities that address goals/objectives across areas, see Appendix A.

Animal Moves

Children identify and imitate the movements of animals. The activity can be introduced by reading a story about animals or looking at pictures of different animals. Opportunities can be provided for the children to practice balancing and jumping skills by choosing stories or pictures of animals that jump (e.g., kangaroos) or balance on one foot (e.g., storks).

Example: Survival in the wild also depends on "standing" absolutely still. Alice enjoys the game because she has an opportunity to practice balance by using the muscles of her trunk when sitting and when on her hands and knees. Alice has a chance to play on the floor with the other children without her wheelchair, and balancing with her trunk improves her posture and gives her more endurance. (GM B:1.3, adapted)

Pop Goes the Weasel

This activity involves the children reciting the rhyme "Pop Goes the Weasel" and jumping up in the air whenever the word "Pop!" is sung.

All around the cobbler's bench, the monkey chased the weasel.
The monkey thought that it was fun. POP! goes the weasel.

A penny for a spool of thread. A penny for a needle.
That's the way the money goes. POP! goes the weasel.

As the children recite the song, they walk in a circle until it is time to jump, practicing maintaining balance while walking.

GOAL 2　　Bounces, catches, kicks, and throws ball

Objective 2.1　**Bounces ball**

Objective 2.2　**Catches ball**

Objective 2.3　**Kicks ball**

Objective 2.4　**Throws ball**

CONCURRENT GOALS

Cog A:2	Demonstrates understanding of qualitative and quantitative concepts
Cog A:3	Demonstrates understanding of spatial and temporal relations concepts
Cog C:1	Follows directions of three or more related steps that are not routinely given
Cog F	Play (all goals)
Cog G:1	Counts at least 20 objects
SC B:1	Uses verbs
SC B:5	Uses descriptive words
Soc A:2	Initiates cooperative activity
Soc B	Participation (all goals)

DAILY ROUTINES

Routine events that provide opportunities for children to practice gross motor skills with balls include indoor and outdoor playtimes. Close supervision ensures safety during gross motor activities.

Example: During recess, the interventionist, Mr. Orizo, selects several different sizes of balls for the play area. He places a lighter, medium-size ball in front of him and demonstrates kicking by modeling the action of moving his leg through the ball. Timmy watches and smiles. The interventionist brings a ball over, places it in front of Timmy, and as he says, "Kick it, Timmy," he models by moving his own leg through the action again. (GM B:2.3)

ENVIRONMENTAL ARRANGEMENTS

- Provide balloons, beanbags, beach balls, and other balls of different sizes and weights to create opportunities for practice and to promote mastery in bouncing, catching, kicking, and throwing during indoor and outdoor play periods. Trash cans, boxes, or hoops may become a target for the game.

- The ideal environmental arrangement for ball activities includes not only the close supervision of adults for safety but active participation of family members and classroom personnel to assist in developing the children's awareness of body position in space.

- An understanding of the developmental sequence of throwing, kicking, catching, and bouncing balls promotes environmental arrangements that allow children to successfully practice ball activities at their present skill level while offering opportunities to achieve a higher level of mastery. The maturational sequence of throwing a ball begins with only an arm movement and eventually includes rotation of the body and stepping forward with the leg on the same side as the throwing arm. The sequence of kicking a ball initially involves simply pushing against the ball. Later, the child will stand still and kick at the ball with the leg straight. Finally, as the child learns to kick through the ball, the lower leg will bend, swinging backward and forward with the arms to provide balance. Children learning to catch a ball will initially use both body and hands before learning to catch with only hands. For successful catching activities, use larger balls initially before using smaller balls. After a period of simply chasing balls, a child's attempt to catch a ball with the arms will appear. Modeling and verbal cues help a child to learn how to position the arms for catching. For a 3- to 4-year-old, fear of a thrown ball (turning the head away) is not unusual.

INTERVENTION ACTIVITIES

Two examples of how to embed this goal and the associated objectives within activities are presented next. For a list of intervention activities that address goals/objectives across areas, see Appendix A.

Basketball

Children can play basketball with a child-size hoop (e.g., a trash can, laundry basket) and child-size "basketballs" (e.g., red rubber balls, plastic beach balls). This activity provides opportunities for the children to practice bouncing, catching, and throwing balls. Rules are modified depending on the skill level of the children participating; other modifications may include special equipment to ensure participation and the optimal combination of physical assistance and verbal cues. It is important to emphasize developmentally appropriate motor skill acquisition, rather than winning, when children participate in sports activities.

Example: The interventionist and Alice have designed a "breakaway" basketball play. When Alice's team has the ball, she propels her wheelchair as fast as she can to the basket. Her teammates practice bouncing, throwing, and catching the ball down the court. When Alice is in position, her friends pass her the ball and Alice shoots. (GM B:2.2, 2.4, adapted)

One Fly Up

This game is played with small groups of children in a field or in a gym. One child becomes the "thrower." The other children are assisted in finding their own special spot away from each other and a few feet from the thrower. The interventionist selects a ball of appropriate size and weight for the gross motor skill level of the group. The "thrower" throws the ball. The "catchers" cannot move their feet, and whoever catches the ball gets to be the "thrower." The interventionist should make sure that the children are facing the "thrower" and have their hands ready to catch the ball. Children will require different combinations of physical assistance and verbal cues to catch and throw the ball.

Example: The interventionist selects a ball of medium size and weight that makes a sound when it moves. She reminds the "thrower" to signal the "catcher" by saying, "Ready, Eric, hold your arms out to catch," before throwing the ball. The sound of the ball approaching and the verbal cues give everyone, including Eric, who has a visual impairment, a greater chance to successfully catch the ball and become the "thrower." (GM B:2.2)

GOAL 3   Skips

Objective 3.1   Hops

CONCURRENT GOALS

Cog A:2   Demonstrates understanding of qualitative and quantitative concepts
Cog A:3   Demonstrates understanding of spatial and temporal relations concepts
Cog C:1   Follows directions of three or more related steps that are not routinely given
Cog F   Play (all goals)
SC B:1   Uses verbs
SC B:5   Uses descriptive words
Soc A:2   Initiates cooperative activity
Soc B   Participation (all goals)

DAILY ROUTINES

Daily routines that provide opportunities for children to practice hopping and skipping include the following:

• Indoor and outdoor playtimes

• Transitions (moving from one activity or place to another)

Close supervision ensures safety during gross motor activities.

Example: Manuel and his family have been playing tag in the park. The game has been modified to allow Manuel and his brothers and sisters to practice jumping, hopping, running, and skipping. The person who is "it" calls out the gross motor skill. When Manuel's father is "it," he points to a child skipping in the park and says, "Look at that boy skipping, Manuel. Do you want to try?" Manuel's father allows time out from the tag game for the whole family to practice skipping. After observing Manuel and his brothers and sisters skipping, Manuel's father continues the tag game with skipping as the targeted gross motor skill. (GM B:3)

ENVIRONMENTAL ARRANGEMENTS

- Arrange the classroom into activity areas, including a gross motor area. Use a safe, open space where children have space to hop and skip and an outdoor play area. Sometimes long hallways free of obstacles provide the space to practice hopping and skipping.

   Example: During recess, the interventionist introduces skipping to a group of interested children. Standing in front of the group and facing away from the children, the interventionist models the action of skipping and calls out, "Step hop, step hop," to assist the children in development of the appropriate timing and movement sequence for skipping. Children practice skipping by following the leader (the interventionist). After a rest, children take turns leading the skipping activity. (GM B:3)

- Environmental arrangements should allow children to successfully participate in hopping and skipping activities at their present skill level while promoting higher levels of mastery and independence in games involving hopping and skipping.

INTERVENTION ACTIVITIES

Two examples of how to embed this goal and the associated objective within activities are presented next. For a list of intervention activities that address goals/objectives across areas, see Appendix A.

Simon Says

The interventionist (or a child) is "Simon" and leads the children in movement activities. Simon directs and models a specific gross motor skill and direction of movement, such as "Simon says hop forward." Children imitate the leader's movement and follow the designated direction. The interventionist might take one or more turns being Simon to offer the children an equal opportunity to participate in a variety of movement experiences.

Skip, Skip, Skip, to My Lou

Children skip or dance during group circle time while singing the song "Skip, Skip, Skip, to My Lou."

> Skip, skip, skip, to my Lou,
> Skip, skip, skip, to my Lou,
> Skip, skip, skip, to my Lou,
> Skip to my Lou, my darlin'.

GOAL 4   Rides and steers two-wheel bicycle

Objective 4.1   Pedals and steers two-wheel bicycle with training wheels

CONCURRENT GOALS

Cog C:1   Follows directions of three or more related steps that are not routinely given
SC B:1   Uses verbs
SC B:5   Uses descriptive words
Soc A:2   Initiates cooperative activity
Soc B   Participation (all goals)

DAILY ROUTINES

Routine activities that provide opportunities for children to practice riding and steering a two-wheel bicycle include outdoor playtimes. Close adult supervision and use of a child's bicycle helmet ensure a safe biking experience.

   Example: Latifa's mother and Joey's mother bring their children's bikes to the park so the children can practice riding their two-wheel bicycles with training wheels. (GM B:4.1)

ENVIRONMENTAL ARRANGEMENTS

• Include a range of bicycle-riding equipment to create opportunities for children to practice at their existing level of bicycle-riding ability. Provide small and large tricycles for children learning bike skills, and introduce obstacles (e.g., cones, chairs, blocks) as children become adept at pedaling and steering. Two-wheel bikes with and without training wheels will challenge children to develop more advanced skills. Arrange play areas to include a large open space with a hard surface where children can be adequately supervised.

- A qualified motor specialist can assist in recommendations for tricycle and bicycle adaptations. Tricycles and bicycles may be modified with a safety belt, an addition to the back of the seat, or both to provide increased support of a child's trunk; adaptations to the pedals offer assistance with foot position while pedaling. Modifications to the pedaling system create an opportunity for children to use a variety of arm and leg patterns to pedal, steer, and turn.

INTERVENTION ACTIVITIES

Two examples of how to embed this goal and the associated objective within activities are presented next. For a list of intervention activities that address goals/objectives across areas, see Appendix A.

Trains

Children line up with different vehicles (e.g., bikes, tricycles, wagons) and form a "train." Children take turns wearing a hat and pretending to be the train engineer. The engineer leads the group and blows the horn.

Police Officers

Children ride around on their bicycles pretending to be police officers. This can be planned as an outdoor dramatic play activity, using an outdoor climbing structure or a large cardboard box as a police station. Children can use blue shirts for uniforms, make "tickets" and "badges" from paper, and label different outdoor bikes and tricycles with the words "police car." Opportunities to ride bicycles occur as children ride around handing out "tickets" or helping adults or peers in trouble.

Example: The interventionist selects Latifa, Joey, and Maria to be the police officers. Joey's police car is a two-wheel bicycle with training wheels. Latifa feels safer patrolling the streets on a tricycle. Maria's adapted tricycle has a seat belt and an additional back support to assist her with balanced sitting while she concentrates on pedaling and steering with her arms. Eric travels downtown in his wagon, and Manuel offers to pull the wagon. Latifa notices them traveling too quickly and gives them a ticket for speeding. Eric receives a warning for not wearing a seat belt in the wagon. (GM B:4, 4.1, adapted)

Gross Motor

AEPS™

Adaptive Area
Three to Six Years

Adaptive

Newborns are almost totally dependent on their caregivers to provide them with necessary nutrition, warmth, safety, and emotional support. For several months following birth, infants are dependent on caregivers to be fed, clothed, and kept clean. Gradually, as infants mature and develop motor skills, they begin to exercise partial control over these activities. Preschoolers are typically able to conduct many activities of daily living independently. The Adaptive Area is focused on selected daily living skills, including mealtime, personal hygiene, and dressing and undressing. The ability to independently meet personal needs contributes to children's positive self-image and fosters autonomy.

Initially, caregivers spend considerable time feeding, changing, and protecting their infants from harm. Although infants are dependent on adults, they are competent in a number of ways that help ensure their survival. At birth, infants are able to eat, eliminate body waste, and regulate their body temperature, which is subject to frequent variation. Newborn infants exhibit reflexive behaviors when they orient to a food source, close their lips around a nipple, suck, and swallow. Some of these early reflexes remain, but others disappear as higher brain functioning and learning provide the 3- to 4-month-old infant with new responses needed for interaction with the environment.

Through the continuing interaction between infants and environments, along with neurological maturation, fine and gross motor skills develop. As infants become familiar with caregiving routines, they begin to cooperate, to anticipate, and to perform actions independently; for example, a child may pull an arm out of a sleeve during undressing or open his or her mouth on seeing a spoon full of food. The caregiver should maintain a balance between encouraging the development of new skills and still providing assistance as necessary. With each developing skill, caregivers should reduce the amount of assistance yet still provide enough support for children to successfully complete tasks. Children should always be encouraged to move toward independent performance of an activity, even when it initially takes the child longer to complete the activity without assistance.

During the preschool years, mealtime, personal hygiene, and dressing skills are refined as children's motor, cognitive, and social skills develop. Many preschool children are able to meet most of their personal needs but may need practice with more intricate aspects of a task (e.g., buttoning buttons). Children learn to eat and drink a variety of foods, handle utensils, and prepare simple foods for mealtimes. Most children learn to use the toilet during the preschool years.

Adaptive

In the area of dressing, children initially learn to pull off clothing, particularly shoes, socks, and hats. This requires less refinement of motor skills than putting on the same items. Next, children learn to pull off and wiggle out of jackets, sweaters, shirts, and pants. Caregivers often find that toddlers resist putting on clothes but are gleeful in removing them from their bodies. As preschoolers gain independence, most develop an intense desire to dress themselves, which may be frustrating for them and their caregivers. With practice, most preschoolers are able to dress and undress independently.

Children's ability to perform adaptive skills is dependent on other areas of their development. Adaptive skills generally have motor, social, and cognitive components. A goal that requires a child to select appropriate clothing and dress independently at designated times requires the gross and fine motor skills necessary to have access to the clothing and manipulate fasteners. In addition, this goal requires the cognitive and social skills necessary to discriminate which clothing will meet the child's physical needs in a socially appropriate way (e.g., choosing a sweater to wear when it is cold outside). The goals in the Adaptive Area require children to coordinate a variety of skills and information. Consequently, these goals address multiple targets, are functional, and can usually be addressed in routine activities throughout the day.

The Adaptive Area is composed of three strands. Strand A (Mealtime) focuses on the child's ability to eat and drink a variety of foods using utensils and prepare and serve food. Strand B (Personal Hygiene) focuses on the child's ability to conduct toileting functions and to wash and groom him- or herself. Strand C (Dressing and Undressing) examines the child's ability to fasten and unfasten fasteners on garments, as well as the ability to select appropriate clothing and dress independently. Earlier eating, toileting, and dressing skills are targeted in the AEPS Curriculum for Birth to Three Years.

The Adaptive Area curriculum is divided into four sections: 1) Intervention Considerations, 2) Suggested Activities, 3) Using Activity-Based Intervention, and 4) Area Goals. Intervention Considerations addresses important factors that an interventionist may wish to consider prior to and when working with children at risk for or who have disabilities. Suggested Activities provides a selected list of activities that may be particularly helpful when working on adaptive skills. This section also provides suggestions for additional materials that increase the opportunities for children to practice targeted adaptive skills. The third section provides an illustration of how to target IFSP/IEP goals in the Adaptive Area using an activity-based intervention approach. The final section, Area Goals, discusses suggestions for Concurrent Goals, Daily Routines, Environmental Arrangements, and Intervention Activities in the home and classroom for each goal and associated objectives identified in the Adaptive Area of the AEPS Test for Three to Six Years.

INTERVENTION CONSIDERATIONS

General considerations when working on adaptive goals are discussed next.

- Adaptive skills should be practiced throughout children's daily routines in a variety of settings, with a variety of people. Routines such as dressing and undressing, mealtimes, and children's unstructured playtimes are natural contexts for children to learn adaptive skills.

- An occupational or physical therapist can help assess children to determine if an adaptive goal is functional or realistically attainable for children with motor impairments. Children with motor impairments may demonstrate a variety of feeding difficulties that require intervention from a qualified specialist. Children may need additional support to improve their oral-motor control and their self-feeding skills. In addition to providing information concerning the modification of activities and utilization of adaptive equipment, a therapist may recommend therapy to help normalize a child's muscle tone.

- Children with motor skill impairments may require compensatory strategies such as modification to the environment or adaptive equipment to increase their independence. Adaptive equipment such as hand splints, non-slip surfaces, shortened or built-up utensils, Velcro fasteners, and handrails for toilets and sinks can provide the support necessary for children to participate in a variety of activities. Consult a qualified specialist to obtain information concerning special equipment and adaptations to the environment, activities, or materials.

- Positioning is an important consideration for children with motor impairments. To participate in activities such as mealtimes, the child needs to be upright and well supported. Adaptive equipment such as a wheelchair, however, often places the child higher than other children, and lap trays create a physical barrier between a child and peers. Whenever possible, particularly during activities that are social events, such as mealtimes, children should be seated in regular chairs or adapted chairs (if extra support is required).

- Plan adequate time for children to complete tasks. During busy schedules at home and school, adults often find themselves rushing children through mealtime, dressing, and toileting routines to keep on schedule. When possible, allot the necessary time for children to complete tasks independently or with minimal assistance. Creating sufficient opportunities to practice is necessary if a child is to achieve independence in personal care.

- Children with visual impairments may benefit from adaptations to materials during activities. The use of brightly colored, high-contrasting materials may assist a child with limited vision. In addition, keeping materials (e.g., clothing, washcloths, soap, cups, plates, utensils, food items) in predictable locations and using modified materials (e.g., bowls and plates with a lip) help the child acquire independence.

SUGGESTED ACTIVITIES

Art activities provide opportunities for adaptive skills such as dressing and undressing, washing, and grooming when children put on and take off smocks and wash up after the activity. The following list of activities and materials may be particularly helpful for eliciting skills within the Adaptive Area. For a complete list of intervention activities, see Appendix A.

Dramatic Play Activities

Children can practice mealtime, personal hygiene, and dressing and undressing skills as they act out dramatic play scenarios. House play is particularly helpful for embedding adaptive goals.

Other Activities

- Cooking
- Exploratory activities
- Messy art activities
- Painting
- Restaurant
- Shoe store
- Teddy bear picnic
- Washing babies

USING ACTIVITY-BASED INTERVENTION

An illustration of how an interventionist can incorporate activity-based strategies to enhance the development of a child's adaptive skills is provided next. The child's targeted IFSP/IEP objective is to use any functional means to fasten buttons/snaps/Velcro fasteners when dressing.

- The interventionist observes Maria playing in the dramatic play center. She *follows the child's lead* by joining Maria in her play and encourages peers to join. The interventionist *expands on the child's initiation* by opening up the chest with dress-up clothing such as aprons with snaps, brightly colored shirts with oversize buttons, and shoes and slippers with Velcro fasteners.

- The interventionist *models* how to fasten buttons by putting on a shirt, using *self-talk* to comment on her own actions (e.g., "I'm going to put on this pretty shirt. First I'll line up the buttons and holes . . .").

- The interventionist draws Maria's attention to peers who are displaying more advanced skills (e.g., "Look at Latifa! She's putting on an apron and snapping the snaps"). The classroom consists of a *heterogeneous* group of children, providing opportunities for Maria to learn new skills by observing peer models or to enhance skills by assisting children with different strengths.

- The interventionist uses additional strategies to encourage Maria to practice targeted goals. She comments, "Don't forget to wear an apron," when Maria is playing at the stove, providing an opportunity for her to practice fastening the snaps or ties on the apron.

- The interventionist provides the *least amount of assistance* necessary for Maria to fasten fasteners while playing in the dramatic play center.

AREA GOALS

This section provides suggestions for concurrent goals, daily routines, environmental arrangements, and intervention activities for all of the adaptive goals listed in the AEPS Test for Three to Six Years. If an objective has been targeted, then the interventionist can turn to the corresponding goal and determine which suggestions are relevant to facilitate that objective. A standard format is used for each goal: 1) Strand, 2) Goal, 3) Objective(s), 4) Concurrent Goals, 5) Daily Routines, 6) Environmental Arrangements, and 7) Intervention Activities. Concurrent Goals list AEPS goals from other developmental areas that can often be addressed at the same time that the child works on the target goal or associated objectives. Daily Routines present a list of routine activities that provide opportunities to practice targeted skills. Environmental Arrangements should be considered when designing children's programs around child-initiated, routine, and planned intervention activities. Finally, the Intervention Activities offer examples of how to embed targeted goals within the context of intervention activities. Additional information on daily routines, environmental arrangements, and planned intervention activities is provided in Chapter 3.

Adaptive

Mealtime

GOAL 1   Eats and drinks a variety of foods using appropriate utensils with little or no spilling

Objective 1.1   Puts proper amount of food in mouth, chews with mouth closed, swallows before taking another bite

Objective 1.2   Takes in proper amount of liquid and returns cup to surface

Objective 1.3   Eats a variety of food textures

Objective 1.4   Selects and eats a variety of food types

Objective 1.5   Eats with utensils

CONCURRENT GOALS

FM A:1   Uses two hands to manipulate objects, each hand performing different movements
Cog A   Concepts (all goals)
Cog B:1   Groups objects, people, or events on the basis of specified criteria
SC A   Social-communicative interactions (all goals)
SC B   Production of words, phrases, and sentences (all goals)
Soc B   Participation (all goals)
Soc C   Interaction with environment (all goals)
Soc D:1   Communicates personal likes and dislikes

DAILY ROUTINES

Routine events that provide opportunities for children to eat and drink a variety of foods using appropriate utensils include the following:

- Mealtime or snack time

- Unstructured playtime

- Visit to restaurant

Example: During mealtime and snack time, a variety of foods with different textures are provided. The interventionist encourages children to try new foods and to eat using the appropriate utensils. (Adap A:1.3, 1.4, 1.5)

ENVIRONMENTAL ARRANGEMENTS

- Arrange the classroom into activity areas including a dramatic play center. Although a dramatic play center usually uses pretend foods, as a special treat the interventionist may want to provide real foods for the children to serve and eat. Include forks, spoons, cups, and bowls to provide opportunities for children to practice handling utensils, with or without real food.

- Whenever possible, mealtimes and snack times should occur at a consistent time and location with consistent expectations for children. Provide child-size tables and chairs, cups, and food that is in small pieces or easily cut up by a child.

- Provide foods from the different food groups (e.g., dairy, meat, fruit, vegetables, breads) as well as foods with different textures. A range of foods helps children learn to use a variety of utensils.

- To encourage children to practice eating with a fork and spoon, offer foods during mealtime and snack time that can be scooped (e.g., applesauce, yogurt, pudding, ice cream) or speared (e.g., meat, vegetables, chunks of fruit). Provide utensils that can be easily managed by children.

- Positioning is an important consideration for children with motor impairments. Make sure that the child is upright and well supported during mealtimes.

- Adaptations to utensils may be necessary for children with special needs to perform this skill independently; for example, children with motor impairments may benefit from the use of nonslip surfaces to stabilize bowls or plates or from the use of utensils with built-up or shortened grips. Adapted utensils are available commercially or can be fabricated. Contact a qualified specialist for adaptation needs of children with sensory and/or motor impairments.

Example: During snack time, Maria uses an adapted spoon and places the elbow and forearm of her free hand on the table to provide balance and support to her upper body. Her interventionist sits close by and uses verbal cues and the least level of assistance necessary for Maria to successfully eat her pudding. Maria grasps her spoon, scoops pudding, brings it to her mouth, removes the food from the spoon with her mouth, and returns the spoon to the bowl. The interventionist fades assistance as soon as possible. (Adap A:1.5)

INTERVENTION ACTIVITIES

Two examples of how to embed this goal and the associated objectives within activities are presented next. For a list of intervention activities that address goals/objectives across areas, see Appendix A.

Adaptive

Super Soup

A nutritious soup can be made for lunch or snack. Children can actively participate by washing and cutting (with adult assistance) the vegetables and then combining the vegetables, broth, and spices. The five senses are used throughout the process by looking, touching, smelling, listening (e.g., to the snap of celery being broken), and tasting the ingredients. Opportunities can be provided for children to sample foods of different textures (e.g., cooked meat, raw and cooked vegetables, raw and cooked macaroni, vegetable broth). The soup can be served with dairy products and fruits to encourage children to select and eat foods from different food groups. The interventionist should observe children's ability to use utensils when eating soup or when scooping or spearing other food items.

Fruit Salad

Children can prepare fruit salad for a snack. The interventionist can provide fruits with different textures (e.g., bananas, pineapple, raisins, oranges, apples) and let the children take an active part in preparing the food by washing, peeling, slicing, and scooping foods into bowls. Yogurt, granola, ground nuts, or wheat germ can be added to the salad if desired. The interventionist should encourage children to sample foods of different textures while preparing the snack and offer foods from the different food groups during snack. Children use utensils while preparing foods (e.g., spoons to scoop yogurt, forks to spear fruits) and while eating their snack.

Example: The interventionist allows Eric, who has a visual impairment, time to explore his food and utensils through touch. The interventionist provides a deep bowl with a lip that Eric and the other children can use to practice scooping. When it is time to eat the fruit salad, the interventionist provides brightly colored utensils that contrast with the placemat, helping Eric to locate his spoon. The interventionist also provides verbal feedback as to where utensils and food are located and places them in predictable locations (e.g., the spoon on the right-hand side of his plate). (Adap A:1.5, adapted)

GOAL 2   Prepares and serves food

Objective 2.1   Prepares food for eating

Objective 2.2   Uses knife to spread food

Objective 2.3   Pours liquid into a variety of containers

Objective 2.4   Serves food with utensil

CONCURRENT GOALS

FM A:1   Uses two hands to manipulate objects, each hand performing different movements
SC A   Social-communicative interactions (all goals)
SC B   Production of words, phrases, and sentences (all goals)
Soc A:2   Initiates cooperative activity
Soc C   Interaction with environment (all goals)
Soc D:1   Communicates personal likes and dislikes

DAILY ROUTINES

Routine events that provide opportunities for children to prepare and serve food include the following:

- Mealtime or snack time

- Unstructured playtime

Example: During snack, Latifa peels a banana, spreads peanut butter on bread, and pours juice from a small pitcher into her cup. Latifa's mother sits by her, providing verbal cues and the least level of physical assistance necessary for Latifa to prepare her snack. (Adap A:2)

ENVIRONMENTAL ARRANGEMENTS

- Arrange the classroom into activity areas that include a dramatic play center. Although a dramatic play center usually uses pretend foods, as a special treat the interventionist might provide real foods for the children to serve and eat. Include forks, spoons, knives, pitchers, and cups for children to practice preparing and serving food, with or without real food.

- Present materials during snack or mealtimes that provide opportunities for children to practice the following:

  - Preparing food (e.g., wrapped crackers, foods in containers, bananas with peel, hardboiled eggs with shell, cheese with plastic wrappers)

  - Using a knife to spread (e.g., dull knives to spread peanut butter on bread, cream cheese on crackers, jam on toast)

  - Pouring liquid into containers (e.g., juice from a child-size pitcher into a cup, milk from a small bottle into a cup)

  - Serving food with a utensil (e.g., scooping applesauce or yogurt into a bowl, spearing melon with a fork and transferring to a bowl or plate)

Adaptive

Example: Alice uses a knife to practice spreading cream cheese on a cracker. The interventionist uses verbal cues and the least level of physical assistance to prompt Alice to stabilize the cracker with her left hand while she spreads the cheese with her right hand. (Adap A:2.2)

- Positioning is an important consideration for children with motor impairments. Make sure that the child is upright and well supported during mealtimes.

- Adaptations to materials may be necessary for children with special needs. Contact a qualified specialist for adaptation needs of children with sensory and/or motor impairments. Children with motor impairments may benefit from the use of nonslip surfaces to stabilize materials (e.g., bowls, plates) or by using utensils with built-up or shortened grips.

INTERVENTION ACTIVITIES

Two examples of how to embed this goal and the associated objectives within activities are presented next. For a list of intervention activities that address goals/objectives across areas, see Appendix A.

Animal Cookies

Children make cookies from a sugar cookie dough and animal cookie cutters. They can actively participate in making the cookies by opening containers, transferring ingredients from containers to the bowl, pouring liquids into the bowl, and stirring ingredients together. When the cookies have been baked, children can use dull knives to spread frosting or jam on them. Close supervision during cooking activities will ensure safety.

Fruit Animals

Children practice preparing and serving food while making animals from fruit. The interventionist can provide canned fruit such as pineapple slices, maraschino cherries, and pear halves, as well as sliced bananas, oranges, raisins, grapes, and apricot halves. Children create animals on paper plates using the pineapple rings or pear halves as faces, cherries or raisins for eyes, wedges of oranges or apricot halves for ears, and bananas for mouths. Children practice preparing food as they peel bananas, remove raisins from boxes, and spoon or spear fruit while transferring it from bowls to paper plates. Children eat their creations during snack time.

STRAND B

Personal Hygiene

GOAL 1   Carries out all toileting functions

Objective 1.1   **Uses toilet paper, flushes toilet, washes hands after using toilet**

Objective 1.2   **Uses toilet**

Objective 1.3   **Indicates need to use toilet**

CONCURRENT GOALS

FM A:1   Uses two hands to manipulate objects, each hand performing different movements

Adap A:1   Eats and drinks a variety of foods using appropriate utensils with little or no spilling

Adap C:3   Fastens fasteners on garments

SC A   Social-communicative interactions (all goals)

SC B   Production of words, phrases, and sentences (all goals)

Soc C   Interaction with environment (all goals)

DAILY ROUTINES

When children are first learning to use the toilet, it may be useful to incorporate consistent and frequent visits to the bathroom into their daily routine. It is important not to pressure children about toilet training and to avoid punishing them for noncompliance. Caregivers and interventionists should realize that toilet training is a gradual process, so even if a child is toilet trained, accidents may occur if a child is busy, tired, or upset. With some conditions, such as spina bifida, toilet training may not be an appropriate goal because of the child's lack of bowel and bladder sensation and control. A developmental psychologist may provide useful suggestions to promote the emotional and psychological well-being of older children working on toileting goals.

ENVIRONMENTAL ARRANGEMENTS

• Children require access to a toilet, toilet paper, a sink, hand soap, paper towels, and a garbage can to independently carry out toileting functions.

• Clothing that is easily removed by the child (e.g., skirts, dresses, pants that have a stretch waist, fasteners that are easily engaged) may facilitate a child's independently carrying out toileting functions. As the child increases independence in toileting, this activity can provide opportunities to embed goals addressing manipulation of more complex fasteners.

- Children who use augmentative communication systems should be provided with a means to communicate their need to use the toilet (e.g., a sign for toilet, a picture of a toilet on the communication board).

- Some children require adaptations to successfully reach this goal. The following considerations may influence the child's ability to independently carry out toileting functions: the size/model of the toilet (child-size toilets, toilets that flush by hand or foot levers, potty chairs), handrails on the side of the toilet, the location/type of toilet paper roll dispenser, the size/model of the sink (a step stool, handrails, or both may be necessary for the child to have access to the sink), and the type of dispensers provided for soap and paper towels. Children with visual impairments will benefit from consistent and predictable location of all necessary materials. Consult qualified specialists for programming suggestions.

INTERVENTION ACTIVITIES

Although planned activities are not appropriate for this goal, subskills such as washing hands or dressing can be targeted within activities (e.g., washing hands before cooking or after messy play, changing clothes during pretend play). For a list of intervention activities that address goals/objectives across areas, see Appendix A.

GOAL 2　Washes and grooms self

Objective 2.1　**Uses tissue to clean nose**

Objective 2.2　**Brushes teeth**

Objective 2.3　**Bathes and dries self**

Objective 2.4　**Brushes or combs hair**

Objective 2.5　**Washes and dries face**

CONCURRENT GOALS

FM A:1　Uses two hands to manipulate objects, each hand performing different movements

Adap C:3　Fastens fasteners on garments

SC A　Social-communicative interactions (all goals)

SC B　Production of words, phrases, and sentences (all goals)

Soc C:1　Meets physical needs in socially appropriate ways

Soc D:1　Communicates personal likes and dislikes

DAILY ROUTINES

Routine events that provide opportunities for children to wash and groom themselves include the following:

- Bath time
- Bedtime
- Dressing
- Mealtime or snack time
- Transition times
- Unstructured playtime

Example: Eric, who has a visual impairment, has a goal to bathe and dry himself. Eric's mother keeps towels, soap, and shampoo in consistent locations in the bathroom. She guides Eric's hand and talks to him, familiarizing him with the hot and cold knobs and how to test the water before getting into the tub. (Adap B:2.3)

Example: Children practice brushing their teeth after snack at school. (Adap B:2.2)

ENVIRONMENTAL ARRANGEMENTS

- Present materials in the home and classroom environments that provide opportunities for children to independently wash and groom themselves; for example, provide a child-size sink (or a step stool) in the bathroom and a mirror at the child's height. Children should have access to their own toothbrushes, brushes or combs, washcloths or paper towels, and tissues. To prevent the spread of infection, children should not share any items they use while washing and grooming themselves. Consult qualified specialists for adaptations to materials for children with disabilities.

INTERVENTION ACTIVITIES

Two examples of how to embed this goal and the associated objectives within activities are presented next. For a list of intervention activities that address goals/objectives across areas, see Appendix A.

Trip to the Police Station

Children may enjoy going on a trip to the local police station. Reading a story or discussing police officers prior to the trip will help prepare children for the visit. Children can practice grooming skills by getting ready for the trip, washing their faces, and brushing their hair (mirrors should be provided). Before leaving, let children eat a small snack so they do not get hungry on the trip. Children may brush their teeth afterward. The interventionist should carry tissues and provide the least amount of assistance necessary for children to clean their noses when necessary.

The Fire Station

The children can set up a fire station in the dramatic play center. The station can reflect the daily life of firefighters and where they sleep, eat, and work. The interventionist may want to facilitate a discussion on how community helpers are careful about their grooming and try to stay neat and clean when not fighting fires. Provide a mirror in the dress-up area, uniforms (e.g., white shirts, fire hats, yellow raincoats, boots), individual children's brushes or combs, tissues, and dining materials (e.g., utensils, cups, pitchers, napkins, pretend food, small table and chairs).

Dressing and Undressing

GOAL 1   Unfastens fasteners on garments

Objective 1.1   Unfastens buttons/snaps/Velcro fasteners on garments

Objective 1.2   Unties string-type fastener

Objective 1.3   Unzips zipper

CONCURRENT GOALS

FM A:1   Uses two hands to manipulate objects, each hand performing different movements
Adap C:3   Fastens fasteners on garments
Cog F:1   Engages in cooperative, imaginary play
Soc C:1   Meets physical needs in socially appropriate ways

DAILY ROUTINES

Routine events that provide opportunities for children to manipulate different types of fasteners include the following:

- Arrival/departure

- Bath time

- Bedtime

- Dressing/undressing

- Unstructured playtime

Example: Timmy arrives at school and walks over to the children playing with playdough. His interventionist leads him back to his cubby and says (signing), TAKE OFF YOUR COAT, TIMMY. THEN YOU CAN GO PLAY WITH THE PLAY-DOUGH. When Timmy does not respond, the interventionist points to the zipper and says, FIRST YOU NEED TO UNZIP YOUR COAT. Timmy unzips his coat, and the interventionist provides verbal cues and the least amount of physical assistance for Timmy to detach the zipper. (Adap C:1.3)

ENVIRONMENTAL ARRANGEMENTS

- Present a large selection of materials that provide opportunities for the children to manipulate different types of fasteners (e.g., dolls with doll clothes that have different types of fasteners such as snaps, laces, zippers, buttons, or Velcro fasteners; dress-up clothes with different types of fasteners). Arrange the classroom into activity areas that include a dramatic play center, and arrange materials so children have easy access. Dress-up clothes should include clothing with buttons, snaps, Velcro fasteners, string-type fasteners, and zippers.

- Consultation with a qualified motor specialist may assist the interventionist in designing activities to include children with sensory and/or motor impairments. Adaptations for manipulating fasteners to maximize a child's potential for functional independence should include a discussion of position (standing or sitting), sequence of activity, type of fastener or modification of clothes, assistive devices for the arm or hand, and the optimal combination of modeling, physical assistance, and verbal cues.

- Children who have limitations in fine motor control may require the assistance of peers, family members, or classroom personnel. Typically, children with motor impairments require significantly greater amounts of time to complete dressing activities. Interventionists and caregivers should schedule adequate time to manipulate fasteners during dressing and play activities rather than simply offering assistance to save time.

INTERVENTION ACTIVITIES

Two examples of how to embed this goal and the associated objectives within activities are presented next. For a list of intervention activities that address goals/objectives across areas, see Appendix A.

Doctor's Office

Children can set up a doctor's office in the dramatic play center of the classroom. The interventionist can provide props such as bandages, pretend stethoscopes, cots for the patients, a wagon for an ambulance, and uniforms. Opportunities can be provided for children to unfasten fasteners on garments as they engage in this dramatic play. Patients can untie their shoes or unzip their coats before lying on the cot, and doctors and nurses can take off their uniforms, unfastening buttons/snaps/Velcro fasteners after "surgery" (smocks make excellent "scrubs").

Body Tracing

Children paint an outline of their body. This activity can begin by having children put on smocks with fasteners. The outline is created by having a child lie down on a piece of butcher paper while either the interventionist or another child outlines the child's body with a marker or chalk. The outline is taped to the wall, and the children are allowed to paint in their facial features, clothing, and background decorations. The interventionist should prepare the paint before the activity, making sure it is quite thick to keep it from dripping down the wall. Children practice unfastening fasteners when they complete the activity and take off their smocks.

GOAL 2   Selects appropriate clothing and dresses self at designated times

Objective 2.1   Puts on long pants

Objective 2.2   Puts on front-opening garment

Objective 2.3   Puts on pullover garment

Objective 2.4   Puts on shoes

Objective 2.5   Puts on underpants, shorts, or skirt

Adaptive

CONCURRENT GOALS

FM A:1	Uses two hands to manipulate objects, each hand performing different movements
Adap C:3	Fastens fasteners on garments
Cog A:1	Demonstrates understanding of color, shape, and size concepts
Cog A:3	Demonstrates understanding of spatial and temporal relations concepts
Cog C:1	Follows directions of three or more related steps that are not routinely given
Soc C:1	Meets physical needs in socially appropriate ways
Soc D:1	Communicates personal likes and dislikes

DAILY ROUTINES

Routine events that provide opportunities for children to practice selecting appropriate clothing and dressing themselves at designated times include the following:

- Bedtime

- Departure

- Dressing

- Unstructured playtime

Example: Timmy can put on his shoes without assistance but sometimes puts his shoes on the wrong feet. Timmy's interventionist puts a small red sticker on the inside edge of each sneaker, near the toes. Timmy puts on his shoes before going outside to play, and if necessary, the interventionist reminds Timmy to make the two stickers touch. She also draws Timmy's attention to the way the shoes curve at the toes and as soon as possible fades the use of the stickers. (Adap C:2.4)

ENVIRONMENTAL ARRANGEMENTS

- Children should be able to independently retrieve clothing in the home and school environment. Cubbies or lockers provide a location for personal belongings at school, and child-size dressers or low shelves provide opportunities for children to select clothing and dress themselves at home.

- Offer clothing that is simple to put on when children are first learning to dress (e.g., pants with an elastic waist, oversize tops). As children become more competent in dressing, other types of clothing can be introduced.

- Include a dramatic play center in the classroom and provide interesting clothing or uniforms that allow opportunities for children to practice skills (e.g., sweatshirts, post office shirt and pants, ruffled blouses, fancy shoes).

Example: Joey sits in a chair, and his interventionist hands him (in the correct position) a pair of "police" pants. She draws his attention to the label in the back of the pants. Joey sits in the chair until the pants are at his knees and then stands to pull them up all the way. The interventionist helps him fasten the button. (Adap C:2.1)

- Consultation with a qualified motor specialist may assist the interventionist in designing activities to include children with sensory and/or motor impairments. Adaptations for selecting clothing and dressing self to maximize a child's potential for functional independence should include a discussion of position (standing or sitting); sequence of activity; type of fastener or modification of clothes; assistive devices for the arm or hand; and the optimal combination of modeling, physical assistance, and verbal or visual cues. Some children may need additional adaptations to the environment to make clothing accessible (e.g., lowering a coat hook for a child who uses a wheelchair, returning clothing to predictable locations for a child with a visual impairment).

- Children who have limitations in fine motor control may require the assistance of peers, family members, or classroom personnel. Typically, children with motor impairments require significantly greater amounts of time to complete dressing activities. Interventionists and caregivers should schedule adequate time during dressing and play activities rather than simply offer assistance to save time.

INTERVENTION ACTIVITIES

Two examples of how to embed this goal and the associated objectives within activities are presented next. For a list of intervention activities that address goals/objectives across areas, see Appendix A.

Forest Ranger

The interventionist reads a book to children or facilitates a discussion on what forest rangers do at work (e.g., teach people about the environment, maintain campgrounds, watch for forest fires). A campground is set up in the dramatic play center with props such as a tent (tarps or sheets draped over chairs), a campfire (stones that form a ring with sticks for wood), cooking pots and utensils, backpacks, water bottles and canteens, old blankets or bed rolls, and pictures of the forest and animals. Materials should be included that allow the children to select clothing and dress themselves, such as flannel shirts, raincoats, pants, rain or snow boots, and a forest ranger's uniform (e.g., green dress shirt, green pants, ranger hat, belt, boots).

Let's Go Fishing!

Children go fishing and bring the fish to the "market" to sell. Fishing poles can be created by attaching one end of a string to the end of a dowel and attaching a magnet to the other end of the string for the "hook." The children make fish from construction paper, with a paper clip attached to each fish so that it will be attracted to the magnet. Children practice selecting clothing (e.g., overalls, boots, raincoats, sweaters, coats, socks, smocks, shirts, skirts) and dressing themselves while they pretend to be fisherpeople, market workers, or shoppers. Set up a marketplace with small tables, cash registers, pretend money, and grocery sacks.

Adaptive

GOAL 3   Fastens fasteners on garments

Objective 3.1   Ties string-type fastener

Objective 3.2   Fastens buttons/snaps/Velcro fasteners

Objective 3.3   Threads and zips zipper

CONCURRENT GOALS

FM A:1   Uses two hands to manipulate objects, each hand performing different movements

SC B:5   Uses descriptive words

Soc C:1   Meets physical needs in socially appropriate ways

DAILY ROUTINES

Routine events that provide opportunities for children to practice fastening fasteners on garments include the following:

- Bedtime

- Departure

- Dressing

- Unstructured playtime

Example: Eric, who has a visual impairment, gets dressed in the morning before breakfast. Eric chooses his clothes, which are kept in consistent locations but needs assistance buttoning the buttons on his shirt. His mother first guides Eric's hands to feel all of the buttons and holes, starting at the top and moving to the bottom. She then provides verbal cues and the least level of physical assistance for Eric to button his shirt. (Adap C:3, 3.2)

ENVIRONMENTAL ARRANGEMENTS

- Present a large selection of materials that provide opportunities for the child to manipulate different types of fasteners (e.g., dolls with doll clothes that have different types of fasteners such as snaps, laces, zippers, buttons, or Velcro fasteners; dress-up clothes with different types of fasteners). Arrange the classroom into activity areas with easy access that include a dramatic play center and store materials. Dress-up clothes should include clothing with buttons, snaps, Velcro fasteners, string-type fasteners, and zippers.

- Consultation with a qualified motor specialist may help the interventionist design activities to include children with sensory and/or motor impairments. Possible adaptations for manipulating fasteners to maximize a child's potential for functional independence should include a discussion of position (standing or sitting); sequence of activity; type of fastener or modification of clothes; assistive devices for the arm or hand; and the optimal combination of modeling, physical assistance, and verbal cues.

- Children who have limitations in fine motor control may require the assistance of peers, family members, or classroom personnel. Typically, children with motor impairments require significantly more time to complete dressing activities. Interventionists and caregivers should schedule adequate time to manipulate fasteners during dressing and play activities rather than simply offering assistance to save time.

INTERVENTION ACTIVITIES

Two examples of how to embed this goal and the associated objectives within activities are presented next. For a list of intervention activities that address goals/objectives across areas, see Appendix A.

Going on a Picnic

Children prepare food and invite family members to a picnic. It may be helpful to hold this event after school or on a weekend so that working family members can participate. Before inviting family members to a picnic, the children can practice holding picnics during school hours by eating their snack outside. Children can practice fastening fasteners as they get ready for the picnic, either dressing up in special clothing or putting on coats in cool weather. If the weather is warm, then children may enjoy taking off their shoes in a grassy area and can practice tying a string-type fastener when they put their shoes on.

Washing Babies

Children wash their "babies" (washable baby dolls) in tubs of water. The interventionist should provide shampoo, soap, soft brushes, washcloths, towels, and baby clothing that has different types of fasteners (e.g., snaps, buttons, Velcro fasteners, zippers). Children practice their fastening skills as they get ready (e.g., putting on smocks with fasteners) and participate in (e.g., dressing their baby dolls after their bath, fastening the dolls' shoes) this activity.

AEPS™

Cognitive Area
Three to Six Years

LIST OF AEPS TEST ITEMS

Cognitive

Cognitive

Cognition refers to thinking and learning processes used by humans to obtain desired goals, solve problems, and adapt to environmental demands. The development of cognitive abilities in children appears to result from the interaction between their genetic and physiological characteristics and their experiences. Clearly, the development of cognitive abilities is fundamentally important to the well-being of children and their success in becoming independent and functional individuals.

The Cognitive Area of this curriculum is designed to enhance and expand the reciprocal interactions between children and their social and physical environments. The activities and strategies are designed to encourage children to actively engage their environment and to capitalize on children's inherent motivation to explore and expand their repertoires. Piaget's (1970) constructivist theory of cognitive development provided the general framework to organize the series of goals and intervention activities in this area. A brief review of early cognitive development is offered before the introduction to these goals and activities.

During the early stages of the *sensorimotor period* of cognitive development described by Piaget, an infant's interactions with the environment are governed by sensory and primitive motor behaviors such as sight, sound, and touch. The infant learns by reaching, grasping, mouthing, and acting on objects and then processing the feedback received from these actions. During the entire sensorimotor period, which lasts from birth to approximately 2 years, children gradually acquire the ability to make associations; use symbols to represent objects, events, and social agents; and to manipulate these symbols mentally; for example, the development of *object permanence* during the second year is dependent on the child's ability to form and maintain mental representations or images of objects not present in the visual field. Children who master mental manipulation of symbols move into a period of cognitive development not tied to concrete and immediate experiences. Children learn to perform actions "in their head" and to anticipate outcomes before they occur.

The transition from the sensorimotor to the *preoperational period*, which generally occurs between 24 and 36 months, shows children learning to mentally represent objects and events and learning to "think" about past, current, and future activities. They learn to use symbols, beginning with those that are concrete and moving to those that are increasingly abstract; for example, a child may first learn that a toy cat represents an actual cat and then that a black and white sketch represents a cat.

Three- to five-year-old children who are in the preoperational stage come to understand that the world operates in a predictable fashion. Children learn numerous concepts that allow them to recognize invariants of objects even though the conditions of size, shape, placement, and other dimensions may change. They also recognize invariants of functions (e.g., there are several ways to retrieve an object out of reach). Language is used to exchange information, and children in the preoperational period can learn from the communication of others. Extensive dialogues are managed on topics not immediately present or that happened earlier. Grammar expands and becomes more refined. Children are able to seek feedback by using questions or restatements and are able to follow complex instructions.

Associated with the development of concepts and symbolic thinking is children's growing ability to imitate responses observed earlier and to engage in pretend play; for example, children can pretend to be someone or something else observed previously, can use objects to substitute for other objects (e.g., a block becomes a train), and can conduct pretend activities (e.g., give a doll a drink from an imaginary cup). During this period, categories of concepts are developed and understood, indicating that children are learning to organize information so that it is applicable not only to a specific entity but also to similar constellations of objects, people, and events. Children learn to appreciate

Cognitive

the differences and similarities between entities, which permits them to classify and arrange items along a number of dimensions (e.g., size, color, use). In addition, children begin to learn number, time, and spatial relations concepts.

The growth in cognitive abilities of the young child during the sensorimotor and preoperational periods is remarkable. Appreciation of and knowledge about the substantial qualitative changes in the cognitive skills of young children are necessary if interventionists and caregivers are to develop and deliver effective intervention services to children whose cognitive development is delayed or atypical. Those who would benefit from additional information on cognitive growth and development in young children are referred to Flavell, Miller, and Miller (1993) and McCormick (1990).

There are three important reasons for observing children across a range of settings and activities before drawing firm conclusions about their cognitive abilities. First, children with disabilities often have uneven repertoires so that they may perform differently as conditions vary; for example, a child may show more advanced problem-solving skills when engaged in familiar activities than when engaging in unfamiliar activities. Second, cognitive skills do not develop in isolation. Rather, early cognitive, communication, motor, and social processes appear to develop interdependently in young children, and the lack of development in one area can adversely affect development in another area; for example, acquisition of means–ends and causality concepts might be significantly delayed in children with severe motor impairments because of their reduced opportunity to physically act on the environment, not because of inherent cognitive limitations. Third, many activities and tasks require children to draw on skills from more than one behavioral area; for example, a child's ability to follow a three-step direction (e.g., clean up your toys, put on your coat, and line up at the door) requires gross and fine motor (e.g., walking and zipping), adaptive (e.g., putting on a coat), language (e.g., understanding words), and cognitive (e.g., attention and memory) skills. The child may have adequate attention and memory skills but be unable to follow the directions because of deficient language skills.

Children with disabilities often require adaptation of activities if meaningful participation is to occur. The challenge is to design activities that maximize children's independent participation but still provide ample opportunity for children to practice targeted goals/objectives. Providing alternative methods of responding, working in conjunction with specialists, and being sensitive to children's subtle cues can lead to the successful adaptation of activities so that participation and benefits are maximal for children with disabilities.

The Cognitive Area is composed of eight strands. Strand A (Concepts) involves the child's ability to follow directions, answer questions, or identify objects according to color, shape, size, qualitative, quantitative, spatial, or temporal dimensions. Strand B (Categorizing) involves the child's ability to group objects, people, or events on the basis of category, function, or physical attribute. Strand C (Sequencing) involves the child's ability to follow directions, place objects in a series according to length or size, and retell events in sequence. Strand D (Recalling Events) involves the child's ability to recall events with or without contextual cues. Strand E (Problem Solving) examines the child's ability to evaluate solutions to problems as well as reasoning skills.

Strand F (Play) involves the child's ability to engage in cooperative and imaginary play and games with rules. Strand G (Premath) involves the child's ability to count objects and identify printed numerals. Strand H (Phonological Awareness and Emergent Reading) examines the child's phonological awareness as well as the ability to sound out words, write words, and read words by sight.

The Cognitive Area curriculum is divided into four sections: 1) Intervention Considerations, 2) Suggested Activities, 3) Using Activity-Based Intervention, and 4) Area Goals. Intervention Considerations addresses important factors an interventionist may wish to consider prior to and when working with children at risk for or who have disabilities. Suggested Activities provides a selected list of activities that may be particularly helpful when working on cognitive skills. This section also provides suggestions for additional materials that will increase opportunities for children to practice targeted cognitive skills. The third section provides an illustration of how to target IFSP/IEP goals in the Cognitive Area using an activity-based intervention approach. The final section, Area Goals, discusses suggestions for Concurrent Goals, Daily Routines, Environmental Arrangements, and Intervention Activities in the home and classroom for each goal and associated objectives listed in the Cognitive Area of the AEPS Test for Three to Six Years.

INTERVENTION CONSIDERATIONS

General considerations when working on cognitive goals/objectives are discussed next.

- Some preschool special education programs emphasize school skills (e.g., numbers, letters, colors, writing skills). If the child does not understand the concepts that underlie academic skills, then working on these skills can be frustrating for both the child and the interventionist. In addition, other nonacademic skills such as communication, social interactions, following directions, attention, and the ability to move easily from one activity to the next are as important for success in public school environments as academic skills.

- When choosing goals/objectives for a child, consider their immediate functionality. How many times a day will the child actually use the targeted goal? Will it give him or her more independence? Because children with cognitive impairments may take longer to learn new skills, it is particularly important to target goals that will be functional and generalizable in their immediate and future environments.

- Observe children carefully and work with familiar adults to determine each child's methods of communication, and provide nonverbal children with alternative forms of communication when assessing cognitive skills (see Social-Communication Area).

- Observe children carefully across a range of settings and activities as well as across developmental areas before drawing firm conclusions about their cognitive abilities. Children may show more advanced problem-solving skills when engaged in familiar activities or in the presence of familiar adults, peers, and settings.

- Children with disabilities may require additional considerations to facilitate generalization of responses. Observe children's learning styles carefully to determine their strengths (e.g., visual, auditory, kinesthetic, a combination of styles). Many examples of objects, people, and events across different activities and settings may need to be explored by children to understand different concepts (e.g., these round objects are all balls, but they have features such as size, color, shape, texture, and weight that are different).

- Spatial concepts are particularly difficult for children with visual impairments. When applicable, it is helpful to go from three-dimensional objects (e.g., a sphere) to two-dimensional objects (e.g., a picture with raised graphics).

- The inability of a child to move freely in the environment can inhibit cognitive development. The interventionist should work closely with specialists to determine adaptations to the environment, activities, and materials that allow the child to actively explore and manipulate objects, participate in activities, and interact with peers.

- Be aware of the amount of noise and distraction in the environment. Some children may have difficulty attending to the appropriate stimuli (e.g., a direction, a book being read) with other distractions occurring (e.g., peers talking, loud noises).

SUGGESTED ACTIVITIES

The following list of activities and materials may be particularly helpful for eliciting skills within the Cognitive Area. For a list of complete intervention activities, see Appendix A.

Dramatic Play Activities

Dramatic play is an excellent context for children to practice cognitive skills. When selecting props, include materials that will provide opportunities for children to practice targeted goals/objectives; for example, if a child has a target skill to sort objects on the basis of physical attribute, then include materials such as different socks, utensils, and coins that can be sorted by color, shape, or size. The following themes are particularly helpful when embedding cognitive goals: house play, shoe store, post office, and airplane.

Other Activities

- Art activities
- Board games

- Books/book making
- Collages
- Construction/manipulation activities
- Cooking
- Expressive arts
- Marble painting
- Planting a garden
- Playdough
- Ramps
- Teddy bear counting game
- Water/sand play
- What's missing?

USING ACTIVITY-BASED INTERVENTION

An illustration of how an interventionist can incorporate strategies to enhance the development of a child's cognitive skills is provided next. Alice's targeted IFSP/IEP goals/objectives are to 1) indicate solutions to problems (adult can provide general cues) and 2) correctly count five objects.

- The interventionist observes Alice choosing to play with playdough. She *follows the child's lead* by joining Alice in her play and encourages peers to join. The classroom consists of a *heterogeneous* group of children, providing opportunities for Alice to learn new skills by observing peer models or to enhance skills by assisting children who are less able.

- The interventionist *forgets* to put rolling pins with the playdough, providing an opportunity for Alice to recognize the missing materials and indicate a solution to the problem.

- During the activity, Alice says, "Me making hot dogs." The interventionist *expands on the child's initiation,* providing an opportunity for Alice to practice counting by commenting, "Hmm—I wonder how many hot dogs you have?"

- If necessary, the interventionist *models* counting for Alice (e.g., "I'm going to count my hot dogs . . . 1, 2, 3, 4, 5") or encourages a child with more advanced skills to model by asking, "How many hot dogs do you have, Maria?"

- The interventionist encourages Alice to practice counting different materials such as rolling pins, cookie cutters, colors of playdough, or the number of people participating in the activity.

Cognitive

- The interventionist *violates the child's expectations* by using a cookie cutter incorrectly (upside down) and commenting, "Hmm—This isn't working!" Alice may be able to recognize the problem and offer a solution or may learn by observing a peer's solution to the problem.

- Throughout the activity, the interventionist uses the *least amount of assistance* necessary for Alice to successfully practice counting or solving problems.

AREA GOALS

This section provides suggestions for concurrent goals, daily routines, environmental arrangements, and planned intervention activities for the cognitive goals listed in the AEPS Test for Three to Six Years. If an objective has been targeted, then the interventionist can turn to the corresponding goal and determine which suggestions are relevant to facilitate that objective. A standard format is used for each goal: 1) Strand, 2) Goal, 3) Objective(s), 4) Concurrent Goals, 5) Daily Routines, 6) Environmental Arrangements, and 7) Intervention Activities. Concurrent Goals list the AEPS goals from other developmental areas that can often be addressed at the same time that the child works on the target goal or associated objectives. Daily Routines present a list of routine activities that may provide opportunities to practice targeted goals/objectives. The Environmental Arrangements should be considered when designing children's programs around child-initiated, routine, and planned intervention activities. Finally, the Intervention Activities section offers examples of how to embed targeted goals within the context of intervention activities.

Concepts

GOAL 1 Demonstrates understanding of color, shape, and size concepts

Objective 1.1 Demonstrates understanding of eight different colors

Objective 1.2 Demonstrates understanding of five different shapes

Objective 1.3 Demonstrates understanding of six different size concepts

CONCURRENT GOALS

FM A:2	Cuts out shapes with curved lines
FM B	Emergent writing (all goals)
Adap C:2	Selects appropriate clothing and dresses self at designated times
Cog A:2.1	Demonstrates understanding of 10 different qualitative concepts
Cog B	Categorizing
Cog C:2	Places objects in series according to length or size
SC A:1	Uses words, phrases, or sentences to inform, direct, ask questions, and express anticipation, imagination, affect, and emotions
SC B:5	Uses descriptive words
Soc D:1	Communicates personal likes and dislikes
Soc D:3	Relates identifying information about self and others

DAILY ROUTINES

Routine events that provide opportunities for children to demonstrate understanding of color, shape, and size concepts include the following:

- Arrival and departure
- Bath time
- Bedtime
- Circle time
- Dressing
- Mealtime or snack time
- Transition time
- Travel time
- Unstructured playtime

Example: While caregivers help children get dressed, they reinforce color concepts by commenting about, describing, and requesting clothing by color. (Cog A:1.1)

Example: Manuel's father often describes shapes they see while driving in the car. One day Manuel points to a traffic sign and says, "Look, a triangle." (Cog A:1.2)

Example: During clean-up time, the interventionist asks Joey to pick up all of the long blocks and Latifa to pick up all of the short blocks. (Cog A:1.3)

ENVIRONMENTAL ARRANGEMENTS

- Arrange the classroom into activity areas that include an art center and dramatic play area and provide age-appropriate and appealing materials of different colors:

  - Art materials with different colors, such as markers, crayons, paints, and paper

  - Materials of different colors, such as playdough, Legos, and Tinkertoys, counting bears, small colored blocks, and clothing in the dress-up area

  - Materials of different colors used in daily routines, such as cups and bowls, food items, chairs, carpet squares

- Include special color days or weeks in the classroom plan; for example, Monday is blue day, and the color blue is highlighted throughout the day with special activities such as painting with different shades of blue, eating blueberries for snack, and having a scavenger hunt to find blue objects.

- Include materials of different shapes and sizes during unstructured playtimes and routine events that provide opportunities for the child to learn shape and size concepts:

  - Art materials such as shape stencils; sponges cut into different shapes to use as paint stamps; thin and fat markers, crayons, or paintbrushes; big and little scissors; and various sizes and shapes of construction paper

  - Collage materials such as beans, macaroni, yarn, and buttons

  - Snack items of varying shapes (e.g., crackers, cheese cut into shapes) and sizes (e.g., tiny crackers and big cookies; fruit, cups, plates, utensils, pitchers of different sizes)

  - Materials of different shapes (e.g., parquetry blocks, shape sorters, puzzles, playdough rolled and cut with cookie cutters) and sizes (e.g., blocks, stacking /nesting cups, plastic people/animals, cars and trucks, big and small hats for dress-up, books, balls, and bikes; water table materials of various sizes such as cups, pitchers, and big and little tables and chairs)

- Display pictures or decorations in the environment that provide examples of different shapes. Include books about shapes in the library area. Labeling tables/chairs/activity areas with shapes may make transitions more smooth and reinforce children's shape concepts (e.g., "When you get inside, go to the star table for the painting activity").

- Include books in the library and story audiotapes in the music area that are about colors, shapes, and sizes (e.g., *Goldilocks and the Three Bears*).

- Paint the classroom or home environment in bright, appealing colors. Hang pictures or include decorations in the environment that provide examples of different colors, shapes, and sizes.

INTERVENTION ACTIVITIES

Three examples of how to embed this goal and the associated objectives within activities are presented next. For a list of intervention activities that address goals/objectives across areas, see Appendix A.

Butterfly Blots

Children use construction paper and paint in squeeze bottles (e.g., plastic ketchup or mustard bottles) to make "butterflies." They 1) choose colored paper, 2) fold the paper in half lengthwise, 3) open the paper, 4) choose paint colors, 5) squirt small blobs of paint on one half of the paper, 6) fold the paper in half, 7) press and smooth out, and 8) open up the butterfly and let it dry. The interventionist facilitates a discussion of what colors appear when the paints mix as they are flattened.

Water Music

Children experiment with tones by tapping jars filled with colored water. Use food coloring or paint to make a variety of colors of water. Glass jars provide the clearest tones, but safety should be considered when choosing containers. The interventionist should provide several sizes of water containers and items to tap with (e.g., spoons, chopsticks, wooden sticks). Children vary the amount of water in each jar and tap the jar to produce different sounds. (The interventionist should model how to tap softly.) Children demonstrate understanding of size and color concepts as they get ready for the activity (e.g., "Use the big bucket to get some water"), follow directions (e.g., "See what sound the smallest jar makes"), and participate in the activity ("The blue jar makes a lower sound than the pink jar"). The interventionist reinforces concepts by labeling, commenting, and describing materials by size, shape, and color.

Shape Search

Children search the classroom for examples of different shapes. Depending on the skill level of children, the interventionist can 1) tell the children what to

Cognitive

look for (e.g., "Find something shaped like a circle"); 2) show the children a model of a circle and then have the children look for one; or 3) have the children hold the model while looking for another object shaped like a circle.

Example: The interventionist provides a tactile model of a circle for Eric, who has a visual impairment. Eric "feels" the circle and finds a puzzle that has a circle piece to match. (Cog A:1.2)

GOAL 2	Demonstrates understanding of qualitative and quantitative concepts

Objective 2.1   **Demonstrates understanding of 10 different qualitative concepts**

Objective 2.2   **Demonstrates understanding eight different quantitative concepts**

CONCURRENT GOALS

Adap A:1   Eats and drinks a variety of foods using appropriate utensils with little or no spilling
Adap A:2   Prepares and serves food
Adap C:2   Selects appropriate clothing and dresses self at designated times
Cog B   Categorizing
Cog G   Premath (all goals)
SC A:1   Uses words, phrases, or sentences to inform, direct, ask questions, and express anticipation, imagination, affect, and emotions
SC B:5   Uses descriptive words
Soc D:1   Communicates personal likes and dislikes

DAILY ROUTINES

Routine events that provide opportunities for children to demonstrate understanding of qualitative concepts include the following:

* Arrival and departure

* Bath time

* Bedtime

* Circle time

* Dressing

* Mealtime or snack time

* Transition time

- Travel time

- Unstructured playtime

Example: During dinner, Joey takes a bite of his food and says, "Ow!" His mother prompts him by asking, "Is it hot, Joey?" and Joey responds, "Yeah, hot." (Cog A:2.1)

Example: Joey plays with plastic cups during bath time. His father plays too, filling a cup and saying, "My cup is full," and emptying the cup with, "Oops, now it's empty." Joey says, "Mine full!" (Cog A:2.2)

ENVIRONMENTAL ARRANGEMENTS

- Arrange the classroom into activity areas that include a science and nature center where children can explore objects with different qualitative attributes. Children add to the table by bringing natural objects that they find outside, such as pine cones, rocks, shells, and feathers. Provide materials with different qualitative features:

  - Art materials such as cotton balls, fabrics such as velvet and denim, paper products such as sandpaper and tissue paper, and paint that has been given a rough texture by adding sand

  - Food and snack items with contrasting qualitative features, such as sweet and sour tastes, hot and cold temperatures, smooth and rough surfaces (e.g., apple, pineapple), and wet and dry qualities

  - Materials such as blocks (heavy/light), musical instruments (loud/soft), clay and playdough (hard/soft), and sand or water table filled with different materials (e.g., sand, cornmeal, flour, warm or cold water)

- Provide a weather chart with pictures depicting sunny, rainy, cloudy, or snowy days. Discuss the weather during group time. Pictures help children visualize concepts such as wet/dry, light/dark, and hot/cold. Whenever possible, go outside or look out a window to see the clouds, feel the warm sun, and touch the wet rain or cold snow.

- Provide materials during free play and routine events that have many parts to count, as well as materials that can be poured and measured according to volume:

  - Art supplies with many pieces, such as collage materials (e.g., beans, buttons, scraps of paper, pieces of yarn), crayons, pencils, and markers

  - Food and snack items in many pieces (e.g., mini crackers, raisins) as well as liquid or semi-liquid items (e.g., juice, applesauce) that can be poured or scooped into cups or bowls

  - Materials with many pieces, such as blocks, Tinkertoys, Legos, plastic animals and people, and cars; sorting materials, such as counting bears, nuts, and bolts

Cognitive

- Present materials that provide opportunities for children to make comparisons according to number and volume, and demonstrate use of quantitative concepts; for example, provide activity areas that include art, manipulative, and dramatic play areas.

  Example: Latifa and Manuel are pretending to have dinner in the play house. Manuel holds up a bowl of pretend food and tells Latifa, "I have a lot of cake—want some?" (Cog A:2.2)

- Include pictures, books, and tapes that give children opportunities to learn about or demonstrate understanding of quantitative concepts; for example, a picture of a family eating dinner provides opportunities to compare food quantity using concepts such as more, empty, full, or a lot.

INTERVENTION ACTIVITIES

Two examples of how to embed this goal and the associated objectives within activities are presented next. For a list of intervention activities that address goals/objectives across areas, see Appendix A.

Nature Collage

Children go outside on a scavenger hunt and later make collages with the items that they found. The interventionist specifies the characteristics of items ahead of time (e.g., hard/soft, prickly/smooth, light/heavy), and children go in teams to hunt for items with those characteristics. Children should be encouraged to gather only items that have fallen to the ground so that plants can continue to grow! Children demonstrate understanding of qualitative concepts as they get ready for the activity (e.g., "What's the weather like outside? Yes, it's cold, so we need to wear our coats"), follow directions (e.g., "Find something smooth"), and participate in the activity. The interventionist reinforces the concepts by labeling, commenting on, and describing objects, people, or events according to qualitative concepts. After finding several items, the children can glue items onto a piece of cardboard.

Example: After Jose completes his project, his interventionist encourages him to talk about his collage, prompting him to use qualitative terms, "How does the moss feel? Is the pebble rough or smooth?" (Cog A:2.1)

Bubbles

This activity is fun to do outside. The recipe for bubbles is ¼ cup glycerine (available in drug stores), ¼ cup dishwashing liquid, and 8 cups water. Children pour about ¼ cup of this mixture into a cup and use straws to blow bubbles. Children should practice blowing through straws because some children suck through the straw by mistake. Children practice using quantitative concepts as they get ready for the activity (e.g., "Pour the bubbles in the big cup"), follow directions (e.g., "Let Joey have some"), and participate in the activity (e.g., "I made more bubbles than you!"). The interventionist reinforces the quantitative concepts by using such terms to describe objects, people, or events.

GOAL 3   Demonstrates understanding of spatial and temporal relations concepts

Objective 3.1   Demonstrates understanding of 12 different spatial relations concepts

Objective 3.2   Demonstrates understanding of seven different temporal relations concepts

CONCURRENT GOALS

GM B   Play skills (all goals)
Adap C   Dressing and undressing (all goals)
Cog C:3   Retells event in sequence
Cog D   Recalling events
SC A:1   Uses words, phrases, or sentences to inform, direct, ask questions, and express anticipation, imagination, affect, and emotions
SC A:2   Uses conversational rules
SC B:5   Uses descriptive words
Soc A:2   Initiates cooperative activity

DAILY ROUTINES

Routine events that provide opportunities for children to demonstrate understanding of spatial and temporal relations concepts include the following:

- Arrival and departure

- Bath time

- Bedtime

- Circle time

- Dressing

- Mealtime or snack time

- Transition time

- Travel time

- Unstructured playtime

Example: Getting in the car, Manuel's father asks him, "Do you want to sit in front or back?" Manuel replies, "Front" and goes to open the front door of the car. (Cog A:3.1)

Example: Maria's mother asks her, "What would you like to do after dinner?" and waits for Maria to respond with her communication board. Maria points to the picture of books. (Cog A:3.2)

ENVIRONMENTAL ARRANGEMENTS

- Present materials during free play and routine events that provide opportunities for the child to demonstrate an understanding of different spatial relations concepts:

  - Blocks, cars, and trucks with little people or animals to move in relation to each other

  - Sand/water table with cups, scoops, funnels, pitchers, and water wheels

  - Dolls, playhouse with people, and barn with animals

  - Bikes, wagons, and other vehicles

  - Slides, tunnels, and climbing structures

Example: While playing with the barn and animals, Alice puts all of the cows in the barn. The interventionist says, "I wonder where the cows are?" and Alice points and says, "In barn." (Cog A:3.1)

- Provide children with choices about where they want to sit or stand during activities such as circle time, snack time, and transition times. Comment on the relative position of the children (e.g., "Eric's sitting next to Maria").

- Spatial concepts are particularly difficult for children with visual impairments and should be emphasized. When applicable, it is helpful to go from three-dimensional objects (e.g., a sphere) to two-dimensional objects (e.g., a picture with raised print).

- Present materials during free play and routine events that provide opportunities for the child to demonstrate an understanding of different temporal relations:

  - Sequenced story cards

  - Sand/water tables, block play, and other exploratory activities that provide opportunities for children to anticipate or recall events

  - Art, construction, and cooking activities that require several steps to accomplish

  - Pets and other animals, particularly interesting animals to observe such as those that metamorphose (e.g., polliwog into a frog, caterpillar into a butterfly)

- Establish a predictable routine to the classroom day that includes an opening and closing circle time. During opening circle, the daily schedule and special events (e.g., birthdays, holidays, field trips, unusual activities) are discussed. A calendar is a visual means to discuss events of yesterday, today, and tomorrow. Closing circle gives children an opportunity to discuss the day's events.

- Present pictures, posters, books, and magazines that give children opportunities to demonstrate understanding of spatial relations and recall events on the basis of temporal relations.

Example: At school, while looking at a picture in a book, Latifa says, "I go on school bus." (Cog A:3.2)

INTERVENTION ACTIVITIES

Two examples of how to embed this goal and the associated objectives within activities are presented next. For a list of intervention activities that address goals/objectives across areas, see Appendix A.

My Town

Children make a town on a tabletop by creating houses using milk cartons and boxes, tunnels of paper tubes or boxes with ends cut off, ponds or rivers with blue paper, and roads with masking tape. The children decorate their houses with markers, crayons, and construction paper and choose a spot on the table to tape their creation. Children decide together where the roads, tunnels, and ponds should be located. After the town is created, small cars, animals, and people can be added. Children demonstrate knowledge of spatial relations as they get ready for the activity (e.g., "I want to sit next to Eric"), follow directions (e.g., "Put the rest of the paper under the table"), and participate in the activity (e.g., "My dog's in the pond"). The interventionist reinforces spatial concepts by commenting about and describing objects, people, or events using spatial relations concepts.

Example: Alice's interventionist says, "Look, Alice. The boy is standing in front of his house, but where is his dog?" Alice responds, "In back," while pointing to the back of the house. (Cog A:3.1)

Leaf Rubbings

The children take a walk and gather leaves in small bags. They make rubbings by placing a leaf under a piece of lightweight paper and rubbing with the side of a crayon or pencil over the paper. The imprint of the leaf will appear. Children describe how and when they made their leaf rubbings during closing circle or to a parent.

Cognitive

Categorizing

GOAL 1 Groups objects, people, or events on the basis of specified criteria

Objective 1.1 Groups objects, people, or events on the basis of category

Objective 1.2 Groups objects on the basis of function

Objective 1.3 Groups objects on the basis of physical attribute

CONCURRENT GOALS

Adap A:1   Eats and drinks a variety of foods using appropriate utensils with little or no spilling

Cog A   Concepts (all goals)

SC A:1   Uses words, phrases, or sentences to inform, direct, ask questions, and express anticipation, imagination, affect, and emotions

SC B:5   Uses descriptive words

Soc D:1   Communicates personal likes and dislikes

DAILY ROUTINES

Routine events that provide opportunities for children to group objects, people, or events on the basis of devised criteria include the following:

- Cleanup time

- Mealtime or snack time

- Transition time

- Unstructured playtime

Example: During cleanup time, the interventionist asks Joey to put all of the toy animals in one basket and Latifa to put all of the toy people in another. (Cog B:1.1)

ENVIRONMENTAL ARRANGEMENTS

- Present materials during free play and routine events that are interesting and appealing to the children, and provide opportunities to group objects, people, or events on the basis of specified criteria; for example, present toys and materials that can be sorted according to the following:

- Different functions (e.g., art materials, tools, toys that go in the water, things to eat, things to wear)

- Different categories (e.g., food from different food groups)

- Physical attributes (e.g., blocks of different sizes, foods with different textures such as crunchy or sweet, crayons of different colors)

Example: While playing in the house play area, Manuel cleans house, putting away the food in the refrigerator and clothing in the dresser. (Cog B:1.2)

- Include pictures, posters, books, and magazines in the environment that give children opportunities to group objects, people, or events on the basis of certain criteria; for example, posters of children playing could be categorized on the basis of sex, age, hair color, or any other criterion selected by the children or interventionist.

INTERVENTION ACTIVITIES

Two examples of how to embed this goal and the associated objectives within activities are presented next. For a list of intervention activities that address goals/objectives across areas, see Appendix A.

What Am I Thinking Of?

One child thinks of an animal and other children try to guess what it is. The interventionist provides miniature objects that represent different categories (e.g., animals that fly, animals that live in water, animals of different colors, farm or zoo animals). Other children each ask a question to narrow the possibilities. A child might ask, "Does it live in the water?" and, if the answer is yes, then all animals that do not live in water are removed. If each child has made a guess about the animal and no one has guessed correctly, then the first child gives another clue. The interventionist should provide the least level of assistance necessary for children to think up questions and subsequently categorize the objects.

Animal Books (see Books/Book Making in Appendix A)

Children cut pictures of animals from magazines and paste them in their books (use large sheets of paper for the books). Encourage children to glue on the same page animals that can be categorized together. Some children may come up with their own categories, whereas others need more assistance (e.g., "See if you can find pictures of animals with feathers for this page").

Example: Eric's interventionist provides him with pictures of animals with tactile surfaces glued on (e.g., birds with feathers, mammals with furry material, fish with smooth surfaces). Eric glues animals that go together on different pieces of paper in his book. (Cog B:1.3)

Sequencing

GOAL 1 Follows directions of three or more related steps that are not routinely given

Objective 1.1 Follows directions of three or more related steps that are routinely given

CONCURRENT GOALS

GM B   Play skills (all goals)
Soc B   Participation (all goals)
Soc C:2   Follows context-specific rules outside home and classroom

DAILY ROUTINES

Routine events that provide opportunities for children to follow directions include the following:

- Arrival and departure
- Bath time
- Bedtime
- Circle time
- Clean-up time
- Dressing
- Mealtime or snack time
- Transition time
- Travel time
- Unstructured playtime

Example: Latifa's mother tells her, "It's time for bed, Latifa. Turn off the television, brush your teeth, and get in bed. Then, I'll come read you a story." (Cog C:1.1)

ENVIRONMENTAL ARRANGEMENTS

- Provide children with independent access to materials that they use during free play and routine activities. Place coat hooks at the child's height, a child-size sink (or sink with a step stool) and soap and towels within reach, and free choice materials at the child's level. The caregiver or interventionist facilitates by providing opportunities for children to follow directions.

Example: During free play, Joey asks the interventionist if he can paint. The interventionist says, "Sure you can. First, get a smock. Then, get a piece of paper, and bring it to the easel." (Cog C:1)

INTERVENTION ACTIVITIES

Two examples of how to embed this goal and the associated objective within activities are presented next. For a list of intervention activities that address goals/objectives across areas, see Appendix A.

Simon Says

The interventionist is "Simon" and gives three-step directions to the children. Children enjoy doing silly things, so be creative!
Example: Simon says, "Put your hands on your head, make a funny face, and say 'hamburger.'" (Cog C:1)

My Body

Children lie down on large pieces of paper, and another person traces their bodies. Children color in their skin color, features, and clothing with markers, crayons, or paint. Children follow directions getting ready for the activity, participating in the activity, and cleaning up.
Example: Timmy's interventionist signs him a three-step direction, YOU AND JOEY CAN GET A BIG PIECE OF PAPER AND CRAYONS AND PUT THEM ON THE FLOOR. (Cog C:1, adapted)

GOAL 2   Places objects in series according to length or size

Objective 2.1   Fits one ordered set of objects to another

CONCURRENT GOALS

Adap A:2   Prepares and serves food
Cog A:1   Demonstrates understanding of color, shape, and size concepts
Cog B:1   Groups objects, people, or events on the basis of specified criteria
SC A   Social-communicative interactions (all goals)
SC B:5   Uses descriptive words

Cognitive

DAILY ROUTINES

Routine events that provide opportunities for children to place objects in a series according to length or size include the following:

- Cleanup time

- Mealtime or snack time

- Transition time

- Unstructured playtime

Example: While getting ready to go outside, children line up from shortest to tallest (and from tallest to shortest to come inside). (Cog C:2)

ENVIRONMENTAL ARRANGEMENTS

- Present materials in the environment of varying length and size that provide opportunities for children to make comparisons (e.g., blocks, Legos, cups, pitchers, paint brushes, crayons, balls). In addition, provide objects of different sizes that have two or more parts that children can fit together (e.g., bowls with lids, nuts and bolts, dolls with doll clothes, cars and "garages").

- Arrange the classroom into activity areas and encourage children to return materials in an orderly way to designated locations. Children place objects in a series according to length or size while cleaning up.

INTERVENTION ACTIVITIES

Two examples of how to embed this goal and the associated objective within activities are presented next. For a list of intervention activities that address goals/objectives across areas, see Appendix A.

Goldilocks and the Three Bears

Children work together to make a flannelboard set of *Goldilocks and the Three Bears.* The interventionist provides stencils or outlines for three bowls, chairs, beds, and bears (small, medium, and large) and Goldilocks. Children help cut out the figures, decorate them, or make a stage for the play. The interventionist models the story of *Goldilocks and the Three Bears* and provides opportunities for children to sequence the props while they retell the story.

Driving Cars

Have a set of cars of varying sizes available (i.e., small, medium, large). Also have a set of "garages" (cardboard boxes of varying sizes). Children work together to drive their cars into the "right" garage.

GOAL 3   Retells event in sequence

Objective 3.1   Completes sequence of familiar story or event

CONCURRENT GOALS

Cog A:3.2   Demonstrates understanding of seven different temporal relations concepts
Cog C:1   Follows directions of three or more related steps that are not routinely given
Cog D   Recalling events
SC A   Social-communicative interactions (all goals)
SC B   Production of words, phrases, and sentences (all goals)

DAILY ROUTINES

Routine events that provide opportunities for children to retell events in sequence include the following:

- Arrival and departure
- Bath time
- Bedtime
- Circle time
- Dressing
- Mealtime or snack time
- Transition time
- Travel time
- Unstructured playtime

Example: Manuel helps his mother make cookies. During dinner, she asks him, "Manuel, can you tell your father how you made cookies?" and Manuel responds, "I stirred the cookies, and then we scooped them on the cookie sheet and put them in the oven." (Cog C:3)

Cognitive

ENVIRONMENTAL ARRANGEMENTS

- Provide opportunities to retell events or complete a familiar story in sequence, and present activities and materials in the environment that are interesting and appealing to children:

  - Sequenced story cards

  - Books, flannelboard materials, and story audiotapes

  - Pictorial descriptions of activities (e.g., a painting activity uses pictures of a child putting on a smock, getting a piece of paper, painting a picture on the easel, and hanging the picture up on the wall)

  - Art, construction, cooking, or science activities that require several steps to accomplish

- Arrange the classroom into activity areas that include a science center and dramatic play center. Experiments such as growing seeds can be ongoing in the science area, allowing children to track progress from day to day and retell events in sequence. Dramatic play centers provide opportunities for children to role play familiar situations or stories.

- Establish a predictable routine to the classroom day, including an opening and closing circle time. During opening circle, the daily schedule and special events (e.g., birthdays, holidays, field trips, unusual activities) are discussed. Establishing a predictable daily routine will help the children respond appropriately to questions about the sequence of events in the classroom (e.g., "What do we do next?"). Closing circle provides opportunities for children to discuss the day's events in the sequence in which they occurred.

INTERVENTION ACTIVITIES

Two examples of how to embed this goal and the associated objective within activities are presented next. For a list of intervention activities that address goals/objectives across areas, see Appendix A.

Planting a Garden

Planting a garden involves several steps (e.g., hoeing the ground, planting the seeds, watering the ground, weeding) and provides opportunities for the child to retell events in sequence. Reading a story about growing things (e.g., *The Carrot Seed*), discussing the sequence of steps ahead of time, or making sequenced cards of the event may help children answer questions about the sequence of the event or retell the event in correct sequence.

Making Popcorn

The interventionist makes popcorn using a heavy pan with a lid or an electric popper, ⅓ cup popcorn, 2 tablespoons oil, salt, and a large bowl. The children can examine the corn kernels before popping them. Oil and popcorn are added to the saucepan or electric popper. The popcorn can be served once it cools, and children can retell the event.

Recalling Events

GOAL 1   Recalls events that occurred on same day, without contextual cues

Objective 1.1   Recalls events that occurred on same day, with contextual cues

Objective 1.2   Recalls events immediately after they occur

CONCURRENT GOALS

Cog A:3   Demonstrates understanding of spatial and temporal relations concepts
Cog C   Sequencing (all goals)
SC A   Social-communicative interactions (all goals)
SC B   Production of words, phrases, and sentences (all goals)

DAILY ROUTINES

Routine events that provide opportunities for children to recall events include the following:

- Arrival and departure

- Bath time

- Bedtime

- Circle time

- Dressing

- Mealtime or snack time

- Travel time

- Unstructured playtime

Example: On the drive home from school, Timmy's mother asks, "What did you do at school today?" Timmy takes a picture from his bag and signs, PAINT. (Cog D:1)

ENVIRONMENTAL ARRANGEMENTS

- Provide materials and activities in the environment that are age appropriate and appealing to children. Field trips to community sites such as the post office, fire station, zoo, or museum provide topics for later discussions.

- Include group times in the daily routine, when children come together to share special events in their home lives and discuss classroom events.

   Example: Eric arrives at group time after the other children. They say, "We missed you, Eric. Where have you been?" Eric replies, "At Grandma's house." (Cog D:1.2)

- Keep a notebook for each child and send it from school to home with the child. The child's caregivers describe special events that occurred at home, and the school staff describe the activities at school. This information is then used to prompt the child to recall past events.

INTERVENTION ACTIVITIES

Two examples of how to embed this goal and the associated objectives within activities are presented next. For a list of intervention activities that address goals/objectives across areas, see Appendix A.

Sharing Time

Children take turns telling about something they did or something special that occurred during the day at school. Whereas some children will be able to recall events without contextual cues, the interventionist may need to provide cues (e.g., examples of artwork, materials that the child played with) to prompt them. Limiting the number of children who share each day to two or three helps keep the other children from becoming restless.

Handprints

Children make handprints by pressing a hand in a tray with paint (Styrofoam trays work well) or by having a friend paint the palm of one hand; then press the painted hand on paper. The interventionist provides opportunities to recall events by asking the children what activity they just came from (e.g., "Hi, Joey. What were you just doing?") or by asking questions during the activity about events that occurred earlier in the day (e.g., "What did you have for snack?"). At the end of the day, during group time, the interventionist holds up a few handprints and asks children what they did during art.

Cognitive

Problem Solving

GOAL 1   Evaluates solutions to problems

Objective 1.1   Suggests acceptable solutions to problems
Objective 1.2   Identifies means to goal

CONCURRENT GOALS

Cog E:2   Makes statements and appropriately answers questions that require reasoning about objects, situations, or people
SC A   Social-communicative interactions (all goals)
SC B   Production of words, phrases, and sentences (all goals)
Soc A:3   Resolves conflicts by selecting effective strategy

DAILY ROUTINES

Routine events that provide opportunities for children to evaluate solutions to problems include the following:

- Arrival and departure
- Bath time
- Bedtime
- Circle time
- Dressing
- Mealtime or snack time
- Transition time
- Travel time
- Unstructured playtime

As children follow directions and get ready for and participate in activities, caregivers or interventionists reinforce the ability to solve problems by discussing reasons why and how routine activities are conducted, answering "why" or "how" questions that children ask about routine events, and providing reasons for requests made of children. Eventually, caregivers begin to question children, providing opportunities for children to evaluate their own solutions to problems.

Example: When Latifa's mother helps her get dressed in the morning, she talks about the weather. If Latifa complains about wearing her sweater, then her mother reminds her that when it is cold, a sweater keeps her warm. (Cog E:1.1)

ENVIRONMENTAL ARRANGEMENTS

- Provide materials and activities during routine and planned intervention activities that are interesting and appealing to children. Activities should be child directed and open ended whenever possible, providing opportunities for the child to explore materials and evaluate solutions to problems as they arise during play.

- Arrange the classroom into activity centers and keep materials in predictable locations accessible to children.

  Example: Timmy and Joey are going shopping at the "grocery store" in the dramatic play center. The interventionist asks, "How will you carry your groceries?" Joey runs to get a paper bag from the art center. (Cog E:1.2)

- Do something deliberate to interfere with the conduct of an activity (e.g., unplug the record player prior to a group music activity). This strategy should be used sparingly and with caution; when employed selectively, it provides opportunities for children to solve problems.

- "Forget" to provide necessary equipment or overlook an important component of a routine or familiar activity; for example, do not have food immediately available for snack time or books for storytime.

- Place objects that are desirable or necessary to complete an activity within sight but out of reach of the child.

- Omit or change a familiar step or element in a well-practiced or routine activity; for example, provide children with popsicle sticks to draw with instead of crayons.

- Provide the least level of assistance necessary when helping a child solve a problem. Encourage children to provide an acceptable solution to the problem (e.g., "What can you try?"). If necessary, go to the next level of assistance; for example, set a cup of water near a child who "can't make the paint work."

INTERVENTION ACTIVITIES

Two examples of how to embed this goal and the associated objectives within activities are presented next. For a list of intervention activities that address goals/objectives across areas, see Appendix A.

Pine Cone Bird Feeders

Children spread peanut butter on large pinecones and then roll the pinecones in birdseed to make bird feeders. The interventionists can have children direct the activity and use problem-solving skills by asking them questions such as, "What we can use to spread the peanut butter on the pine cones?" "How can we keep the table clean?" "Where should we put the feeders so the birds can get to them?" When the class goes outside to hang the bird feeders, have children suggest solutions about how to hang them on high branches (you might have a step stool nearby). Often, children will suggest solutions to problems that do not work. If possible, their solutions should be tried even if they will not work. This provides children with the necessary information to re-evaluate their suggestions and come up with new ideas that do work.

Bug Search

Children look for insects on the playground and collect them to observe briefly. Before searching, children can suggest possible containers to hold the insects and evaluate whether the containers will work. Children look around the classroom for containers, or the interventionist provides containers to choose from. Once the class is outside, the interventionist can ask children where they can find bugs and how they will collect them. Throughout the activity, opportunities can be provided for children to solve problems (e.g., the problem of how to overturn a heavy rock). After observing collected bugs for a few minutes, children return the bugs to their homes.

GOAL 2   Makes statements and appropriately answers questions that require reasoning about objects, situations, or people

---

Objective 2.1   Gives reason for inference

Objective 2.2   Makes prediction about future or hypothetical events

Objective 2.3   Gives possible cause for some event

CONCURRENT GOALS

Adap C:2   Selects appropriate clothing and dresses self at designated times
Cog E:1   Evaluates solutions to problems
SC A   Social-communicative interactions (all goals)
SC B   Production of words, phrases, and sentences (all goals)
Soc A:3   Resolves conflicts by selecting effective strategy
Soc C:1   Meets physical needs in socially appropriate ways
Soc D:2   Understands how own behaviors, thoughts, and feelings relate to consequences for others

DAILY ROUTINES

Routine events that provide opportunities for children to use reasoning skills include the following:

- Arrival and departure

- Bath time

- Bedtime

- Circle time

- Dressing

- Mealtime or snack time

- Storytime

- Transition time

- Travel time

- Unstructured playtime

The caregiver or interventionist reinforces this skill by modeling 1) making inferences (e.g., "That must have hurt. You fell down hard"); 2) making predictions (e.g., "If you walk in that puddle, your shoes will get wet"); and 3) giving possible causes for events (e.g., "You hurt your knee. Did you fall off your bike?").

Example: While giving Manuel a bath, his father asks him, "What do you think would happen if you never took a bath?" Manuel answers, "I'd get real dirty." (Cog E:2.2)

ENVIRONMENTAL ARRANGEMENTS

- Provide materials and activities during routine and planned intervention activities that are interesting and appealing to children. The activities should be open ended, allowing children opportunities to experiment and problem solve. Provide opportunities for children to brainstorm solutions to problems as they arise (e.g., "What will happen if you let go of the block?"). Take time with children after activities to evaluate solutions that were chosen, how they worked, and how other solutions might have worked.

- Arrange the classroom into activity centers that include a science and nature area where children can observe plants, animals, objects, or events and use reasoning skills to explain what they see. Interesting events to observe include watching ice cubes melt, insects eat a leaf, fish swim in a tank, or seeds grow day by day.

Cognitive

Example: While watching the school bunny eat a carrot, Timmy signs, HUNGRY. The interventionist asks, "How do you know the rabbit is hungry?" Timmy signs his answer. (Cog E:2.1)

- Have a plentiful selection of new books in the library. While reading books to children, stop during an exciting moment and ask what they think will happen next. Provide magazines, posters, and pictures of objects (e.g., space-ships), situations (e.g., thunderstorm), or people (e.g., smiling child) that are interesting and provide opportunities for children to make statements or answer questions that require reasoning.

- Deliberately "sabotage" or interfere with the conduct of an activity; for ex-ample, remove a piece of track from a train set or unplug the record player prior to a group music activity.

- "Forget" to provide necessary equipment or overlook an important com-ponent of a routine or familiar activity; for example, do not have food im-mediately available for snack time or books for storytime, and allow chil-dren to solve the problem.

INTERVENTION ACTIVITIES

Two examples of how to embed this goal and the associated objectives within activities are presented next. For a list of intervention activities that address goals/objectives across areas, see Appendix A.

Fire Truck

Large boxes such as refrigerator boxes can be transformed into make-believe structures, in this case a fire truck. Opportunities can be provided for children to solve problems by asking questions such as, "Can anybody think of how we can make a fire truck out of this box?" What do we need?" Throughout the ac-tivity, opportunities can be provided for children to use reasoning skills by asking questions such as, "What might happen if we don't put smocks on while we paint the fire truck?" or "How do you think the fire started?"

Doctor's Office

A doctor's office is set up in the dramatic play center of the classroom. The in-terventionist reads a story about doctors to provide information to get the chil-dren actively involved. Children direct the activity by providing suggestions for what props are needed (e.g., bandages, a cot, white shirts), how the office should be arranged, and what roles they can play. Opportunities can be provided for children to use their reasoning skills in different roles (e.g., "Why is she crying, Doctor?" "What happened to your leg?" "What can you do to make it better?").

STRAND F

Play

GOAL 1 Engages in cooperative, imaginary play

Objective 1.1 Enacts roles or identities

Objective 1.2 Plans and acts out recognizable event, theme, or storyline

Objective 1.3 Uses imaginary props

CONCURRENT GOALS

SC A Social-communicative interactions (all goals)
SC B Production of words, phrases, and sentences (all goals)
Soc A Interaction with others (all goals)
Soc B Participation (all goals)

DAILY ROUTINES

Routine events that provide opportunities for children to engage in imaginary play include the following:

- Bath time
- Bedtime
- Mealtime or snack time
- Unstructured playtime

Example: At bedtime, Eric's mother brings him a glass of water and Eric offers his imaginary friend a drink. (Cog F:1.3)

ENVIRONMENTAL ARRANGEMENTS

- Arrange the classroom into activity areas that include a dramatic play center. Provide materials during free play and routine events that facilitate the child's engagement in imaginary play:
  - Dramatic play props
  - Puppets

- Dolls of all shapes, sizes, and ethnic origins; doll clothing, diapers, bottles, cribs, blankets

- Dollhouses with little people and furniture

- Blocks and Legos with little people, animals, cars

- Stuffed animals

- Outdoor equipment such as climbing structures, wagons, bicycles, tricycles, and big boxes for houses or trains

Example: In the "post office," Latifa scribbles a note on some paper, stuffs it in an envelope, puts a "stamp" on the envelope, and mails it in the mailbox. (Cog F:1.2)

- Include books, pictures, and posters in the home or classroom environment that depict children engaging in imaginary play.

INTERVENTION ACTIVITIES

Two examples of how to embed this goal and the associated objectives within activities are presented next. For a list of intervention activities that address goals/objectives across areas, see Appendix A.

All Up, All Down

Children pretend to be different animals. They first lie down quietly on the floor, and the interventionist calls, "All up . . . ducks." Children get up and pretend to be ducks, quacking and waddling around the room until the interventionist calls, "All down." Children lie down quickly on the floor and then take turns choosing the animal that they will be next.

Paper Bag Animals

Children make animal puppets out of small lunch sacks and materials such as colored construction paper, fabric, buttons, and yarn. Children make their puppets "talk" by putting a hand in the sack and moving the "mouth" (the bottom flap) up and down. The interventionist should encourage the children to suggest animals and, if necessary, provide models of different animals. When children are finished making their puppets, the interventionist can encourage them to make their animals talk to each other or have a puppet show.

Example: Joey makes a puppet with feathers, a big trunk, and big teeth, and he names him Max. When he finishes, the interventionist asks him, "Does Max want a cookie?" and hands a pretend cookie to Max. Joey says, "Yes," and pretends to have Max eat the cookie. (Cog F:1.3)

GOAL 2   Engages in games with rules

Objective 2.1   Maintains participation

Objective 2.2   Conforms to game rules

CONCURRENT GOALS

GM A:1   Runs avoiding obstacles
GM B:2   Bounces, catches, kicks, and throws ball
SC A   Social-communicative interactions (all goals)
SC B   Production of words, phrases, and sentences (all goals)
Soc A:2   Initiates cooperative activity
Soc B:2   Watches, listens, and participates during small group activities
Soc B:3   Watches, listens, and participates during large group activities
Soc C:2   Follows context-specific rules outside home and classroom

DAILY ROUTINES

Routine events that provide opportunities for children to participate in games with the following rules include:

- Unstructured playtime

- Bath time

- Bedtime

- Mealtime or snack time

- Transition time

   Example: Maria's parents play cards together, and sometimes Maria wants to join them. If Maria asks to play a game of cards, then her mother says, "Okay, let's play Go Fish, but you need to stay and play the whole game, okay?" If Maria forgets a part of the game, then a parent reminds her of the rules. (Cog F:2.1)

ENVIRONMENTAL ARRANGEMENTS

- Arrange the classroom into activity centers that include one for children to play games. Have materials available during unstructured playtimes that provide opportunities for children to participate in games with rules:
  - Board games such as Candyland and Color Bingo

- Age-appropriate games with rules, such as Please Don't Break the Ice, and card games, such as Old Maid

- Basketballs, kickballs, soccer balls, hoops, and nets

• Arrange for children to participate in small group activities with peers who have slightly advanced abilities.

Example: Manuel, Latifa, and Timmy are playing Candyland together. When Timmy moves his marker without picking a card first, Manuel says, "Wait, Timmy. You need to pick a card first!" (Cog F:2.2)

INTERVENTION ACTIVITIES

Two examples of how to embed this goal and the associated objectives within activities are presented next. For a list of intervention activities that address goals/objectives across areas, see Appendix A.

Hug Tag

One child is chosen to be "it." That child "freezes" other children by tagging them. The children who are frozen stand absolutely still until another child (one who is not "it" and is not yet frozen) gives them a hug. The children can be allowed to take turns being "it," and they should give gentle hugs. The interventionist should observe the children's ability to follow the rules of the game and provide the least level of assistance if children are forgetting rules.

Doggie, Doggie, Who's Got the Bone?

The children sit together in a group and choose one child to be the "doggie." While the doggie hides his or her eyes, a child who is sitting is chosen to hold the "bone" (the bone can be any small object). All children place their hands behind their backs and chant, "Doggie, doggie, who's got the bone?" The doggie opens his or her eyes and gets three chances to guess which child is hiding the bone.

Premath

GOAL 1   Counts at least 20 objects

Objective 1.1   Counts at least 10 objects

Objective 1.2   Counts three objects

CONCURRENT GOALS

FM A:2   Cuts out shapes with curved lines
Cog A:2.2   Demonstrates understanding of eight different quantitative concepts
SC A:1   Uses words, phrases, or sentences to inform, direct, ask questions, and express anticipation, imagination, affect, and emotions

DAILY ROUTINES

Routine events that provide opportunities for children to count objects include the following:

- Arrival and departure

- Bath time

- Bedtime

- Circle time

- Dressing

- Mealtime or snack time

- Transition time

- Travel time

- Unstructured playtime

Example: After buttoning Latifa's shirt, her mother says, "Let's see how many buttons you have: one, two, three. Now you count!" (Cog G:1.2)

Example: During snack time, Timmy's interventionist has him pass out one napkin to each of his friends and count as he does so. (Cog G:1.1)

ENVIRONMENTAL ARRANGEMENTS

- Provide materials during free play and routine events that have many pieces to count:
  - Art supplies such as collage materials (beans, buttons, scraps of paper, pieces of yarn), crayons, pencils, markers
  - Food/snack items in many pieces (e.g., mini crackers, raisins)
  - Blocks, Tinkertoys, Legos, plastic animals and people, cars
  - Sorting materials such as counting bears, beans, nuts and bolts
- Include posters and books in the environment that provide opportunities for the children to count.

INTERVENTION ACTIVITIES

Two examples of how to embed this goal and the associated objectives within activities are presented next. For a list of intervention activities that address goals/objectives across areas, see Appendix A.

Valentine Cookies

Children help make heart-shaped cookies with a sugar cookie recipe, cookie cutters, and colored frosting for decoration. The children can participate in all aspects of this process by making the dough, rolling it out, cutting the shapes, and decorating and eating the cookies. The activity provides opportunities for children to count objects (e.g., counting children in the group to determine how many chairs are needed, counting number of cookies on a tray, counting napkins).

Potato Prints

Potato prints are made by cutting a raw potato in half, drawing a design on the flat surface (e.g., a heart), and carving around the design with a knife (so the design is raised on the potato surface). Potatoes should be carved by an adult. Children help with the design, watch the carving, and use the potatoes to print. To print, children press the potato in a thin layer of paint, press the painted potato onto a piece of paper, and lift the potato off to see the print. Counting can be incorporated throughout this activity (e.g., count the number of potatoes before and after cutting, count the paint colors, and count the number of prints made on the paper).

GOAL 2   Demonstrates understanding of printed numerals

Objective 2.1   Labels printed numerals up to 10
Objective 2.2   Recognizes printed numerals

CONCURRENT GOALS

Cog A	Concepts (all goals)
Cog B:1	Groups objects, people, or events on the basis of specified criteria
Cog C:2	Places objects in series according to length or size
Cog H:3	Reads words by sight
SC A	Social-communicative interactions (all goals)
SC B	Production of words, phrases, and sentences (all goals)
Soc B	Participation (all goals)

DAILY ROUTINES

Routine events that provide opportunities for children to recognize and label printed numerals include the following:

- Arrival and departure
- Bath time
- Bedtime/naptime
- Books and storytime
- Circle time
- Driving in the car
- Mealtime or snack time
- Music activities
- Transition time
- Unstructured playtime

Example: Ramona's aunt asks her to sort number and letter stickers into separate bins after they make invitation cards for her birthday party. Her older brother labels each number and letter that he recognizes as Ramona sorts and offers corrections if she makes a mistake. (Cog G:2.2)

Example: Ricco's teacher asks him to "Find room number 6" when they are going to observe the kindergarten that he will attend the following year. (Cog G:2.1)

Cognitive

Example: While driving in the car, Rochelle's mother points out the sign for exit number 12, and asks "What exit comes next?"(Cog G:2)

ENVIRONMENTAL ARRANGEMENTS

- Arrange the classroom into activity areas that include housekeeping and dramatic play. Number the areas and post a large sign with the name and number of each center in a prominent location.

    - Provide materials during free play and routine events that have printed numerals.

    - Placemats with numbers printed on them

    - Board games with number cards, decks of playing cards

    - Magnetic board and numbers

    - Number stencils, stamp pad and numbered stamps, variety of number stickers

    - Science-related materials such as timers, scales to weigh items, rulers, and old calculators

    - A calendar with detachable numbers

    - Dramatic play materials such as telephones, toy clocks, play money, signs denoting cost of items, a microwave or stove with numbered controls, cash registers, stamps, and restaurant menus with prices

- Include colorful and appealing posters, books, and magazines in the environment that have printed numerals.

- Integrate printed numerals throughout the classroom environment.

Examples: Have numbered bins of manipulatives ("Let's use bin number 6 for art today"), numbers on each computer ("Ken can use computer number 2, and Kay can use computer number 3"), numbers on each shelf ("Remember that the vehicles go on the shelf with the number 4"), and numbered sign-in lists ("Chuck is number 7 to sign in this morning"). (Cog G:2.2)

- Assign each child a number at the beginning of the day and numbers on chairs or floor mats that children use throughout that day. Ask children to match their number for the day with the correct chair or mat whenever they sit down to snack, circle, or an activity.

Example: The adult gives Kate a card with the numeral 8 for the day, and asks her periodically throughout the day "What number do you have today, Kate?" The teacher also asks Kate to "Find the chair with number 8 on it." (Cog G:2.1, 2.2)

- At home and in the classroom, provide number symbols in different formats. Make sure that children have experiences seeing, recognizing, and labeling numbers in a variety of materials such as felt board, puzzle pieces, and magnetic numbers; handwritten numbers in pen, pencil, chalk, marker, and paint; numbers on paper, on blackboards, on calendars, in magazines, on signs, on clocks, and written on the mirror or in shaving cream.

- Provide materials that pair printed numerals and sets of objects for counting so children can look at the numeral and count the objects.

Example: At school and at home, Pam has picture books that cover the numbers 1–10, showing one printed numeral and a group of objects to count on each page. Pam's parents show her the number, name it, and help her to count. (Cog G:1.1, 1.2)

- Introduce a printed numeral at the beginning of each day. Name the number and ask for volunteers to select the correct number card. Distinguish the printed numerals from letters that might look similar by giving and asking for examples of when the number is used and when the letter is used (e.g., number 3 and letter E; number 2 or 5 and letter S). Place the number card in a prominent location, and have children count many times throughout the day to the number represented by the printed numeral by arranging activities that make use of the number.

Example: The number of the day is 5, and the teacher opens morning circle by having children identify the numeral on a card, count to 5, and look at similarities and differences between the number 5 and the letter s. During the day, the number 5 comes up as each child is asked to take 5 crackers at snack, make an art project using 5 shapes or colors, point out number 5 in written and printed materials, and count 5 minutes on the clock. (Cog G:1.2, 2.2)

- Use the calendar at home or in the classroom to introduce children to number symbols and patterns. Have them identify the number for the date and put a sticker for the weather on each day (e.g., sunny, cloudy, rainy, snowy); count the weather stickers at the end of the week or month to identify the most and least frequent types of weather.

INTERVENTION ACTIVITIES

Two examples of how to embed this goal and the associated objectives within activities are presented next. For a list of intervention activities that address goals/objectives across areas, see Appendix A.

Cognitive

Cooking

Find or make a simple recipe with numerals and pictures of ingredients and utensils for a cooking project. Write the recipe on a large sheet of paper so it is easy for children to see the numerals. Ask them to identify any numbers they can recognize or label on the recipe. In the process of using the recipe, be sure that children label each numeral and count as they measure ingredients. Introduce concepts of empty/full, heavy/light, big/little, weight, and volume with respect to the numerals in the recipe ("Are there more cups of flour or sugar?" "Are the cups or the spoons going to hold more?" "Which will be heavier, the one cup of sugar or the half cup of milk?").

Shape Collage

Provide a number of shapes that children can use to create collages, having precut them from a variety of papers in a variety of sizes, textures, and colors. Give the children time to decide what they will be making, and have them generate ideas about which shapes will be used (e.g., circles and ovals for faces, triangles for hats, rectangles for houses). Ask each child to estimate how many of each shape they will need and to determine whether the estimate was too few, too many, or just enough. Have the children analyze their completed collages to determine which shapes, sizes, and colors were used the most or the least, as well as to compare the size and number of shapes used with the size and form of the completed collage.

STRAND

H

Phonological Awareness and Emergent Reading

GOAL 1 Demonstrates phonological awareness skills

Objective 1.1 Uses rhyming skills

Objective 1.2 Segments sentences and words

Objective 1.3 Blends single sounds and syllables

Objective 1.4 Identifies same and different sounds at the beginning and end of words

CONCURRENT GOALS

GM B   Play skills (all goals)
Cog B:1   Groups objects, people, or events on basis of specified criteria
Cog H:3   Reads words by sight
SC A   Social-communicative interactions (all goals)
SC B   Production of words, phrases, and sentences (all goals)
Soc B   Participation (all goals)

DAILY ROUTINES

Routine events that provide opportunities for children to demonstrate skills in segmenting, blending, rhyming, and alliteration include the following:

- Arrival and departure

- Bath time

- Bedtime/naptime

- Books and storytime

- Circle time

- Driving in the car

- Mealtime or snack time

- Music activities

- Transition time

- Unstructured playtime

Example: When riding in the car, Coral's parents and brother play rhyming word games. They ask, "What's a word that rhymes with *bee*?" and sing songs with rhyming words and repetitive sounds, some of which are nonsense words (e.g., rhyming/alliterative name song such as *Coral, Coral, Bo-boral, banana fana-fo-foral*). They also ask each other to find objects that start with the same sound. (Cog H:1, 1.1, 1.4)

Example: At bedtime, Jack's parents say prayers with him, emphasizing the last word of one line and leaving out the rhyming word of the next line. They say in unison, "Now I lay me down to *sleep;* I pray the Lord my soul to _____." Jack fills in the word *keep.* (Cog H:1.1)

Example: While driving to school, Tolan's grandmother passes the time by asking him to "Tell me each word you hear." Then she makes simple sentences that reflect immediate events, such as "We are in the car." Tolan identifies each word, although at first not necessarily in sequence. (Cog H:1.2)

Example: At transition times and while waiting in line, the teacher gives children the opportunity to blend sounds and segment words. She asks, "Who can tell me what word these sounds make? G – o – ing." Stephanie says "going!" and the teacher responds by asking Stephanie to think of a word and break it into sounds for other children to identify. (Cog H:1.2, 1.3)

Example: While reading stories, Jamal's mother says each syllable of words separately and asks him to identify the word. She refers to the pictures and begins with compound words: "What does this guy do? This word says cow – boy." Jamal says "He's a cowboy!" (Cog H:1.2)

ENVIRONMENTAL ARRANGEMENTS

- Arrange the classroom into activity areas that include a library/literacy/listening center. Providing a quiet, cozy, and comfortable space invites children to spend time with books, CDs, and tapes and helps associate listening and playing with the sounds of the language with reading and writing. Headphones allow some children to listen to music or stories without disturbing others who are looking at books. Provide materials that encourage children to listen for and reproduce words that rhyme and begin/end with the same sounds and to blend sounds and syllables into words and words into sentences.

  - Audiotape recorders

  - Audiotapes of stories

  - Audiotapes of songs and rhymes

  - Picture books with text on audiotape

  - Nursery rhyme books

  - Alphabet picture and word books

  - Picture cards

- Design the schedule at school and home to include a regular storytime, and select books, stories, and poems that emphasize compound words and words that are easily divided into syllables. Use the titles to have children segment and blend words and build anticipation for the story.

Example: At storytime, the teacher is reading *Cloudy with a Chance of Meatballs.* She says, "Let's see who can figure out the title of today's story. The first word sounds like this: cloud-y." After Toni identifies the first word of the title as Cloudy, the teacher states, "The last word has the sounds meat-ball," and asks for someone else to put the syllables together into a word. After either blending sounds or segmenting each word in the title, the teacher asks children to identify each separate word in the title. (Cog H:1.2, 1.3)

- Make an audiotape of words that rhyme and begin/end with the same sounds. Children are generally quite enthusiastic about listening to themselves and their peers on tape and will follow an adult model to make a round-robin recording.

Example: An adult begins a recording by saying, "This is a tape of our class rhyming. First we will each say *hop,* and then a word that rhymes with *hop.*" Ryan says "Hop, pop"; Maryah says "Hop, top"; Jennell says "Hop, cop," and so forth. If a child says a word that doesn't rhyme, then wait and let peers recognize it as a mistake. Repeat the sequence for words that begin or end with the same sounds, and give peers a chance to recognize errors in alliteration. The teacher introduces a new stimulus word when children begin to run out of ideas or repeat words used earlier. (Cog H:1.1, 1.4)

- During circle time, use the morning greeting as a time to blend and segment sounds in each child's name.

Example: Before each chorus of the "Good Morning Song" for each child, the teacher asks the group to identify the next child's name by blending sounds. "Next we'll greet Kar – na. Let's say the name together—Karna." Each child can also segment their own name into syllables and/or sounds. (Cog H:1.2, 1.3, 2.2)

INTERVENTION ACTIVITIES

Two examples of how to embed this goal and the associated objectives within activities are presented next. For a list of intervention activities that addresses goals/objectives across areas, see Appendix A.

Spring Walk

The children go on a walk to look for signs of spring. The interventionist provides opportunities for children to rhyme words by thinking up rhyming words for the different things they find. The interventionist also prompts children to sound out words and introduces similar beginning and ending sounds.

Example: The class is taking a walk outside, looking at trees, plants, insects, and flowers. The children notice a bee, and when the teacher asks them to think of rhyming words, they come up with *tree, see,* and *me.* The teacher then sounds out the name of a tree: "I see a tree with a funny name: d-o-g w-o-o-d" and asks children to blend the sounds to form the words. She then follows the children's lead as they begin to rhyme the word *dogwood: dog could, dog good, dog hood,* and asks them to think of other words that start with the same sound as dog. They then make sentences using the rhyming phrases and words that start with the letter d. (Cog H:1)

Spring Flowers

Children paint a mural of flowers with bright colors on a large piece of paper. The interventionist can draw the stems ahead of time if desired. To provide opportunities for children to blend sounds, the interventionist says, "I have something behind my back. I'm going to say the sounds and see if you can guess what it is." Examples of words to use are *flower, green, blue, paint, paintbrush,* and *marker.* Throughout the activity, the interventionist encourages children to rhyme, blend, segment, and identify words with the same beginning and ending sounds.

GOAL 2   Uses letter–sound associations to sound out and write words

Objective 2.1   Writes words using letter sounds

Objective 2.2   Sounds out words

Objective 2.3   Produces correct sounds for letters

CONCURRENT GOALS

FM B:1	Writes using three-finger grasp
FM B:3	Prints first name
Cog H:3	Reads words by sight
SC A	Social-communicative interactions (all goals)
SC B	Production of words, phrases, and sentences (all goals)
Soc B	Participation (all goals)

DAILY ROUTINES

Routine events that provide opportunities for children to sound out and write words include the following:

- Arrival and departure
- Bedtime/naptime
- Books and storytime
- Circle time

- Mealtime or snack time

- Transition time

- Unstructured playtime

Example: At morning circle, the teacher selects a letter of the day and asks children to identify peers whose names begin with that letter. "Today we have the letter B. Whose name starts with B?" Children say "Ben, Brit." For introducing new letters, the teacher shows name cards for Kris and Kenny, asking, "These names start with the letter k. What sound does the letter k make?" (Cog H:1.4, 2.3)

Example: Walter's grandfather is going to read *The Rainbow Fish* by Marcus Pfister before putting his grandson to bed. Walter is familiar with the book and his grandfather says, "Let's sound out the title." He points to each letter while encouraging Walter to make the associated sounds in sequence. (Cog H:2.2, 2.3)

Example: The teacher looks at Violet's picture and asks her, "Tell me about your picture." Violet says the picture is of a pumpkin farm she visited over the weekend. The teacher asks Violet to label her picture, helping her to sound out the words *pumpkin* and *farm* as she writes. (Cog H:2.1, 2.2)

ENVIRONMENTAL ARRANGEMENTS

- Arrange the classroom into activity areas that include a reading/writing center. Provide materials in the center that are interesting and appealing to children and provide opportunities for reading and writing letter sounds. Make the library center cozy and comfortable, with carpet, soft pillows, or a minicouch. Decorate the area with posters or children's pictures and locate the library center in a quiet part of the classroom. If possible, replenish the area with new books from a local library every week or two.

  - Audiotapes or CDs that sound out words as children read along in books

  - Picture books with read-along text on audiotape or CD

  - Books with pictures and simple text

  - Age-appropriate books, magazines, catalogs

  - Art materials for children to make their own books

  - Dramatic play props such as open/closed signs, street signs, menus, patients' charts, labels on grocery store items

  - Picture cards with labels

  - Magnetic board and letters

- Display examples of written language in the classroom wherever appropriate. Cubbies are labeled with children's names, labels for materials are

Cognitive

posted on shelves, and a menu is created for snack. Pairing written language and pictures (e.g., a picture of Lego toys with the word Legos) will assist children who are just learning to read. Post written labels for common items in the classroom and at home, and encourage children to sound out the words both in context and separate from the labeled items.

Example: Manuel's parents have made copies of the labels in his classroom for *door, wall, window, table, chair,* and *sink,* and have added *bed, toys,* and *books* as labels in his room at home. Manuel's father shows him the same words on another set of cards and helps him sound or write out the words. (Cog H:2)

- Have children routinely label drawings and paintings by writing word approximations, using letter–sound associations. Invented spellings are acceptable during these earliest attempts to write using letter sounds.

  Example: Helene labels a picture of her birthday party, saying "My party," while writing MI PARDE. Her teacher reads it back, "My party." (Cog H:2.1, 2.2)

- Label children's drawings with the words they dictate, asking for beginning letters of words and drawing attention to each letter–sound combination as it is written.

  Example: Laurence has drawn a picture of his pony and dictates a caption: "This is my pony, Patches." The teacher writes Laurence's caption word for word, asking him for the letter that makes the "p" sound for the words *pony* and *Patches.* (Cog H:2.3)

- Hang colorful alphabet pictures and posters with both upper- and lower-case letters in the classroom and in children's rooms.

  Example: Rochelle's favorite pictures in the classroom are the alphabet posters that have a child's picture and name for each letter. She proclaims her favorites to be "Michelle because her name sounds almost like mine and Rocky because his name starts with the same sound as mine." (Cog H:2.3)

INTERVENTION ACTIVITIES

Two examples of how to embed this goal and the associated objectives within activities are presented next. For a list of intervention activities that address goals/objectives across areas, see Appendix A.

Alphabet Soup

Children make alphabet soup from any soup recipe, using alphabet noodles. Children are given many opportunities to sound out words or produce the phonetic sounds for letters while they make the soup and eat the finished product. The interventionist puts together words consisting of three phonetic units and prompts children to sound out the words, especially encouraging them to sound out words and letters that surface in their soup.

Example: The class is engaged in a cooking activity—making soup for lunch. The teacher has provided a surplus of alphabet noodles so that there are enough for manipulating and for the soup. She gives each child a word to spell that relates to the activity and they search the noodles for letters to make their words: *cook, soup, spoon, stir.* Children sound out consonant–vowel–consonant words on simple recipe cards: *put, can, pat, top, pan, mix.* (Cog H:2.1, 2.2)

Oatmeal Cookies

Children make oatmeal cookies from a recipe. The interventionist writes out the recipe in simple, easy-to-read words and prompts children to sound out words throughout the activity. Words consisting of consonant-vowel-consonant units that can be included in the recipe are *mix, cup,* and *top.*

Example: Manuel's teacher starts to read, "Sprinkle sugar on . . ." and pauses, pointing to the word *top* to encourage Manuel to sound it out. (Cog H:2.2)

GOAL 3 Reads words by sight

Objective 3.1 Identifies letter names

CONCURRENT GOALS

FM B:3 Prints first name
SC A   Social-communicative interactions (all goals)
SC B   Production of words, phrases, and sentences (all goals)
Soc B   Participation (all goals)
Soc D:3 Relates identifying information about self and others

DAILY ROUTINES

Routine events that provide opportunities for children to identify letters and read words by sight include the following:

- Arrival and departure

- Books and storytime

- Circle time

- Community outings

- Travel time

- Transition times

Example: As Dustin and his mother are waiting for the bus, the child is reminded that "Our bus is the one that says *DOWNTOWN;* remember to look for the first letter D." (Cog H:3, 3.1)

Example: While Margarite and her father go to the store, he encourages his daughter to, "Find a sign that says *OPEN;* it will start with the letter O." (Cog H:3, 3.1)

Example: Brett needs to use the bathroom and wants to go there on his own. His teacher reminds him, "Be sure to go in the one that says *BOYS;* that is the one that starts with the letter B, just like your name." (Cog H:3, 3.1)

Example: When reading Joey a book at bedtime, his mother sometimes names different letters and asks Joey to identify them in the text. She also points out the words in titles such as *Hop On Pop,* and encourages him to "read" the titles as she points to each word. (Cog H:3, 3.1)

ENVIRONMENTAL ARRANGEMENTS

- Arrange the classroom into activity areas that include a reading/writing center. Provide materials in the center that are interesting and appealing to children and provide opportunities for reading and writing letter sounds and sight words.

  - Audiotapes or CDs that sound out words as children read along in books

  - Picture books with read-along text on audiotape or CD

  - Books with pictures and simple text

  - Age-appropriate books, magazines, and catalogs

  - Art materials for children to make their own books

  - Dramatic play props such as open/closed signs, street signs, menus, patients' charts, labels on grocery store items

  - Picture cards with labels

  - Alphabet picture/word books

  - Flannelboards with flannel letters and numbers

  - Alphabet puzzles

- Display examples of written language wherever appropriate in the classroom environment. Cubbies are labeled with children's names, names of materials are posted on shelves, and a menu is created for snack. Pairing written language with pictures (e.g., a picture of Lego toys with the word Legos) will assist children who are just learning to read. Encourage children to "read" the labels where they are posted and have a separate set of cards with the same words for children to read by sight and/or match with posted labels.

Example: Jared has great confidence in his ability to read because he recognizes common words from his classroom. He amazes his parents by recognizing by sight most of the same words on a set of cards he brings home. (Cog H:3)

• At circle time, have each child's name written on a card and show the name card during circle each day. Use the names to have children identify letter sounds and to read peers' names by sight.

Example: It is morning circle time, and the teacher holds up a card with the name *HECTOR*, asking "Whose name is this?" Hector recognizes his own name and one or two other children recognize his name also. The teacher then prompts the children to say the sound the letter *h* makes, then goes on to ask, "Who else's name starts with the *h* sound?" Helen answers, "My name does!" (Cog H:3, 3.1)

• Teach children how to spell their first names, and then have them match those letters to words they commonly see in print.

Example: Becca can identify each letter of her name, and when she sees the words *BOYS*, *EXIT*, *CAT*, and *ALPHABET*, she points to each of the first letters and says, "This letter is in my name." (Cog H:3.1)

• Take pictures of familiar objects, events, and people at home and in the classroom, and label them with simple sight words. Have a matching set of cards with the words only, to make a matching card game.

Example: Daniel is playing with a set of cards that his mother made for him. He picks up the picture of his father and reads *DAD* on the caption and sorts through the pile of word cards until he finds the one that says *DAD*. (Cog H:3)

INTERVENTION ACTIVITIES

Two examples of how to embed this goal and the associated objectives within activities are presented next. For a list of intervention activities that address goals/objectives across areas, see Appendix A.

Name Cards

Children make name cards on a piece of cardboard and decorate them with crayons, markers, stickers, glitter, and so forth. The interventionist provides the least level of assistance necessary for each child to have a legible model of his or her name. Opportunities can be provided for children to identify letters

Cognitive

in their names and other children's names. The cards can be used at different times of the day to provide opportunities for children to recognize their names.

Example: During circle time, the teacher shows name cards that the children have made as a way to take attendance. She shows each card and asks, "Is this person here today?" and each child takes his or her name card and posts it on the attendance board. The group is encouraged to read all of the names at the end of the circle. (Cog H:3)

Note: Children may seem to be reading their name cards but may at first be attending to other stimuli (e.g., the length of their name, the decorations on their cards). To determine if the child is actually recognizing his or her name, the interventionist can have the child identify each letter in his or her name.

Letter Search

Children look through magazines, catalogs, and newspapers for specific letters. They cut out and identify letters and glue them on a piece of paper. The teacher can ask children for words that they would like to find letters for and then print those words in large letters. The interventionist can encourage children to find and identify letters that are in their names or for words that reflect other high interest objects, events, people. As children find letters, they can paste them above or below the letters the teacher has printed.

AEPS™

Social-Communication Area
Three to Six Years

LIST OF AEPS TEST ITEMS

Social-Comm

The ability to communicate effectively is fundamental to satisfying relationships and independent functioning throughout life. *Communication* refers to the exchange of symbolic or nonsymbolic messages or information between speaker and listener. *Symbolic communication* is generally referred to as *language* and requires the exchange of words, pictures, tokens, or signs that stand for or represent the actual thing, action, setting, concept, or person. Language is a conventional system that employs a code that represents ideas about the world for the purpose of communication (Bloom & Lahey, 1978). Nonsymbolic communication also conveys messages and information from speaker to listener through gestures, facial expressions, and other actions; however, this form of communication is generally not a conventional system that uses a code to represent ideas about the world.

Infants enter the world as communicators. Their initial communicative efforts are nonsymbolic and indicate to caregivers their pleasure, displeasure, interest, or physiological state. Over time, most children learn to understand and use the symbolic communication or the language code of their environment. Acquisition of both nonsymbolic and symbolic communication permits children to become increasingly independent and effective problem solvers. Children who lack effective communication skills are dependent on caregivers to satisfy their needs and solve their problems.

The Social-Communication Area of the AEPS Curriculum was designed to systematically build and enhance children's symbolic and nonsymbolic communication skills as they use them in daily communicative transactions.

Social-Comm

This area provides strategies that will move children from simple early symbolic and nonsymbolic skills to understanding and using increasingly complex language and socially appropriate communication. The preferred approach is to embed training into the activities and routines that occur throughout the child's day.

The Social-Communication Area is composed of two strands. Strand A (Social-Communicative Interactions) focuses on the child's use of words, phrases, and sentences to develop and enhance social interactions. Learning conversational roles and rules is essential to developing positive and meaningful communicative interactions with peers and adults. Strand B (Production of Words, Phrases, and Sentences) addresses the grammatical structures children need for effective communication.

The pervasiveness of social-communicative behavior and its strong association with cognitive processes are strong arguments not to view these behaviors as independent of other behavioral areas. Team members should observe the child's use of social-communicative behaviors across a range of settings and activities in order to determine whether an impairment is related to or the result of other problems; for example, a child's ability to name colors is dependent on understanding questions such as, "Show me the green one," or "What color is this?" as well as being able to discriminate between colors, which is a cognitive skill. In addition, communicative behaviors can be classified in more than one area; for example, a smile directed to a familiar caregiver can be a social-communicative, cognitive, and social behavior.

The Social-Communication Area Curriculum is divided into four sections: 1) Intervention Considerations, 2) Suggested Activities, 3) Using Activity-Based Intervention, and 4) Area Goals. Intervention Considerations addresses important factors that an interventionist may wish to consider prior to and when working with children who are at risk for or who have disabilities. Suggested Activities provides a selected list of activities that may be particularly helpful when working on social-communication skills. This section also provides suggestions for additional materials that will increase the opportunities for children to practice targeted social-communication skills. The third section provides an illustration of how to target IFSP/IEP goals in the Social-Communication Area using an activity-based intervention approach. The final section, Area Goals, provides suggestions for Concurrent Goals, Daily Routines, Environmental Arrangements, and Intervention Activities in the home and classroom for each goal and associated objectives identified in the Social-Communication Area of the AEPS Test for Three to Six Years.

INTERVENTION CONSIDERATIONS

General considerations when working on social-communication goals and associated objectives in the Social-Communication Area are discussed next.

- The influence of cultural values on children's social-communication behavior should be considered when developing intervention goals and plans; for example, in some cultures, establishing eye contact is not appropriate behavior. In other cultures, children may not be encouraged to communicate openly. Work closely with family members when targeting social-communication goals for the child.

- A hearing evaluation is a critical first step in assessing communication abilities and determining appropriate goals for children. If the child wears a hearing aid, then the adult should make certain it is operating properly. Consultation with a communication specialist is recommended for any child for whom a communication goal has been selected.

- The inability to communicate his or her wants, needs, and feelings can be an extremely frustrating and isolating experience for a child. In many cases, behavior problems in the classroom or at home can be attributed to inappropriate or unsuccessful attempts at communication (e.g., grabbing to get a toy, pushing another child to get a turn). Adults should observe children with hearing/communication problems closely to determine communicative intent, target communication skills that will effectively replace inappropriate behaviors, and develop appropriate intervention plans. It is important to create an environment in which a child needs to use communication to make his or her needs known during routine, child-initiated, and planned intervention activities; for example, placing a juice pitcher within sight but out of the reach of a child may encourage the child to request "juice." Make sure that the child's attempts to speak are consistently rewarded with events that are reinforcing to the child and are logical consequences to the child's language (e.g., if a child says, "Mo," then the adult responds, "Oh, you want more juice," and hands the child juice). Model appropriate communication for the child, without sounding punitive.

- Provide opportunities for children to communicate but do not make repeated demands on children to respond that might intimidate them and actually stifle communication. If a child becomes frustrated or is unwilling to make any attempt to communicate, then it is necessary to re-evaluate programming strategies, taking into consideration individual children's learning styles.

- Positioning of a child with a hearing or communication impairment is critical for optimal use of sensory information. The adult should ensure that the child is facing a speaker and is in proper position to see lips, signs, or pictures, particularly during large group activities such as circle time or storytime. The child may benefit from the addition of visual or kinesthetic cues (e.g., pictures, gestures, objects) to help him or her interpret information. During activities, seating children across from and next to each other (as opposed to facing an empty space or sitting alone) may facilitate communication.

- The adult–child ratio and the positioning of adults in the classroom may influence the frequency or types of child-to-child interactions. Be aware of the amount of "adult talk" in a classroom, as well as the number of adult–child interactions that occur and whether these interactions stifle communicative attempts between peers.

Social-Comm

- Some children may be sensitive to noise or certain sounds. Sounds that seem normal to an adult may be uncomfortably loud to some children; certain frequencies may be painful; and combinations of sounds or too much noise may be uncomfortable or distracting. Be aware of how the environment affects children.

- Children with visual impairments may need additional encouragement to look at or orient to the direction of the person to whom they are speaking. Children may need to be taught what is appropriate personal space (e.g., there are times when it is okay to reach out and touch a friend and times when it is not).

Bilingual Learners

Young children acquiring more than one language simultaneously initially learn vocabulary without distinguishing between languages. The number of words in a child's vocabulary, therefore, should be counted as the *total* number of words or word approximations that the child is using in *both* languages. This principle holds for toddlers learning English as a second language, as well as for children from bilingual and multilingual homes. Typically developing children do not reliably and consistently sort languages into separate systems until they acquire cognitive skills of categorization and classification, usually after the third birthday.

Young children from bilingual homes or who are learning English as a second language should always be assessed for comprehension in both languages and, if possible, in multiple settings. Children may use the family's native language predominantly at home and English at a center-based program, even if they have more sophisticated skills in the native language. An accurate measure of comprehension, therefore, includes presenting AEPS test items in any language to which the child is regularly exposed.

Augmentative Communication

If a child is unable to produce intelligible speech, then it may be necessary to choose an augmentative communication system. Continue to encourage the speech a child does have while pairing that speech with another system. Several systems such as picture communication symbols, language boards, computer-operated systems, or sign language are available. Consultation with parents and a communication specialist will assist in determining the best method for each child. Considerations include the following:

- Portability

- Cost

- Ease of use

- How understandable the system is to people in the child's environment (e.g., Do caregivers, siblings, and peers know the sign for *water*?)

- How much the system will interfere with the child's activities (e.g., Is it difficult to move from activity to activity with the system?)

After determining which communication system is most appropriate for the child, guidelines for deciding what vocabulary to target should be considered. These decisions will also be important when considering what vocabulary to target with children with limited speech. Guidelines for choosing vocabulary items include 1) functionality, 2) frequency of use, and 3) ease or difficulty in pronouncing words. Examples of words/phrases to be included are 1) preferred words (e.g., a picture for "tickle me"); 2) questions or requests (e.g., "I want water"); 3) words used by peers (e.g., "awesome"); 4) funny words (e.g., "okey dokey"); and 5) feeling words (e.g., "sad").

SUGGESTED ACTIVITIES

The following list of activities and materials may be particularly helpful for eliciting skills within the Social-Communication Area. For a complete list of intervention activities, see Appendix A.

Dramatic Play Activities

Dramatic play centers provide excellent places for children to experiment with forms of communication that they have been exposed to at home and in their community. Ideas for dramatic play are endless, and the children may enjoy providing suggestions for themes that are interesting to them. The following themes may be particularly helpful when embedding social-communication goals:

- Camping
- House play
- Restaurant
- Spaceship
- Veterinary office

Other Planned Activities

- Audiotape recorder/CD player
- Book time
- Books/book making

Social-Comm

- Construction toys (with small figures)

- Expressive art

- Flannelboard

- Playdough

- Singing/chants

- Water table

- Zoos and barns

USING ACTIVITY-BASED INTERVENTION

An illustration of how an interventionist can incorporate strategies to enhance the development of a child's social-communication skills is provided next. The child's targeted IFSP/IEP objective is to use words to inform (e.g., describe objects, actions, and events).

- During free play at school, the interventionist notices that Joey is watching a bird through a window. The interventionist follows the child's lead and uses the strategy of delay (e.g., "Look, a . . ."), providing an opportunity for Joey to say, "Bird." If he is unable to verbalize "Bird," then the interventionist models "A bird. It's a bird," or encourages peers who have more advanced verbal skills to describe what they see.

- The interventionist uses parallel talk, commenting on what Joey is doing (e.g., "You're watching the bird"). Joey vocalizes, "Fly." The interventionist expands on the child's initiation with, "Yes, fly. Birds fly."

The interventionist asks open-ended questions that are related to Joey's activity, such as, "What does the bird look like?" If Joey has difficulty answering, then the interventionist provides him with a choice to encourage him to use words to describe the bird, asking, "Is the bird big or little?"

AREA GOALS

This section provides suggestions for concurrent goals, daily routines, environmental arrangements, and intervention activities for the social-communication goals listed in the AEPS Test for Three to Six Years. If an objective has been targeted, then the interventionist can turn to the corresponding goal and determine which suggestions are relevant to address that objective. A standard format is used for each goal: 1) Strand, 2) Goal, 3) Objective(s), 4) Concurrent Goals, 5) Daily Routines, 6) Environmental Arrangements, and 7) Intervention Activities. Concurrent Goals list the AEPS goals from other developmental areas that can often be addressed at the same time the child works on the target goal or associated objectives. Daily Routines present a list of routine activities that may provide opportunities to practice targeted skills. The Environmental Arrangements should be considered when designing children's programs around child-initiated, routine, and planned intervention activities. Finally, the Intervention Activities offer examples of how to embed targeted goals within the context of intervention activities. Additional information on daily routines, environmental arrangements, and planned intervention activities is provided in Chapter 3.

Social-Comm

Social-Communicative Interactions

GOAL 1 Uses words, phrases, or sentences to inform, direct, ask questions, and express anticipation, imagination, affect, and emotions

Objective 1.1 Uses words, phrases, or sentences to express anticipated outcomes

Objective 1.2 Uses words, phrases, or sentences to describe pretend objects, events, or people

Objective 1.3 Uses words, phrases, or sentences to label own or others' affect/emotions

Objective 1.4 Uses words, phrases, or sentences to describe past events

Objective 1.5 Uses words, phrases, or sentences to make commands to and requests of others

Objective 1.6 Uses words, phrases, or sentences to obtain information

Objective 1.7 Uses words, phrases, or sentences to inform

CONCURRENT GOALS

Adap B:1   Carries out all toileting functions
Cog A   Concepts (all goals)
Cog C:3   Retells event in sequence
Cog D:1   Recalls events that occurred on same day, without contextual cues
Cog E   Problem solving (all goals)
Cog F:1   Engages in cooperative, imaginary play
Cog H:1   Demonstrates phonological awareness skills
Soc A:3   Resolves conflicts by selecting effective strategy
Soc B   Participation (all goals)
Soc C:1   Meets physical needs in socially appropriate ways
Soc D:2   Understands how own behaviors, thoughts, and feelings relate to consequences for others
Soc D:3   Relates identifying information about self and others

DAILY ROUTINES

Routine events that provide opportunities for children to have an active role in conversations include the following:

- Arrival and departure

- Bath time

- Bedtime

- Circle time

- Dressing

- Mealtime or snack time

- Transition time

- Travel time

- Unstructured playtime

Example: During mealtime, family members provide opportunities for children to share what they did during the day. (SC A:1.4)

Example: Maria has a goal to point to a picture on her communication board to make commands to or requests of others. During circle time, the interventionist makes sure her communication board is accessible and includes pictures that represent a request to sing a song, listen to a story, or play a circle game. The interventionist provides an opportunity for Maria to use her communication board to make a request during circle time if necessary. The interventionist or a peer provides assistance. (SC A:1.5, adapted)

Example: In closing circle, the interventionist provides opportunities for children to share what they will do when they leave school (e.g., go shopping, take a nap, ride the bus). (SC A:1.1)

Example: While driving on long trips, family members play the game "I see . . ." and children use words to inform by labeling what they see outside. (SC A:1.7)

ENVIRONMENTAL ARRANGEMENTS

- Provide materials that promote communication, and arrange the classroom into activity areas that include a dramatic play center. In the dramatic play center, roles can be varied so that children have opportunities to inform or direct (e.g., store clerk, police officer, forest ranger) or label their own or others' affects/emotions (e.g., feel bad, feel proud).

Example: While Joey is playing with a doll in the house play area, he says, "No cry. My baby." (SC A:1.2)

Example: When using the play telephone at school, children practice using words, phrases, or sentences to obtain information. (SC A:1.6)

- Include pictures in the classroom or books in the library of children displaying various emotions (e.g., happy, sad, angry) to provide opportunities for children to label others' affect/emotions.

Example: After reading a story about people with different emotions, Maria touches "happy" on her communication board, and her friend says, "Are you happy, Maria?" Maria nods. (SC A:1.3)

- Intervention strategies that involve environmental arrangements include the following:
  - Heterogeneous grouping
  - Choices
  - Forgetfulness
  - Visible but unreachable
  - Violation of expectations
  - Piece by piece
  - Assistance
  - Sabotage
  - Negotiation

Example: (Choices) During transition to free play, the interventionist provides children with a choice of two or three activities. Children who are nonverbal indicate choices by touching a representative object (e.g., block, crayon, puppet, book), pointing to a picture on their communication board, or signing. (SC A:1.5, 1.7)

Example: (Negotiation) In the art center, the interventionist provides children with only one bottle of glue. While sharing the glue, the children use words to request or obtain information. (SC A:1.5, 1.6)

INTERVENTION ACTIVITIES

Two examples of how to embed this goal and the associated objectives within activities are presented next. For a list of intervention activities that address goals/objectives across areas, see Appendix A.

Growing Seeds

Children grow their own plants by planting seeds (e.g., corn, beans, marigolds) in paper cups filled with soil. Reading and talking about growing plants provide opportunities for children to ask questions and provide information necessary for children to express anticipated outcomes. Giving only one spoon or one bowl of soil for every two children gives the opportunity for children to make commands to or requests of others (e.g., "Ask Latifa for the spoon"). The interventionist should allow each child to water and care for his or her own plant and have children describe the process of planting seeds during group time.

Example: While planting seeds, the interventionist says, "I wonder what's going to happen when we plant these seeds?" and pauses to give time for children to respond. (SC A:1.1)

Garden Field Trip

The class takes a field trip to public gardens or a local plant nursery. Reading a book about flowers or springtime prior to the trip may help children prepare for the event. The interventionist should encourage children to ask questions on the field trip and to answer any questions directed at them. The interventionist can model appropriate questions or responses and provide opportunities for children to describe what they saw when the class returns. Children may enjoy drawing pictures of what they saw at the nursery, and the interventionist can use communication strategies to facilitate individual goals while looking at the pictures. Children can be encouraged to tell parents about their experiences, and a small report of the day's events can be sent home to aid communication. Drawing simple pictures to indicate the day's events is particularly helpful for nonverbal children so they can "tell" about their day while pointing to pictures.

GOAL 2   Uses conversational rules

Objective 2.1   **Alternates between speaker/listener role**

Objective 2.2   **Responds to topic changes initiated by others**

Objective 2.3   **Asks questions for clarification**

Objective 2.4   **Responds to contingent questions**

Objective 2.5   **Initiates context-relevant topics**

Objective 2.6   **Responds to others' topic initiations**

CONCURRENT GOALS

Cog C:3   Retells event in sequence
Cog D   Recalling events
Cog E:2   Makes statements and appropriately answers questions that require reasoning about objects, situations, or people
Cog F:2   Engages in games with rules
Soc A:1   Interacts with others as play partners
Soc A:2   Initiates cooperative activity
Soc B:2   Watches, listens, and participates during small group activities
Soc B:3   Watches, listens, and participates during large group activities

DAILY ROUTINES

Routine events that provide opportunities for children to use conversational rules include the following:

- Arrival and departure
- Bath time
- Bedtime
- Circle time
- Dressing
- Mealtime or snack time
- Transition time
- Travel time
- Unstructured playtime

Example: At breakfast, Joey's father says, "We're going to the zoo today!" If Joey does not respond, then his father prompts him by saying, "We'll see tigers and elephants and . . ." (SC A.2.6)

Example: Timmy has a goal to supply relevant information following another person's request for clarification, repetition, elaboration, or confirmation of his previous statement using sign language. When Timmy wakes up, he signs, WANT. His mother faces Timmy and speaks clearly: "What do you want?" Timmy responds, EAT. (SC A:2.4, adapted)

ENVIRONMENTAL ARRANGEMENTS

- Provide materials that promote communication and arrange the classroom into activity areas that include a dramatic play/house play activity center.

Example: While playing in the "hair salon," children alternate between speaker and listener roles during conversations between stylists and clients; for example, one child asks another, "You want your hair cut?" and waits for a response. (SC A:2.1)

Example: Latifa speaks on the "telephone" to her friend Joey and says, "Hi. Who's this?" The interventionist who is close by looks expectantly at Joey and nods, but, when Joey does not respond, the interventionist gives him a more direct prompt by modeling, "It's Joey." Joey responds, "Joey." (SC A:2.4)

- Intervention strategies that involve environmental arrangements include the following:
  - Heterogeneous grouping
  - Choices

- Forgetfulness

- Visible but unreachable

- Violation of expectations

- Piece by piece

- Assistance

- Sabotage

- Negotiation

Example: (Choices) During circle time, the interventionist lets children take turns choosing songs; for example, a child says, "I want duck song!" (SC A:2.5)

Example: (Violation of expectations) During snack time, the interventionist serves "blocks" for the children to eat. A child laughs and asks, "Where snack?" (SC A:2.3)

INTERVENTION ACTIVITIES

Two examples of how to embed this goal and the associated objectives within activities are presented next. For a list of intervention activities that address goals/objectives across areas, see Appendix A.

Family Puppets *(see Puppets in Appendix A)*

Children make puppets of their family members and put on a "show" (a stage can be created from an old refrigerator box or by turning a table on its side). The interventionist models appropriate conversational rules (e.g., turn taking) by communicating through puppets. Opportunities for children to use conversational rules (e.g., respond to topic changes, respond to contingent questions) occur when children "talk" to each other through their puppets or can be prompted by the interventionist if necessary. Encouraging children to play act an event they are familiar with, such as eating dinner, may help them focus on conversational rules.

Example: The interventionist plans an opportunity for children to converse by having two children at a time put on a show for the class. The interventionist may need to prompt the children (e.g., looking at them expectantly, modeling an exchange). (SC A:2)

Going to Grandma's

Children use conversational rules during a pretend visit to Grandma's house. They may dress up for their visit to play the role of "grandma." The interventionist designs opportunities for a child to practice specific goals by playing

Social-Comm

the role of grandma and planning opportunities for targeted skills; for example, the interventionist questions the child during role play to provide opportunities for the child to supply relevant information when responding. The interventionist should be in close proximity when children are play acting to provide prompts if necessary. This activity can be modified for a wide range of events and places.

Example: Timmy's interventionist knows that he enjoys making cookies with his grandmother, so when Timmy comes to "visit," his interventionist says, "I'm going to make cookies." The interventionist pauses to allow Timmy an opportunity to sign, ME HELP? (SCA:2.6, adapted)

GOAL 3   Establishes and varies social-communicative roles

Objective 3.1   Varies voice to impart meaning

Objective 3.2   Uses socially appropriate physical orientation

CONCURRENT GOALS

Cog F:1	Engages in cooperative, imaginary play
Cog H:1	Demonstrates phonological awareness skills
Soc A:1	Interacts with others as play partners
Soc A:3	Resolves conflicts by selecting effective strategy
Soc B:2	Watches, listens, and participates during small group activities
Soc B:3	Watches, listens, and participates during large group activities

DAILY ROUTINES

Routine events that provide opportunities for children to establish and vary social-communicative roles include the following:

- Arrival and departure
- Bath time
- Bedtime
- Circle time
- Dressing
- Mealtime or snack time
- Travel time
- Transition time
- Unstructured playtime

Example: When Latifa comes inside from playing, her mother says, "Remember to whisper, Latifa. Your brother is sleeping." Latifa whispers, "Okay." (SC A:3.1)

Example: Alice uses a wheelchair to get around at home and at school. During mealtime and unstructured playtime at school, Alice uses an adapted chair or is positioned on the floor so she is at the same level as her peers and can look at her friends' faces when communicating. (SC A:3.2)

ENVIRONMENTAL ARRANGEMENTS

- Provide materials that promote communication and arrange the classroom into activity areas that include a dramatic play/house play activity center. Materials such as puppets, dollhouses, construction toys with miniature people or figurines, zoo and zoo animals, barn and barn animals, dolls, and class pets provide opportunities for children to take on different social-communicative roles.

- Take a field trip to a classroom of younger children. Have special days in your classroom for younger siblings to visit.

    Example: As children speak to younger siblings, they have opportunities to use shorter and less complex sentences. (SC A:3)

- Intervention strategies that involve environmental arrangements include heterogeneous grouping.

- Children with visual impairments may need additional encouragement to look at or orient to the person to whom they are speaking. Children may need to be taught what is appropriate personal space (e.g., there are times when it is okay to reach out and touch a friend and times when it is not).

INTERVENTION ACTIVITIES

Two examples of how to embed this goal and the associated objectives within activities are presented next. For a list of intervention activities that address goals/objectives across areas, see Appendix A.

Animal Puppets *(see Puppets in Appendix A)*

Children make puppets of animals or cartoon characters and have a puppet show. Puppet shows provide opportunities for children to vary their social-communicative roles as they interact with their puppets. The interventionist joins in the show by using a puppet, following the children's lead, and providing appropriate models of targeted skills.

Social-Comm

Washing Babies

Children wash their baby dolls in small tubs of water with soap, shampoo, washcloths, soft hairbrushes, and towels. Provide fewer materials than the number of children to provide opportunities for children to share and to communicate their needs. As children take on the "caregiver" role, opportunities arise for them to alter their voices as they talk to their babies.

Production of Words, Phrases, and Sentences

GOAL 1   Uses verbs

Objective 1.1   Uses auxiliary verbs

Objective 1.2   Uses copula verb "to be"

Objective 1.3   Uses third person singular verb forms

Objective 1.4   Uses irregular past tense verbs

Objective 1.5   Uses regular past tense verbs

Objective 1.6   Uses present progressive "ing"

CONCURRENT GOALS

FM A	Bilateral motor coordination (all goals)
FM B	Emergent writing (all goals)
GM A:2	Alternates feet walking up and down stairs
GM B	Play skills (all goals)
Adap A	Mealtime (all goals)
Adap B	Personal hygiene (all goals)
Adap C	Dressing and undressing (all goals)
Cog B:1	Groups objects, people, or events on the basis of specified criteria
Cog C:3	Retells event in sequence
Cog D:1	Recalls events that occurred on same day, without contextual cues
Cog E:1	Evaluates solutions to problems
Cog F:1	Engages in cooperative, imaginary play
Cog G:1	Counts at least 20 objects
Cog H:1	Demonstrates phonological awareness skills
Soc A	Interaction with others (all goals)
Soc C	Interaction with environment (all goals)
Soc D	Knowledge of self and others (all goals)

DAILY ROUTINES

Routine events that provide natural opportunities for children to use verbs include the following:

- Arrival and departure

- Bath time

- Bedtime

- Circle time

- Dressing

- Mealtime and snack time

- Transition time

- Travel time

- Unstructured playtime

Example: While traveling in the car, family members talk to their children about what they see people or animals doing (e.g., walking, playing, running), emphasizing the "ing" ending. (SC B:1.6)

Example: During circle time, Manuel's interventionist says, "I am very happy to see you today!" emphasizing "am," and Manuel says, "I am, too." (SC B:1.2)

ENVIRONMENTAL ARRANGEMENTS

- Provide materials that encourage communication, and arrange the classroom into activity areas that include a dramatic play center. Provide a time for children to talk about what happened during the day and share their experiences.

Example: While Manuel is playing in the "doctor's office," his interventionist follows his lead and gets involved in the play. The interventionist models a third person singular verb form by saying, "Doctor, Joey has a broken leg. What is wrong with Timmy?" Manuel says, "Timmy has a cold." (SC B:1.3)

- Sing songs, do fingerplays, or tell nursery rhymes that use verbs.

Example: In circle, the children sing a familiar song that is full of past tense verbs such as "Jack and Jill went up the hill to fetch a pail of water. Jack fell down and broke his crown and Jill came tumbling after." (SC B:1.4)

- Intervention strategies that involve environmental arrangements include the following:

  - Heterogeneous grouping

  - Choices

  - Forgetfulness

  - Visible but unreachable

  - Violation of expectations

  - Piece by piece

- Assistance

- Sabotage

- Negotiation

Example: (Forgetfulness) The interventionist pours juice during snack time but "forgets" to provide any snack items. A child says, "I'm hungry!" (SC B:1.2)

Example: (Violation of expectations) The interventionist serves the children blocks for snack, and children protest, "We can't eat blocks!" (SC B:1.1)

INTERVENTION ACTIVITIES

Two examples of how to embed this goal and the associated objectives within activities are presented next. For a complete list of intervention activities that address goals/objectives across areas, see Appendix A.

Zoo Field Trip

The interventionist takes the class on a field trip to the zoo. Field trips are exciting for children and can be structured to provide opportunities for them to use verbs. Reading a book on the subject of the field trip ahead of time will help children anticipate events. Talking about what the animals are doing and how the child is feeling and providing models of verb forms throughout the field trip facilitates the use of verbs. Back in the classroom, the interventionist can set up a zoo in the dramatic play area, draw pictures of the trip, or write a story to further facilitate the child's use of verbs. The interventionist models the appropriate verb form if necessary.

Example: After returning from the zoo, Latifa's interventionist writes a group story about what happened on the field trip. Latifa shares, "I went to the zoo. Zebras ran around." (SC B:1.4)

Ants on a Log

Children make their own snacks by spreading peanut butter on a piece of celery (log) and placing raisins (ants) in a row on the peanut butter. The interventionist can talk about what he or she is doing (e.g., spreading, placing, eating) and encourage children to talk about what they are doing throughout the activity. Opportunities can be provided for children to explain how they made their snacks to facilitate the use of regular and irregular past tense verbs (e.g., *opened, washed, spread, made, put*).

Example: While spreading peanut butter, the interventionist uses self-talk: "I'm spreading, and you are . . ." (providing an opportunity for a child to say, "spreading"). (SC B:1.6)

Social-Comm

GOAL 2   Uses noun inflections

Objective 2.1   Uses possessive "s"

Objective 2.2   Uses irregular plural nouns

Objective 2.3   Uses regular plural nouns

CONCURRENT GOALS

FM A:1	Uses two hands to manipulate objects, each hand performing different movements
FM B:3	Prints first name
Adap A:1	Eats and drinks a variety of foods using appropriate utensils with little or no spilling
Adap B:2	Washes and grooms self
Adap C:2	Selects appropriate clothing and dresses self at designated times
Adap C:3	Fastens fasteners on garments
Cog B:1	Groups objects, people, or events on the basis of specified criteria
Cog C:3	Retells event in sequence
Cog F:1	Engages in cooperative, imaginary play
Cog G:1	Counts at least 20 objects
Cog H:1	Demonstrates phonological awareness skills
Soc A:2	Initiates cooperative activity
Soc C:1	Meets physical needs in socially appropriate ways
Soc D:1	Communicates personal likes and dislikes

DAILY ROUTINES

Routine events that provide natural opportunities for children to use noun inflections include the following:

- Arrival and departure

- Bath time

- Bedtime

- Circle time

- Dressing

- Mealtime and snack time

- Transition time

- Travel time

- Unstructured playtime

Example: At departure time, Manuel's teacher holds up Maria's coat and jokingly says, "Here's your coat, Manuel!" Manuel responds, "No, that's Maria's coat." (SC B:2.1)

Example: While driving on long trips, family members play the game "I see . . ." and model appropriate regular and irregular plural nouns (e.g., horses, geese) for the child. (SC B:2.2, 2.3)

ENVIRONMENTAL ARRANGEMENTS

- Provide materials that promote communication and arrange the classroom into activity areas that include a dramatic play center. Provide objects as examples of regular plural nouns (e.g., blocks, cars, glasses, horses, cows, coats, hats) and objects as examples of irregular plural nouns (e.g., mice, geese, teeth, feet). Frequently model correct plural forms of both regular and irregular nouns during play with children.

- Place pictures around the classroom and books in the library area that show examples of regular plural nouns (e.g., bubbles, trees, birds) and irregular plural nouns (e.g., feet, geese, mice).

- Sing songs, read nursery rhymes, and do fingerplays that involve both regular and irregular plural nouns, such as the following:

    - "If you're happy and you know it, clap your hands. If you're mad and you know it, stomp your feet . . ."

    - "The wheels on the bus go round and round . . ."

    - "Five little monkeys jumping on the bed . . ."

- Intervention strategies that involve environmental arrangements include the following:

    - Heterogeneous grouping

    - Choices

    - Forgetfulness

    - Visible but unreachable

    - Violation of expectations

    - Piece by piece

    - Assistance

    - Sabotage

    - Negotiation

Example: (Forgetfulness) The interventionist pretends to pour juice on the table, but a child reaches out to stop her. The interventionist asks, "Oh, no. What do I need?" The child says, "Cups." (SC B:2.3)

Social-Comm

Example: (Violation of expectations) The interventionist gives the children popsicle sticks to draw with instead of crayons. Joey looks up and says, "No write." The interventionist asks, "What do you need?" Joey responds, "Crayons." (SC B:2.3)

Example: (Negotiation) The interventionist provides only a few collage materials during a free-choice activity. A child comments, "I need more sticks." (SC B:2.3)

INTERVENTION ACTIVITIES

Two examples of how to embed this goal and the associated objectives within activities are presented next. For a list of intervention activities that address goals/objectives across areas, see Appendix A.

Whose Shoes?

All children take off one shoe and put it in the middle of the circle. One child at a time picks a shoe (not his or her own) and guesses whose shoe it is by looking for the match. The interventionist lets each child have more than one turn and models or reinforces other children's appropriate use of "s" to express possession (e.g., "That's right. It's Timmy's!"). Regular and irregular plural nouns are emphasized throughout the activity (e.g., socks, shoes, children, shoelaces, feet).

Example: The interventionist has Eric, who has a visual impairment, find the matching shoe by feeling the shoes on children's feet. Once he finds the match, the interventionist prompts him by saying, "You found the other shoe on Maria, so whose shoe do you have?" Eric replies, "Maria's." (SC B:2.1)

Body Tracing

The interventionist or a friend traces around children while they lie on butcher paper. Children color their outlines with crayons or markers. The interventionist provides opportunities to use noun inflections throughout the activity by prompting the children to name different body parts that are plural (e.g., eyes, ears, toes, fingers, legs, arms, feet). During the close of the activity, a strategy that provides opportunities for children to use possessive "s" is to "forget" whose picture is whose (e.g., "It's Lisa's").

GOAL 3   Asks questions

Objective 3.1   Asks yes/no questions

Objective 3.2   Asks questions with inverted auxiliary

Objective 3.3   Asks "when" questions

Objective 3.4   Asks "why," "who," and "how" questions

Objective 3.5   Asks "what" and "where" questions

Objective 3.6   Asks questions using rising inflections

CONCURRENT GOALS

Cog A   Concepts (all goals)
Cog B:1   Groups objects, people, or events on the basis of specified criteria
Cog C:2   Places objects in series according to length or size
Soc B:2   Watches, listens, and participates during small group activities
Soc B:3   Watches, listens, and participates during large group activities
Soc C:2   Follows context-specific rules outside home and classroom

DAILY ROUTINES

Routine events that provide natural opportunities for children to ask questions include the following:

- Arrival and departure

- Bath time

- Bedtime

- Circle time

- Dressing

- Mealtime and snack time

- Transition time

- Travel time

- Unstructured playtime

    Example: After dinner, Manuel asks, "Can I have a cookie?" (SC B:3.1)
    Example: During school, some of the children go outside while others do an art project inside. Manuel asks, "Why can't I go outside?" (SC B:3.2, 3.4)

ENVIRONMENTAL ARRANGEMENTS

- Provide materials that promote communication and arrange the classroom into activity areas that include a dramatic play center.

    Example: While talking on the "telephone" to her mother, Latifa asks, "When you come pick me up?" (SC B:3.3)

- Intervention strategies that involve environmental arrangements include the following:

  - Heterogeneous grouping

  - Choices

  - Forgetfulness

  - Visible but unreachable

  - Violation of expectations

  - Piece by piece

  - Assistance

  - Sabotage

  - Negotiation

Example: (Choices) During free play, the children must ask permission to use the computer. A child asks, "I go to computer?" and the interventionist models, "May you go? Yes, you may." (SC B:3.2)

Example: (Forgetfulness) During storytime, the interventionist pretends to read from her hands, and a child comments, "Where book?" (SC B:3.5)

Example: (Negotiation) During snack time, the interventionist provides more crackers at one table than another. When a child asks for more, the interventionist directs him to the other table. "Ask Joey for more crackers." (SC B:3.1)

Example: (Violation of expectations) Serving the children blocks for snack may stimulate questions such as, "Where is the snack?" (SC B:3.5)

INTERVENTION ACTIVITIES

Two examples of how to embed this goal and the associated objectives within activities are presented next. For a list of intervention activities that address goals/objectives across areas, see Appendix A.

Visit from the Vet

A veterinarian is invited to talk to the class about what he or she does at work and about care for pets. The interventionist informs the children about the visitor before the veterinarian arrives and provides opportunities for children to ask questions before, during, and after the visit. The interventionist provides appropriate models of questions or prompts the children to ask questions if necessary.

Example: When a veterinarian comes to visit, Latifa's interventionist prompts her during the question and answer time, "Latifa, would you like to ask a question such as, 'How do you help animals?' " (emphasizing the words *why, who,* or *how*). Latifa asks, "How you help animals?" (SC B:3.4)

Animal Charades

One child chooses a card with an animal (it is helpful to do this after talking about or reading a book about animals), and the other children ask questions about the animal. Children ask questions such as, "What do you eat?" or "Where do you live?" The interventionist provides prompts to facilitate the children asking and answering questions. The children may make animal cards by cutting out pictures of animals from magazines and gluing them on cardboard.

GOAL 4   Uses pronouns

Objective 4.1   Uses subject pronouns

Objective 4.2   Uses object pronouns

Objective 4.3   Uses possessive pronouns

Objective 4.4   Uses indefinite pronouns

Objective 4.5   Uses demonstrative pronouns

CONCURRENT GOALS

FM A	Bilateral motor coordination (all goals)
FM B	Emergent writing (all goals)
GM A:2	Alternates feet walking up and down stairs
GM B	Play skills (all goals)
Adap B	Personal hygiene (all goals)
Adap C	Dressing and undressing (all goals)
Cog A	Concepts (all goals)
Cog B:1	Groups objects, people, or events on the basis of specified criteria
Cog D:1	Recalls events that occurred on same day, without contextual cues
Cog F:1	Engages in cooperative, imaginary play
Cog H:1	Demonstrates phonological awareness skills
Soc A	Interaction with others (all goals)
Soc B:2	Watches, listens, and participates during small group activities
Soc B:3	Watches, listens, and participates during large group activities
Soc D	Knowledge of self and others (all goals)

DAILY ROUTINES

Routine events that provide natural opportunities for children to use pronouns include the following:

- Arrival and departure

- Bath time
- Bedtime
- Circle time
- Dressing
- Mealtime or snack time
- Transition time
- Travel time
- Unstructured playtime

Example: During mealtime, families wait for children to initiate requests for second helpings and model appropriate use of pronouns (e.g., "I want more potatoes, please"). (SC B:4.1)

Example: During outdoor playtime, Manuel comes crying to the interventionist and says, "He hurt me." (SC B:4.1)

ENVIRONMENTAL ARRANGEMENTS

- Provide materials that promote communication and arrange the classroom into activity areas that include a dramatic play/house play center.

  Example: As a child sets the table in the house play center, he or she comments, "This is my cup, and this is your cup." (SC B:4.3)

- Intervention strategies that involve environmental arrangements include the following:
  - Heterogeneous grouping
  - Choices
  - Forgetfulness
  - Visible but unreachable
  - Piece by piece
  - Assistance
  - Sabotage
  - Negotiation

  Example: (Choices) The interventionist asks, "Do you want to wash babies with her or play cars with him?" (SC B:4.2)

  Example: (Visible but unreachable) At snack time, the interventionist puts the juice out of reach and pauses, waiting for children to initiate, "We want juice." (SC B:4.1)

Example: (Piece by piece) While building a fire station with Legos or Duplos, the interventionist gives blocks to the children a few at a time, waiting for the children to ask for more (e.g., "Please give me more"; "Give me all of them"). (SC B:4.4)

INTERVENTION ACTIVITIES

Two examples of how to embed this goal and the associated objectives within activities are presented next. For a list of intervention activities that address goals/objectives across areas, see Appendix A.

Picture Day

Children bring in pictures of their family or use pictures taken at school to share during group time. The interventionist provides a time for other children to ask questions about family members (e.g., "How old is your sister?") to facilitate the children's use of pronouns.

Example: Manuel's interventionist prompts him, "You are with your brother in this picture; he looks really big." Manuel says, "That's José. He is big." (SC B:4.1)

Me Books (see Books/Book Making in Appendix A)

Children make a book by gluing pictures cut from magazines to represent their family members, tracing their handprints, cutting out pictures of favorite toys or foods, and dictating stories about themselves to the interventionist. The interventionist arranges the environment, incorporating strategies such as negotiation to increase opportunities for children to communicate and use pronouns. If necessary, the interventionist models appropriate pronouns for the child.

Example: While dictating his Me Book, Joey says, "Mine brother." The interventionist models while writing "This is my brother," and Joey repeats, "Yeah, my brother." (SC B:4.3)

GOAL 5   Uses descriptive words

Objective 5.1   Uses adjectives

Objective 5.2   Uses adjectives to make comparisons

Objective 5.3   Uses adverbs

Objective 5.4   Uses prepositions

Objective 5.5   Uses conjunctions

Objective 5.6   Uses articles

Social-Comm

CONCURRENT GOALS

FM A	Bilateral motor coordination (all goals)
GM B:2	Bounces, catches, kicks, and throws ball
GM B:4	Rides and steers two-wheel bicycle
Adap A:1	Eats and drinks a variety of foods using appropriate utensils with little or no spilling
Adap B	Personal hygiene (all goals)
Cog A	Concepts (all goals)
Cog B:1	Groups objects, people, or events on the basis of specified criteria
Cog C:2	Places objects in series according to length or size
Cog C:3	Retells event in sequence
Cog D:1	Recalls events that occurred on same day, without contextual cues
Cog E:2	Makes statements and appropriately answers questions that require reasoning about objects, situations, or people
Cog F:1	Engages in cooperative, imaginary play
Cog H:1	Demonstrates phonological awareness skills
Soc A:2	Initiates cooperative activity
Soc A:3	Resolves conflicts by selecting effective strategy
Soc B:2	Watches, listens, and participates during small group activities
SocB:3	Watches, listens, and participates during large group activities
Soc D	Knowledge of self and others (all goals)

DAILY ROUTINES

Routine events that provide opportunities for children to use descriptive words include the following:

- Arrival and departure
- Bath time
- Bedtime
- Circle time
- Dressing
- Mealtime or snack time
- Transition time
- Travel time
- Unstructured playtime

Example: Parents encourage children to use adjectives to describe objects or events during bath time by commenting on the temperature of the water, the "wet" washcloth, or the "slippery" soap. (SC B:5.1)

Example: While playing "dinosaurs" with a friend, a child says, "I have more dinosaurs than you." (SC B:5.2)

ENVIRONMENTAL ARRANGEMENTS

- Provide toys that promote communication, and arrange the classroom into activity areas that include a dramatic play/house play center.

    Example: While playing with blocks and cars, Manuel says to Joey, "I'm in front of you." (SC B:5.4)

    Example: While Latifa is "eating" in the kitchen of the housekeeping area, she says, "Mmm. This tastes good." (SC B:5.3)

- Intervention strategies that involve environmental arrangements include the following:

    - Heterogeneous grouping

    - Choices

    - Forgetfulness

    - Visible but unreachable

    - Violation of expectations

    - Piece by piece

    - Assistance

    - Sabotage

    - Negotiation

    Example: (Choices) The interventionist serves animal crackers for snack, and children choose the ones they want to eat. The interventionist models the use of articles by saying, "I want a horse. What do you want?" Latifa says, "I want a lion." (SC B:5.6)

    Example: (Violation of expectations) Serving children pretend food for snack provides opportunities for them to use descriptive words (e.g., "Bananas taste yummy"). (SC B:5.3)

    Example: (Assistance) When a child is working on a puzzle with shapes or colors, put pieces into a clear container with a lid. The child will have to request the item by describing it (e.g., "I need the blue square"). (SC B:5.1)

INTERVENTION ACTIVITIES

Two examples of how to embed this goal and the associated objectives within activities are presented next. For a list of intervention activities that address goals/objectives across areas, see Appendix A.

Social-Comm

Feely Bag

Children gather small objects from a nature walk (leaves, flowers, pebbles, pine cones, seeds) and put them in a paper bag or large sock. One at a time, children reach into the bag without looking and describe the object they are touching. While children gather objects, the interventionist can encourage opportunities to use prepositions to describe where they found objects (e.g., under a rock, on the stump). Children use adjectives to describe the objects (e.g., "the stone is cold") and to make comparisons (e.g., "the rock is heavier than the feather"), and they use adverbs to modify verbs (e.g., "the feather moves slowly").

Example: While describing a pine cone, Latifa says, "It feels hard." Her interventionist prompts her by saying, "It feels hard and . . ." Latifa continues, "It feels hard and prickly." (SC B:5.5)

How Fast Do They Grow?

Children plant seeds in small planters or paper cups and measure their growth over time. The interventionist can introduce the activity by showing pictures of full-grown plants or flowers, and provide opportunities for children to use adjectives to describe the pictures. Choose seeds for plants that grow quickly, such as grass, corn, or beans. While children plant seeds, the interventionist should encourage them to describe how the soil, water, and seeds feel, to compare the different seeds using descriptive words (e.g., "This one's bigger"), and to use prepositions to describe the process (e.g., "The soil goes in the cup"). To extend this activity over time, children can measure plant growth on a piece of paper taped to the wall behind the plants.

Example: The interventionist has children mark the growth of their plants on pieces of tape placed on a wall. The interventionist guides Eric's hands to feel the pieces of tape and says, "Feel this, Eric. This is your plant's height, and this is Maria's. Her plant is bigger than yours. Now here is your plant, and here is Manuel's. Your plant is . . ." Eric says, "Bigger than Manuel's." (SC B:5.2)

AEPS™

Social Area
Three to Six Years

LIST OF AEPS TEST ITEMS

Social

Social

As children interact with caregivers, siblings, and peers, their social behaviors are shaped by the reactions and guidance of these significant people. As children grow up, they will be expected to function in group settings, to interact in socially appropriate ways, and to follow rules. Adults in children's environments are responsible for teaching and encouraging the development of social skills that will provide the foundation for understanding and participating in increasingly complicated social exchanges.

Infants are born dependent on caregivers to meet all of their essential needs. The relationship that begins as a physiological necessity develops into a social and emotional bond between caregiver and child. Within the context of these first relationships with familiar adults, the infant is introduced to the rules of social initiations and responses; for example, when an infant cries, the caregiver responds by feeding, comforting, or changing the child. When the infant laughs, the caregiver usually responds positively by laughing, smiling, or talking to the baby.

The socialization process entails a progressive movement away from the caregiver as a provider of social stimulation and regulation. The child begins to play independently for short periods of time and to play in the presence of peers or siblings. As children learn to care for themselves, they first master necessary skills (e.g., putting on clothing) and later become aware of the social implications for the activity (e.g., wearing a bathing suit when swimming). As children mature, their sensitivity to social expectations increases, and they become more responsive to subtle cues provided by other social agents.

Interaction with peers requires a group of skills that develop gradually during the first 3 years of life and are refined as the child's experiential base grows. Two babies may begin playing together by pulling and grabbing, but this behavior will evolve into social play as the babies get older and learn how to interact with each other. During the preschool years, children learn to play together cooperatively. Play often originates with children engaging in parallel play. At this stage, children watch and imitate other children as they play, and they increase their overall rate of communication and social interaction. In time, children begin to share ideas or activities; for example, one child shows another how to build a tower or make a waterwheel turn. Eventually, children learn to maintain their communicative interchanges and engage in cooperative play by working together toward a common goal (e.g., building a house together).

It is important to view the Social Area as interdependent with other developmental areas. Social interactions generally have motor, communicative, and cognitive dimensions. When a child asks a peer to help move a large block, he or she is using motor skills (maintaining balance), communication skills (using words to direct others), and cognitive skills (problem solving). In addition, team members should observe children's use of social behaviors across a range of settings and activities in order to determine if their social skills are related to other factors; for example, a child who repeatedly quarrels with one child may actually have the ability to resolve conflicts with other children or with siblings. A child with a motor impairment may have difficulty maintaining participation in gross motor activities but not in circle time.

The Social Area is composed of four strands. Strand A (Interaction with Others) focuses on the child's ability to maintain a relationship with others as play partners, engage in cooperative activities, and resolve conflicts using effective strategies. Strand B (Participation) focuses on the child's ability to initiate and maintain participation in age-appropriate activities, including participation in small and large groups. Strand C (Interaction with Environment) examines the child's ability to meet physical needs in socially appropriate ways and follow rules in different environments. Strand D (Knowledge of Self and Others) focuses on the child's ability to communicate personal likes and dislikes; to understand how their own behaviors, thoughts, and feelings relate to consequences for others; and to relate identifying information about self and others.

The Social Area curriculum is divided into four sections: 1) Intervention Considerations, 2) Suggested Activities, 3) Using Activity-Based Intervention, and 4) Area Goals. Intervention Considerations addresses important factors that an interventionist may wish to consider prior to and when working with children who are at risk for or who have disabilities. Suggested Activities provides a selected list of activities that may be particularly helpful when working on social skills. This section also provides suggestions for additional materials that will increase the opportunities for children to practice targeted social skills. The third section provides an illustration of how to target IFSP/IEP goals in the Social Area using an activity-based intervention approach. The final section, Area Goals, provides suggestions for Concurrent Goals, Daily Routines, Environmental Arrangements, and Intervention Activities in the home and classroom for each goal and associated objectives identified in the Social Area of the AEPS Test for Three to Six Years.

INTERVENTION CONSIDERATIONS

General considerations when working on social skills are discussed next.

- The influence of cultural values on children's social behavior should be considered when developing intervention goals and plans. Understanding a child's social and ethnic environment can help prevent culturally inappropriate expectations; conflicting demands; and frustration and confusion for teachers, family members, and the child; for example, family-oriented cultures may place less importance on a child's ability to interact with peers than more peer-oriented cultures. The best way to understand a family's values is by talking to them and learning about their culture.

- Identify primary adults who interact with the child and include them in the child's program. Young children tend to exhibit the most sophisticated social skills in the presence of familiar adults and peers and in familiar settings.

- Routine events in the child's environment provide many opportunities for learning socially appropriate behaviors. Many of the accepted social conventions we share are grounded in the simple daily routines that we learned as children (e.g., saying hello to friends).

- The range of social styles in young children is broad, and children should be allowed to develop interaction skills that match their temperament. Particular attention should be paid to how children communicate.

- Often, a child's unacceptable behavior can be greatly reduced or eliminated by substituting a more socially acceptable behavior; for example, if children are grabbing toys from each other, instead of reprimanding them for their behavior (e.g., "Don't grab"), provide them with an acceptable way of

Social

accomplishing the goal (e.g., "Ask Joe to share"). Especially when working with children with communicative impairments, it is important to provide frequent models of the language they are lacking, as well as the means to communicate their wants and needs.

SUGGESTED ACTIVITIES

Activities that are child oriented are likely to elicit more social interactions between peers than those that are adult oriented. Activities that require sharing and cooperation among children to complete (as opposed to solitary activities such as puzzles or pegboards) will often encourage spontaneous social interactions among peers. The following list of activities and materials may be particularly helpful for eliciting skills within the Social Area. For a complete list of intervention activities, see Appendix A.

- Birthday party
- Board games
- Body tracing
- Box town
- Grocery store
- Group murals
- Group outdoor games
- Hospital or doctor's office
- Large constructions
- Make-it-move painting
- Mud play
- Post office
- Puppets
- Shoe store
- Tents

USING ACTIVITY-BASED INTERVENTION

An illustration of how an interventionist can incorporate strategies to enhance the development of a child's social skills is provided next. The child's targeted IFSP/IEP target skill is to establish and maintain proximity with peers during unstructured, child-directed activities.

- During a free choice time, the interventionist *observes* Manuel watching another child driving cars on "roads" in the sandbox. She has *arranged the environment* in a way to capitalize on his interests, knowing that Manuel really enjoys playing with cars and trucks.

- The interventionist *follows the child's lead,* noticing Manuel's interest in the cars, and decides to join in the activity, playing with the cars, too. She *prompts* Manuel verbally to join in the activity (e.g., "Come play over here, Manuel!"). If he does not respond, then the interventionist *provides additional guidance to facilitate his play* by taking Manuel by the hand to a spot that is in close proximity to the other child and handing him a car.

- The interventionist *purposefully includes interesting materials* in the sandbox, such as a dump truck and a fire truck, to encourage Manuel and his peers to be involved and close to each other. A *limited number* of toys provides an opportunity for children to negotiate and share, and other children *model* these more advanced social skills for Manuel. The interventionist uses *self-talk* and *parallel talk* during the activity, commenting, "We're driving cars and sitting with our friends."

AREA GOALS

This section provides suggestions for concurrent goals, daily routines, environmental arrangements, and intervention activities for the social goals and associated objectives listed in the AEPS Test for Three to Six Years. A standard format is used for each goal: 1) Strand, 2) Goal, 3) Objective(s), 4) Concurrent Goals, 5) Daily Routines, 6) Environmental Arrangements, and 7) Intervention Activities. Concurrent Goals list related AEPS goals from other developmental areas that can often be addressed at the same time the child works on the target goal or associated objectives. Daily Routines present a list of routine activities that may provide opportunities to practice targeted skills. The Environmental Arrangements section should be considered when designing children's programs around child-initiated, routine, and planned intervention activities. Finally, the Intervention Activities offer examples of how to embed targeted goals within the context of intervention activities. Additional information on daily routines, environmental arrangements, and planned intervention activities is provided in Chapter 3 of this volume.

Interaction with Others

GOAL 1   Interacts with others as play partners

Objective 1.1   Responds to others in distress or need

Objective 1.2   Establishes and maintains proximity to others

Objective 1.3   Takes turns with others

Objective 1.4   Initiates greetings to others who are familiar

Objective 1.5   Responds to affective initiations from others

CONCURRENT GOALS

GM B   Play skills (all goals)
Cog F   Play (all goals)
SC A   Social-communicative interactions (all goals)
SC B   Production of words, phrases, and sentences (all goals)
Soc B   Participation (all goals)

DAILY ROUTINES

Routine events that provide opportunities for children to interact with and re-spond to peers include the following:

- Arrival and departure

- Circle time

- Mealtime or snack time

- Transition time

- Unstructured playtime

Example: At the park, when Manuel's mother encourages him, he approaches another child and asks, "Do you want to play catch with me?" (Soc A:1)

Example: When Latifa enters the classroom, the interventionist whispers to Latifa's friend Alice, "Latifa's here." Alice looks at Latifa. The interventionist models, "Hi, Latifa!" and Alice imitates, "Hi, Latifa!" (Soc A:1.4)

Example: Joey asks to get on the bike Timmy is using. The interventionist sets a timer and lets Joey and Timmy know that it will be Joey's turn when the timer sounds. (Soc A:1.3)

ENVIRONMENTAL ARRANGEMENTS

- Arrange the classroom into activity areas that include a dramatic play center. Providing small, well-defined activity areas increases the frequency of interactions between peers. Cooperation often occurs during pretend play while plans are made, roles assigned, play ideas exchanged, and conflicts negotiated. Provide materials that promote cooperative play:

  - Adult-size wheelbarrows

  - Balls

  - Wagons

  - Oversized blocks

  - Big boxes

  - Seesaws

  - Rocking boats

  - Play sets with many pieces, such as a barn with animals

  - Dramatic play props (e.g., wagon for ambulance, large sheet for tent)

  - Games (e.g., board or card games, group games)

  - Puppets

Example: Maria clings to her interventionist during free play, while carefully watching the children make "cookies" with playdough. The interventionist notices Maria's interest in this activity and brings Maria over to the table. The interventionist joins in the play and encourages Maria; as soon as Maria appears comfortable, the interventionist fades out of the activity. (Soc A:1.2)

- Any activity in which a child is seated at a table or is playing with other children should be arranged so that the child is in a position to make eye contact and interact with peers. Having children face each other or sit next to each other (as opposed to facing an empty space, sitting alone, or sitting next to an adult) encourages social interactions. Children who have physical disabilities should be positioned (with adaptive equipment if necessary) at the same level as their peers. Consult a qualified motor specialist for individual positioning considerations.

- Consider the adult–child ratio in the classroom and whether the number or proximity of adults is influencing the frequency or types of child-to-child interactions. Be aware of the amount of "adult talk" as well as the number of adult–child interactions that occur and whether these factors interfere with social interactions between peers.

Example: Manuel falls down while trying to catch a ball and starts to cry. A classroom assistant starts toward him but the interventionist stops her.

Social

"Wait a second. He's not hurt. Let's see what happens." Manuel's friend Joey runs over, helps him up, and asks, "You okay?" (Soc A:1.1)

- Arrange for the child to participate in small group activities with peers whose social skills are slightly advanced. When grouping children, consider individual peer preferences and make attempts to group children who are compatible. When including children with severe disabilities, make a special effort to group them with children who are willing to include them in play activities. The interventionist may need to provide children with suggestions about how children with severe impairments can participate.

Example: The interventionist pairs Eric, who has a visual impairment, with his friend Joey during a music activity. The children hold hands while marching around the room. (Soc A:1.2)

- Provide an inadequate amount of materials for routine and unstructured play periods. Children will need to "negotiate" with peers to get materials; for example, provide a single glue container at the art center or serve snack family style (i.e., crackers on one plate, fruit in one bowl) to encourage children to request, share, and maintain close proximity during activities.

INTERVENTION ACTIVITIES

Two examples of how to embed this goal and the associated objectives within activities are presented next. For a list of intervention activities that addresses goals/objectives across areas, see Appendix A.

Farm Animals

This activity can be introduced by reading a book on farm animals, showing pictures, talking about different farm animals (e.g., cows, horses, pigs), and singing "Old MacDonald Had a Farm." Materials include a toy barn, small plastic farm animals (one for each child), fences, a pond cut of blue construction paper, and a food trough. Opportunities for children to establish and maintain proximity, greet one another, and respond to affective initiations and distress are facilitated as the children interact through the animals around the barn, pond, and food. If the group has more than four children, then it may be necessary to provide two barns to avoid crowding.

Example: Timmy sits at the edge of the rug holding his cow. The interventionist prompts him, "Look, Timmy, Joey's horse is drinking. Does your cow need a drink of water?" When Timmy does not respond, the interventionist models taking an animal to the pond and gestures to Timmy to bring his cow. The interventionist says, "My chicken is thirsty. Bring your cow, Timmy." Timmy brings his cow next to Joey's horse and begins making slurping sounds. (Soc A:1.2)

Veterinary Office

A veterinarian's office is set up in the dramatic play center. This might be introduced by having a veterinarian come visit the classroom or by reading a book about what happens at the veterinarian's office. Opportunities for social interactions can be increased by having children dress up as cats, dogs, and bunnies instead of using stuffed pets. Ears are made of construction paper and secured with a long strip of paper that circles the child's head, tails are made of strips of fabric, and whiskers are painted on faces with make-up. The interventionist can include a small wagon for an ambulance (requiring cooperation among children to use), cots, a white coat for the vet, a table and chair for the receptionist's office, bandages, and cotton. As children help each other, opportunities arise to interact and practice skills such as responding to peers in distress or need.

Example: Maria, pretending to be a cat, comes crying to the veterinarian's office. Latifa says, "It's okay. I'll help you." (Soc A:1.1)

GOAL 2   Initiates cooperative activity

Objective 2.1   Joins others in cooperative activity

Objective 2.2   Maintains cooperative participation with others

Objective 2.3   Shares or exchanges objects

CONCURRENT GOALS

GM B:2   Bounces, catches, kicks, and throws ball
Cog F   Play (all goals)
SC A   Social-communicative interactions (all goals)
SC B   Production of words, phrases, and sentences (all goals)
Soc B   Participation (all goals)

DAILY ROUTINES

Routine events that provide opportunities for children to initiate cooperative activities include the following:

- Circle time

- Snack time

- Unstructured playtime (indoors and outdoors)

Example: Manuel's mother invites a friend who has a child the same age as Manuel over for coffee. After a few minutes, Manuel's mother suggests, "Why don't you show Emilio your toys?" Manuel takes Emilio to his room and says, "Hey, do you want to make a fort?" Emilio says, "I guess so." (Soc A:2)

Example: Children bring a toy from home to show to other children during circle time and to share during free play. (Soc A:2.3)

ENVIRONMENTAL ARRANGEMENTS

- Arrange the classroom into activity areas that include a dramatic play center. Providing small, well-defined activity areas may increase the frequency of interactions between peers. Cooperation often occurs during pretend play while plans are made, roles assigned, play ideas exchanged, and conflicts negotiated. Provide materials that promote cooperation:

  - Adult-size wheelbarrows
  - Balls
  - Wagons
  - Oversize blocks
  - Big boxes
  - Seesaws
  - Rocking boats
  - Play sets with many pieces, such as a barn and animals
  - Dramatic play props (e.g., wagon for ambulance, large sheet for tent)
  - Games (e.g., board or card games, group games)
  - Puppets

Example: The interventionist models how to make balloons fly in the air while shaking a blanket held by two or more children. During free play, Joey holds a blanket and says to Timmy, "Play balloons! Hold it." (Soc A:2)

Example: Latifa runs to the play kitchen where Alice is washing dishes. "Whatcha doing?" asks Latifa. "Washing dishes," says Alice, "You wanna wash some?" Latifa says, "Yeah," and moves to stand next to Alice. They finish washing dishes and then Latifa asks Alice, "Do you wanna bake a cake?" She and Alice then find the utensils to make a cake. (Soc A:2.2)

- Any activity in which a child is seated at a table or is playing with other children should be arranged so that the child is in a position to make eye contact and interact with peers. Having children face each other or sit next to each other (as opposed to facing an empty space or sitting alone or next to an adult) encourages social interactions. Children who have physical disabilities should be positioned (with adaptive equipment if necessary) at the same level as their peers. Consult a qualified motor specialist for individual positioning considerations.

- Consider the adult–child ratio in the classroom and whether the number or proximity of adults is influencing the frequency or types of child-to-child interactions. Be aware of the amount of "adult talk" as well as the number of adult–child interactions that occur and whether these factors interfere with social interactions between peers.

- Arrange for the child to participate in small group activities with peers whose social skills are slightly advanced. When grouping children, consider individual peer preferences and make attempts to group children who are compatible. When including children with severe disabilities, make a special effort to group them with children who are willing to include them in play activities.

    Example: A small group of children make "cakes" in the sand. Eric stirs in the sand with a stick but is not involved in the other children's play. The interventionist helps Eric have access to the play by commenting, "Hmm, I wonder how Eric could help make a cake." One child hands Eric a spoon and says, "I know—you can stir. Here, Eric." (Soc A:2)

- Provide an inadequate amount of materials for a given activity. Children will need to "negotiate" with peers to get materials; for example, provide only two rolling pins for four children at the playdough table or serve snack family style (i.e., crackers on one plate, fruit in one bowl) to encourage children to request and share during snack time. Children may find it easier to share if they know they can first finish their play and then share. Using the phrase, "Can I use that when you're done?" usually gets positive results. The interventionist provides appropriate language models.

INTERVENTION ACTIVITIES

Two examples of how to embed this goal and the associated objectives within activities are presented next. For a list of intervention activities that address goals/objectives across areas, see Appendix A.

Let's Go Fishing!

Small groups of children take a ride together on a boat and go "fishing." The boat can be a rocking boat that seats four children or a boat constructed of large boxes. Fishing poles are created from yardsticks or branches with a string attached and a small magnet for the "hook." Fish are made of construction paper, decorated, and then made catchable by securing a paper clip to them. This activity provides opportunities for children to play cooperatively by "rowing" together in the boat, sharing poles (provide fewer poles than there are children), sharing fish they catch, and trading roles (e.g., being captain of the boat).

Water Fun

This expansion of water play provides some new twists by introducing novel materials to explore in the water. The interventionist presents an egg beater and a small squeeze-bottle of soap to the children and demonstrates how to use the egg beater and a few drops of soap to make bubbles in the water. These items can be given to children to share. There should still be some standard water play materials in the tub, such as spoons, cups, bowls, waterwheels, and funnels.

  Example: The interventionist watches Eric and Latifa play and notices that Eric is using the beater and Latifa has not had a turn. The interventionist says to Eric, "I wonder if Latifa would like a turn with the beater." When Eric does not respond, the interventionist says, "Ask Latifa, 'Want the beater?'" Eric asks Latifa, "Want the beater?" Latifa says, "Yeah," and Eric gives her the beater. Latifa gives Eric the roller she was using. (Soc A:2.3)

GOAL 3   Resolves conflicts by selecting effective strategy

Objective 3.1   Negotiates to resolve conflicts

Objective 3.2   Uses simple strategies to resolve conflicts

Objective 3.3   Claims and defends possessions

CONCURRENT GOALS

GM B	Play skills (all goals)
Cog E	Problem solving (all goals)
Cog F	Play (all goals)
SC A	Social-communicative interactions (all goals)
SC B	Production of words, phrases, and sentences (all goals)
Soc B	Participation (all goals)

DAILY ROUTINES

Routine events that provide opportunities for children to resolve conflicts include the following:

- Arrival and departure
- Bath time
- Bedtime
- Circle time
- Dressing and undressing

- Mealtime or snack time

- Transition time

- Travel time in car

- Unstructured playtime (indoors and outdoors)

Try to be receptive to children's solutions to conflicts that arise if the solutions do not interfere with established rules.

Example: Manuel's mother wants Manuel to wear his warm red shirt to school, but Manuel wants to wear his dinosaur T-shirt. Manuel asks, "How about if I put this on, too?" indicating a sweatshirt. His mother agrees to his solution. (Soc A:3.1)

Example: On the way to school, Latifa quarrels with her sister about who will sit in the front seat of the car. Latifa's father comments, "I wonder how both of you can get a turn sitting up front." Latifa says, "I know, I'll sit in front now, and you can on the way home." (Soc A:3.1)

ENVIRONMENTAL ARRANGEMENTS

- Provide cubbies or lockers in the classroom where children hang their coats and store personal belongings. Labeling lockers with names and pictures of children helps define a child's private space and personal belongings.

Example: Manuel goes to Timmy's cubby and takes out his coat. Timmy, who communicates through sign language, grabs it from him. The interventionist stoops between the two boys and says, "Tell him it's your coat. Tell him 'mine' [modeling how to sign the word *mine*]." Timmy signs MINE and reaches for his coat. (Soc A:3.3)

- Arrange for children to participate in small group activities with peers whose abilities to negotiate are slightly advanced. When grouping children, consider individual peer preferences and make attempts to group children who are compatible. This arrangement may provide children with effective models to resolve conflicts when peers offer different strategies and may reduce the number of conflicts that arise.

- Provide a safe environment in which children know they can go to an adult for help if they are unable to resolve conflicts with peers.

Example: A child comes crying to the interventionist, "Joey took my truck!" "What did you do?" asks the interventionist. "I told him to give it to me, but he didn't so I hit him." The interventionist says, "It's not okay to hit people. What else can you do?" The child replies, "Tell you." (Soc A:3.2)

- Provide an inadequate amount of materials for a given activity. The children will need to negotiate with peers to get materials.

Social

Example: In the outdoor play area, there are three tricycles for 10 children. The children must negotiate with peers to get turns on the tricycles. Latifa comes crying to the interventionist, saying, "José won't get off!" The interventionist goes with Latifa to talk to José. "Latifa would like a turn, too. In 5 minutes, it will be Latifa's turn." That afternoon the interventionist sees Latifa go to another child on a tricycle and say, "Five more minutes, okay?" (Soc A:3.1)

INTERVENTION ACTIVITIES

Two examples of how to embed this goal and the associated objectives within activities are presented next. For a list of intervention activities that address goals/objectives across areas, see Appendix A.

Washing Babies

Children wash rubber baby dolls in tubs of water. The interventionist may want to introduce the activity by talking about the different things families do for us (e.g., feed us, keep us safe and clean). The number of washtubs can be limited so that children must share (two or three children to a tub) but are not crowded during the activity. The interventionist provides materials such as soap, shampoo, washcloths, soft brushes, towels, baby powder, and doll clothes. Each child is allowed to choose a baby doll of his or her own, but the soap, shampoo, and washcloths are limited to provide opportunities for negotiation among children. Conflicts may arise as children participate in this activity.

Example: Joey lays his doll on a towel and turns to get the baby powder. Latifa picks up her doll, and Joey crys out, "No! Mine!" and the two pull on the baby. Latifa points to Joey's baby and says, "No, it's my baby. There's your baby, Joey." (Soc A:3.3)

House Play

This dramatic play theme is fun for children because they all have experience with what happens around a home. Children enjoy taking on new roles (e.g., mom, dad) and pretending to cook, clean, and play in their own "house." The house can be a commercial playhouse, a house constructed from a large appliance box, or simply a designated area of the classroom. Props include miniature appliances, table and chairs, cups, plates, pretend food, a cot with blankets and a pillow, dress-up clothes, and so forth. The interventionist can limit the number of desirable materials (e.g., portable telephone, fancy dress, hat or jewelry, a play car a child can fit into) that are available and introduce the different roles that children might play to provide opportunities for them to resolve conflicts while negotiating for different materials and roles.

Participation

GOAL 1   Initiates and completes age-appropriate activities

Objective 1.1   **Responds to request to finish activity**

Objective 1.2   **Responds to request to begin activity**

CONCURRENT GOALS

Adap A:1 Eats and drinks a variety of foods using appropriate utensils with little or no spilling

Adap B   Personal hygiene (all goals)

SC A   Social-communicative interactions (all goals)

Soc A:1   Interacts with others as play partners

Soc A:2   Initiates cooperative activity

Soc C:2   Follows context-specific rules outside home and classroom

DAILY ROUTINES

Routine events that provide opportunities for children to participate in activities include unstructured playtimes.

Example: During playtime at home, Latifa's mother says, "I need to start
dinner. Please get your Legos or coloring books to play with." Latifa gets the
Legos from her room and plays with them on the kitchen table. (Soc B:1.2)

ENVIRONMENTAL ARRANGEMENTS

- Provide materials that are age appropriate and appealing, and arrange the
  classroom into activity centers.

  Example: During free play, Joey chooses to work at the water table. After
  10 minutes, the interventionist tells him that in 5 minutes it will be time to
  clean up and go outside. After 5 minutes, the interventionist says, "It's time
  to clean up." Joey finishes pouring water through the waterwheel, puts away
  the water toys in a bucket, and lines up to go outside. (Soc B:1.1)

- Create a daily routine that includes unstructured playtimes. Provide the
  children with opportunities to make choices about activities and materials
  as often as possible during free play and planned intervention activities.

Social

- It may be necessary to adapt materials and/or the environment to make activities accessible to children with special needs. Contact qualified specialists for programming suggestions. Some children may require additional support and guidance from an adult to initially participate in meaningful activities.

INTERVENTION ACTIVITIES

Two examples of how to embed this goal and the associated objectives within activities are presented next. For a list of intervention activities that addresses goals/objectives across areas, see Appendix A.

Leaf Collage

During the fall season, the interventionist and the children take a walk and gather leaves. On returning to school, the children make collages with the leaves that they have gathered, gluing their favorites to construction paper.

Fall Colors

Children paint with fall colors such as red, orange, and yellow on any type of paper. They cut out leaf shapes to paint or to use as stencils. The interventionist cuts out a large tree trunk to put on the wall of the classroom, and the children hang their leaves on the class tree.

GOAL 2	Watches, listens, and participates during small group activities

Objective 2.1   Interacts appropriately with materials during small group activities

Objective 2.2   Responds appropriately to directions during small group activities

Objective 2.3   Looks at appropriate object, person, or event during small group activities

Objective 2.4   Remains with group during small group activities

CONCURRENT GOALS

GM B   Play skills (all goals)
Cog C:1   Follows directions of three or more related steps that are not routinely given

Cog F   Play (all goals)
SC A   Social-communicative interactions (all goals)
Soc A   Interaction with others (all goals)
Soc C   Interaction with environment (all goals)
Soc D:1   Communicates personal likes and dislikes

DAILY ROUTINES

Routine events that provide opportunities for children to participate during small group activities include the following:

- Circle time

- Snack time

Example: During circle time, the interventionist asks children to get a carpet square and come sit in the circle. Timmy watches and imitates the other children as they follow the directions. (Soc B:2.2)

ENVIRONMENTAL ARRANGEMENTS

- Provide materials that are age appropriate and interesting, and arrange the classroom into activity centers.

Example: During a playdough activity, the interventionist models rolling out playdough for Eric, who has a visual impairment, by having him feel the playdough; then she prompts Eric, hand-over-hand, to roll out the playdough. (Soc B:2.1)

- Small chairs or carpet squares for children to sit on during circle time help children define their space and stay with the group. Putting away their chairs or carpet squares signals the end of the activity.

- During circle time, the use of props such as puppets, pictures, or tactile items maintains interest and increases understanding of children in the group (e.g., real flowers to look at and touch when discussing spring, samples of foods to taste and smell when discussing nutrition). Children with visual, communicative, or other impairments should be given special attention, providing opportunities for their participation during circle time. Consult qualified specialists for individual programming suggestions.

Example: While discussing where animals live, the interventionist holds up a picture of a fish and a horse and asks a child who communicates with eye gazes to look at the animal that lives in the water. The child gazes at the fish. (Soc B:2.2)

Social

INTERVENTION ACTIVITIES

Two examples of how to embed this goal and the associated objectives within activities are presented next. For a list of intervention activities that address goals/objectives across areas, see Appendix A.

Snow Painting

Children make "snow" with two cups of soap flakes and one cup of water. Children take turns whipping the mixture with an egg beater or an electric mixer in a large bowl. Then they use paint brushes to create snow pictures (dark construction paper makes a good background), let them dry overnight, and hang them in the classroom or at home.

Example: Latifa is interested in using the electric mixer but is starting to wander away from the table. The interventionist notices Latifa getting restless and reminds the children, "The children who are at the table will get a chance to whip up the snow!" Latifa rejoins the group and gets the next turn to use the mixer. (Soc B:2.4)

Snow Flakes

Children move to music while twirling white scarves or white paper streamers, pretending to be snowflakes. When the music is loud, the "snowflakes" twirl fast; as the music softens, the "snowflakes" slow down; and when the music stops, the "snowflakes" fall to the ground. Children take turns suggesting other things (e.g., birds, leaves) that they will pretend to be.

GOAL 3	Watches, listens, and participates during large group activities

Objective 3.1   Interacts appropriately with materials during large group activities

Objective 3.2   Responds appropriately to directions during large group activities

Objective 3.3   Looks at appropriate object, person, or event during large group activities

Objective 3.4   Remains with group during large group activities

CONCURRENT GOALS

GM B   Play skills (all goals)
Cog F   Play (all goals)

SC A   Social-communicative interactions (all goals)
Soc A:1   Interacts with others as play partners
Soc A:2   Initiates cooperative activity
Soc D:1   Communicates personal likes and dislikes

DAILY ROUTINES

Routine events that provide opportunities for children to participate in large group activities include the following:

- Circle time

- Cleanup time

- Mealtime or snack time

Example: During cleanup, the interventionist gives directions. "When you hear music playing, it's time to clean up; but when the music stops, freeze!" Manuel follows the directions, participating in this game during cleanup time. (Soc B:3.2)

ENVIRONMENTAL ARRANGEMENTS

- Plan activities that are age appropriate and appealing to children during group times.

- Structure the daily routine to include large group activities. Circle time and snack time provide opportunities for large groups of children to participate in activities. Whenever possible, provide children with opportunities to make choices about activities, to direct the activities, and to actively participate in the activities.

Example: During snack time, children pour juice, request preferred food items, and prepare their food (e.g., peel bananas, spread peanut butter on crackers). When Joey gets fidgety and starts to leave the group, the interventionist asks him, "Are you finished Joey, or do you want some more?" (Soc B:3.4)

- Small chairs or carpet squares for children to sit on during circle time may help children define space and stay with the group. Putting away their chairs or carpet squares signals the end of the activity.

Example: Every few minutes, Timmy's interventionist rewards him for sitting in the circle. She rubs Timmy's back, asks him a question, gives him something to hold, or praises him for sitting in the circle. Timmy sits on a carpet square, and if he gets up, the interventionist reminds him, "Stay on your square until we are all finished." (Soc B:3.4)

Social

- During circle time, the use of props such as puppets, pictures, or tactile items maintains interest and increases children's understanding (e.g., real flowers to examine and touch when discussing spring, samples of foods to taste and smell when discussing nutrition). Children with visual, communicative, or other impairments should be given special attention ensuring their active participation during circle time. Consult qualified specialists for individual programming suggestions.

INTERVENTION ACTIVITIES

Two examples of how to embed this goal and the associated objectives within activities are presented next. For a list of intervention activities that address goals/objectives across areas, see Appendix A.

Musical Parade

Children play musical instruments and march in a "parade." They take turns being the leader and lead the other children inside or outside.

Example: Timmy chooses a drum to play during the parade. At first he shakes it up and down to make a noise, so the interventionist models how to hit the drum. Timmy joins the parade, hitting the drum to make noise. (Soc B:3.1, 3.2)

Circus Acrobats

Children gather around a tumbling mat and pretend to be circus acrobats. They go one at a time to the mat and perform a somersault, log roll, or any movement that they can do. Children who are watching clap for each performer.

Example: Manuel watches Maria roll on the mat, claps when Maria finishes, and waits for his turn. (Soc B:3.3)

Interaction with Environment

GOAL 1 Meets physical needs in socially appropriate ways

Objective 1.1 Meets physical needs when uncomfortable, sick, hurt, or tired

Objective 1.2 Meets observable physical needs

Objective 1.3 Meets physical needs of hunger and thirst

CONCURRENT GOALS

GM A:2 Alternates feet walking up and down stairs
Adap A Mealtime (all goals)
Adap B Personal hygiene (all goals)
Adap C Dressing and undressing (all goals)
Cog A:2 Demonstrates understanding of qualitative and quantitative concepts
Cog A:3 Demonstrates understanding of spatial and temporal relations concepts
Cog C:1 Follows directions of three or more related steps that are not routinely given
Cog E Problem solving (all goals)
SC A Social-communicative interactions (all goals)
SC B Production of words, phrases, and sentences (all goals)

DAILY ROUTINES

Routine events that provide opportunities for children to meet physical needs in socially appropriate ways include the following:

- Arrival and departure

- Bath time

- Bedtime

- Circle time

- Mealtime or snack time

- Transition time

- Travel time in car

- Unstructured playtime

Social

Example: As he prepares to go outside, Joey goes to his cubby and gets his sweater. (Soc C:1.2)

Example: Timmy walks into the kitchen and reaches for a glass of water. His mother models the sign, WATER. Timmy imitates her model, and his mother gets him a glass of water. (Soc C:1.3)

ENVIRONMENTAL ARRANGEMENTS

- Arrange the classroom into activity areas that include a quiet area and a dramatic play center. The quiet area should be cozy and comfortable, with carpeting and soft pillows where one or two children can go to engage in quiet activities. In the dramatic play center, children can practice meeting physical needs through role play (e.g., pretend to prepare and eat meals, go to bed, dress and undress, mend injuries in the "doctor's office").

- Provide cubbies or lockers for children to store personal belongings such as sweaters, coats, and a change of clothing. Children with different impairments may need their spaces adapted to make them accessible (e.g., lower a coat hook for a child who uses a wheelchair, label the cubby of a child who has a visual impairment with a strip of wool).

  Example: Manuel whispers, "I peed," to his interventionist. She reassures Manuel, "It's okay. That happens sometimes. Get your clothes from your cubby and change in the bathroom." (Soc C:1.2)

- If possible, provide a child-size sink (with soap and paper towels) in the classroom and bathroom; however, stepping stools make regular sinks accessible to children, or plastic tubs of soapy water make good sink substitutes. Adaptations may be necessary to make sinks accessible to children with motor impairments.

- Provide children independent access to food and water (e.g., a child-size drinking fountain, plastic or paper cups to get water from the sink, healthy snack foods within reach). Adaptations may be necessary for children who have visual or motor impairments. If independent access is not possible, then provide the child a way to meet physical needs (e.g., ask an adult for help).

- Occasionally fail to provide necessary materials or overlook a familiar or important component of a routine or activity; for example, do not have food immediately available for snack time, "forget" to remind children to put on their coats before going outside, or "forget" to remind them to wash their hands before snack time. Observe how children respond to these situations. Provide the least level of assistance necessary for children to meet their physical needs; discontinue this strategy if children become upset or frustrated.

- Place snack items or clothing so that they are visible but out of reach; for example, place preferred foods or drinks in sight but out of reach, requiring children to request items. Do not overuse this technique, and provide children with the skills necessary to meet their physical needs.

INTERVENTION ACTIVITIES

Two examples of how to embed this goal and the associated objectives within activities are presented next. For a list of intervention activities that addresses goals/objectives across areas, see Appendix A.

Making Pancakes

Children can make pancakes for breakfast or snack. Materials include measuring cups, pancake mix, spoons, spatula, water, butter, syrup, bowl, hot plate, and frying pan. Children help measure the pancake mix, stir in water, pour batter into the frying pan, and eat the pancakes when they are cooked. Opportunities to meet physical needs are facilitated by not giving children pancakes until they request them, placing milk or water in small pitchers that children can pour themselves (or can request help from an adult), and having children wash their hands before eating. Close supervision will ensure safety during cooking activities.

Field Trip to a Farm

Children enjoy taking field trips, and a trip to a farm provides information about the source of some foods (e.g., milk from cows, bread from wheat). Field trips also provide opportunities for children to meet their physical needs in socially appropriate ways. Interventionists discuss what children should do if they need to go to the bathroom, are hungry or thirsty, or are not feeling well during the field trip.

   Example: Before the trip, Maria's interventionist tells her, "If you get tired or need anything, tell me what you need, okay?" Occasionally during the trip, the interventionist asks her, "How are you doing? Do you need anything?" Maria's communication board includes pictures of food, water, a toilet, and a bed. (Soc C:1.3)

GOAL 2   Follows context-specific rules outside home and classroom

Objective 2.1   Seeks adult permission
Objective 2.2   Follows established rules at home and in classroom

CONCURRENT GOALS

Adap B   Personal hygiene (all goals)
Adap C:2 Selects appropriate clothing and dresses self at designated times

Social

Cog C:1   Follows directions of three or more related steps that are not rou-
          tinely given
Cog E   Problem solving (all goals)
Cog F:2   Engages in games with rules
Soc B   Participation (all goals)

DAILY ROUTINES

Routine events that provide opportunities for children to follow rules include
the following:

- Appointments and errands (e.g., grocery shopping, doctor's office)

- Arrival and departure

- Bath time

- Bedtime

- Circle time

- Dressing

- Mealtime or snack time

- Transition time

- Travel time

- Unstructured playtime

The interventionist should try to avoid using negative language (e.g., instead of saying, "Don't run," say, "Remember to walk inside"). Children
should be praised whenever they follow rules (e.g., "You did such a nice job
cleaning up your toys. Let's make cookies now").
Example: Before they go shopping, Latifa's mother asks her, "Do you want
to ride in the cart or walk?" Latifa chooses to walk, and her mother reminds
her, "Remember to stay next to me in the store and touch only the things that
we are going to buy. Okay?" Latifa's mother praises her while they shop,
telling her what a good job she is doing and letting her help push the cart or
carry items. (Soc C:2)
Example: During circle time, the interventionist discusses different classroom rules and why they exist. "Remember, raise your hand if you want to say
something. If everyone talks at the same time, then we can't hear anything!"
(Soc C:2.2)

ENVIRONMENTAL ARRANGEMENTS

- Materials should be kept in predictable locations, and rules should be established as to how to use them. Often, a child combines materials from

different activity centers or uses materials in different ways than originally intended. Follow the child's lead and encourage the child's creativity when possible. If a particular use of materials is not okay, then make sure the child understands why it is not acceptable and encourage the child to think of acceptable alternatives.

Example: Manuel wants to bring some blocks up on the climber to make a television set. The interventionist says, "That's a good idea, Manuel, but we don't play with blocks on the climber. If one fell, it might hurt someone. Can you think of another place to build your television set?" (Soc C:2.2)

• Establish a predictable routine at home and in the classroom, and provide children with warnings before making transitions to new activities. A warning such as, "In 5 minutes we're going to clean up and go outside," allows children to complete the activity they are engaged in and prepare for the upcoming activity.

• Arrange the schedule and classroom so that children have opportunities to make choices. Providing children with acceptable choices that fall within established rules often eliminates power struggles between children and adults.

Example: Joey does not want to come sit in circle. The interventionist gives him a choice: "Joey, would you like to bring a chair to circle or sit on the floor?" (Soc C:2.2)

• Arrange for the child to participate in small group activities with peers whose ability to follow rules is slightly advanced.

Example: Manuel and Joey are eating a snack. Manuel finishes his snack, throws away his napkin, and asks (providing a model for Joey), "Can I go outside?" Joey gets up and asks, "Me, too?" The interventionist responds, "Thanks for asking. You both can go outside." (Soc C:2.1)

INTERVENTION ACTIVITIES

Two examples of how to embed this goal and the associated objectives within activities are presented next. For a list of intervention activities that addresses goals/objectives across areas, see Appendix A.

Bug Search

Children search outside for bugs to examine under a magnifying glass. The interventionist provides materials such as magnifying glasses and small plastic tubs with wire mesh lids or plastic lids with holes poked through for collecting the bugs. The interventionist outlines general classroom rules and any spe-

Social

cial rules before the activity begins. Before going outside, the interventionist might ask the children to line up and wait quietly for the rest of their friends. The interventionist might ask the children, "What do you do if you need to go to the bathroom when we're outside?" Rules specific to the activity should be few in number, and the children should be praised for remembering them.

Spiders

Children make spiders of black construction paper, cutting circles for the body and eight black strips for legs that are to be glued or taped to the body. Eyes can be made with glitter, markers, or small circles of a different colored paper. To provide opportunities for children to follow rules, they may need to be reminded of general rules and made aware of any rules specific to the activity. Examples of rules are 1) ask permission if you need to leave the group, and 2) stay at the table while using glue or glitter.

Knowledge of Self and Others

GOAL 1 Communicates personal likes and dislikes

Objective 1.1 Initiates preferred activities
Objective 1.2 Selects activities and/or objects

CONCURRENT GOALS

Adap A:1	Eats and drinks a variety of foods using appropriate utensils with little or no spilling
Adap C:2	Selects appropriate clothing and dresses self at designated times
Cog A	Concepts (all goals)
Cog E:2	Makes statements and appropriately answers questions that require reasoning about objects, situations, or people
Cog F	Play (all goals)
Cog H	Phonological awareness and emergent reading (all goals)
SC A:1	Uses words, phrases, or sentences to inform, direct, ask questions, and express anticipation, imagination, affect, and emotions
SC B	Production of words, phrases, and sentences (all goals)
Soc A:2	Initiates cooperative activity
Soc B:1	Initiates and completes age-appropriate activities

DAILY ROUTINES

Routine events that provide natural opportunities for children to communicate their personal likes and dislikes include the following:

- Bath time
- Bedtime
- Circle time
- Dressing
- Mealtime or snack time
- Unstructured playtime

Example: Latifa's mother teases, "I have a chocolate cake in the kitchen, but I don't know anyone who likes cake." Latifa says, "I do!" (Soc D:1)

Example: While reading a book about animals, the interventionist asks, "Who likes dogs?" Maria doesn't answer, so the interventionist asks her, "Do you like dogs, Maria?" and Maria shakes her head no. (Soc D:1)

Social

ENVIRONMENTAL ARRANGEMENTS

- Have materials available that are fun and interesting for children to play with during unstructured play periods, and arrange the classroom into activity areas that include a dramatic play center. As often as possible, allow children to choose activities. Rotate centers and materials to keep centers exciting and interesting to children.

     Example: The interventionist shows Timmy a block, a ball of playdough, and a crayon and asks, "Timmy, what do you want to do—play with blocks, play with playdough, or draw a picture?" Timmy points to the playdough. (Soc D:1.2)
     Example: Joey rushes to the "fire station" to put on one of the fire hats. (Soc D:1.1)

- Introduce new and unusual foods (e.g., pineapple, avocados, lemons, kiwis, mushrooms) during snack time along with familiar food items (e.g., crackers, cheese, fruit).

     Example: Eric grimaces after taking a bite of a lemon and states, "I don't like it." (Soc D:1)

INTERVENTION ACTIVITIES

Two examples of how to embed this goal and the associated objectives within activities are presented next. For a list of intervention activities that address goals/objectives across areas, see Appendix A.

Tasting Party

This activity is particularly interesting when a classroom is composed of children from different cultural backgrounds. Children can indicate different foods that they enjoy, and the interventionist can ask caregivers what foods the children eat at home. Examples include salsa, curry, sweet rice, and spring rolls. Opportunities for children to communicate personal likes and dislikes occur as children get ready for the activity (e.g., choose who they would like to sit next to at the table), participate in the activity (e.g., select foods that they would like to taste, communicate which foods they like or dislike), and complete the activity (e.g., choose which activity they would like to go to next).

Piñata Party

Piñatas are easy to make and even more fun to break. A large balloon is blown up, and children cover the balloon with thin strips (approximately 1 inch by

12 inches) of newspaper that have been soaked in diluted paste or glue. The balloon is allowed to dry for several days and then painted and decorated. After the paint dries, a small hole is cut in the piñata, the balloon is broken, and the piñata is filled with small bags of nutritious treats. Traditionally, a piñata is hung and children take turns hitting it with a stick until it breaks and the treats spill out. An alternative is to let children pass the piñata at snack time and take out a treat. Children communicate likes and dislikes throughout this process by discussing whether they like the feel of the paste, choosing the color to paint the piñata, and deciding what treats to put inside the piñata.

GOAL 2   Understands how own behaviors, thoughts, and feelings relate to consequences for others

Objective 2.1   Identifies affect/emotions of others

Objective 2.2   Identifies own affect/emotions

CONCURRENT GOALS

Cog E:2	Makes statements and appropriately answers questions that require reasoning about objects, situations, or people
SC A:1	Uses words, phrases, and sentences to inform, direct, ask questions, and express anticipation, imagination, affect, and emotions
SC B:1	Uses verbs
SC B:3	Asks questions
SC B:4	Uses pronouns
SC B:5	Uses descriptive words
Soc A:1	Interact with others as play partners

DAILY ROUTINES

Routine events that provide opportunities for children to understand how their own behaviors, thoughts, and feelings have consequences for others include the following:

- Arrival and departure

- Circle time

- Mealtime or snack time

- Transition time

- Travel time

- Unstructured playtime

Social

Caregivers and interventionists can embed this goal by narrating the child's behavior and its consequences.

Example: During unstructured playtime, Joey grabs Timmy's favorite toy from him and Timmy cries. Joey's interventionist explains the situation by saying, "Timmy is crying because you took his favorite toy." When Joey gives the toy back to Timmy and Timmy stops crying, the interventionist says to Joey, "You made Timmy happy by giving the toy back." (Soc D:2)

Caregivers and interventionists facilitate learning by labeling their own affect/emotions (e.g., "I like the picture you made for me. It makes me happy"). Often, it is possible to read a child's affect and emotion and model for the child (e.g., "You didn't like it when Tom took your car. You must be angry").

Example: During circle time, Manuel's interventionist has each child look at a "feelings" chart/poster/mask and point to or talk about how they feel that day. Manuel points to the angry picture, and his interventionist asks, "Why are you angry?" and Manuel responds, "Latifa won't share." (Soc D:2.2)

Caregivers and interventionists can embed this goal by describing the actions or behaviors of the child that occur during daily activities.

Example: During arrival, the child notices a peer is upset when his or her parent leaves. The child goes to his cubbie and gets his favorite blanket and gives it to the peer. The interventionist says to the child "Thanks for sharing your blanket; it might make him feel better." (Soc D:2)

ENVIRONMENTAL ARRANGEMENTS

- Arrange the classroom into activity areas that include a dramatic play center. Dramatic play centers provide opportunities for children to identify different affect/emotions during pretend play.

  Example: Maria and Latifa are playing in the "doctor's office." The interventionist asks Latifa how her "patient" is feeling. Latifa responds, "She's sad, but I'm fixing her." (Soc D:2.1)

- Provide books and story audiotapes about affect and emotions in the library. Display pictures of children with different emotions in the classroom. Sing songs and do fingerplays that explore affect and emotions (e.g., "If you're happy and you know it, clap your hands").

- Provide books and story audiotapes about how one's behaviors, thoughts, and feelings influence other people. Read those stories and discuss how others' behaviors make them feel.

  Example: During circle time, the interventionist reads a story about how one person's behavior makes others feel. Then, the interventionist asks children how they would feel if the same thing happened to them. (Soc D:2)

INTERVENTION ACTIVITIES

Two examples of how to embed this goal and the associated objectives within activities are presented next. For a list of intervention activities that address goals/objectives across areas, see Appendix A.

Playdough Families

Children create little people out of playdough to represent families, or the interventionist provides big and little gingerbread boy and girl cookie cutters as well as cutters to represent children's pets, such as cats, dogs, and rabbits. While children share materials, the interventionist models for the children, labeling his or her own affect: "Thank you for sharing, Alice. That makes me feel good." As family members are created out of playdough, the interventionist prompts children to communicate how their "people" are feeling and to talk about their own affects and emotions. If children get into conflicts during the activity, then the interventionist asks for identification of other people's emotions: "How do you think Timmy must feel? He doesn't have any playdough. Let's share some with him." If the child is having difficulty sharing the playdough, thus causing other children to become upset or to leave the activity, the interventionist can explain to the child that because he took all of the playdough, his friends became unhappy and chose to play elsewhere.

House Cleaning

Children use sponges, water, paper towels, toy brooms, and a toy vacuum cleaner to clean the house play center. The interventionist prompts children to think about how family members feel when they help around the house and says, "I bet it makes your dad very happy when you help clean up" or "How does your mom feel when you help her at home?" Throughout the activity, as children share, trade, and exchange materials, the interventionist should be aware of opportunities for children to label affect and emotions in themselves or in others.

GOAL 3	Relates identifying information about self and others

Objective 3.1   States address

Objective 3.2   States telephone numbers

Objective 3.3   States birthday

Objective 3.4   Names siblings and gives full name of self

Social

Objective 3.5   States gender of self and others

Objective 3.6   States name and age

CONCURRENT GOALS

FM B:3   Prints first name
SC A   Social-communicative interaction (all goals)
SC B   Production of words, phrases, and sentences (all goals)

DAILY ROUTINES

Routine events that provide opportunities for children to relate identifying information about themselves and others include the following:

- Circle time

- Mealtime or snack time

- Transition time

- Unstructured playtime

   Example: During dinner, Joey looks at his sister and says, "Milk." Joey's mother prompts him, modeling, "Lisa, milk, please . . ." Joey says, "Lisa, milk." (Soc D:3.4)
   Example: When visitors such as parents and volunteers come to the classroom, the interventionist directs children to tell the guests their names and ages. Children communicate with a name sign, talk box with their name and age programmed into it, or other augmentative communication systems. (Soc D:3.6)

ENVIRONMENTAL ARRANGEMENTS

- In the large group area, provide a calendar with removable numbers and symbols to denote special days (e.g., cake symbol for birthdays). In addition to being highlighted on the calendar, birthdays can be an inspiration for classroom decoration. Colorful birthday balloons of construction paper both state a child's name and the child's birthdate. Display balloons at child level so that children can find their balloons and talk about their birthdays.

   Example: When the calendar is discussed in the morning, the interventionist points to the cake and says, "And whose birthday is this?" Alice says, "Mine. 'Cember . . ." The interventionist models, "December 10th," and Alice imitates, "December 10th." (Soc D:3.3)

- Display examples of children's names around the classroom. Label their cubbies, personal belongings, and artwork and include a "star helper" chart in the classroom. Write children's names on a piece of tagboard and place a moveable star next to the helper's name. The star helper for the day assists the staff in such tasks as setting the table for snack or being the leader in lines.

- Arrange the classroom into activity areas that include a dramatic play center and vary "themes" frequently; for example, during one week, create a "post office" where children are encouraged to identify their names and addresses as they write and mail letters. Another week, create a "doctor's office" where the "intake" process facilitates practice in giving identifying information such as name, address, telephone number, age, birthdate, and gender. Many other themes also provide opportunities for children to relay identifying information (e.g., house theme with family photo book; telephone books with children's names, addresses, and telephone numbers).

- Include pictures of children and their families in the classroom. Children share their pictures with the class (perhaps during group time) and hang their pictures in the classroom. Adults provide children with opportunities to name their siblings and themselves by showing an interest in their pictures and asking them to talk about their families.

- Have a telephone with readable numbers in the classroom. Post children's telephone numbers in big numbers on a telephone number list. Children pretend to call home and talk to family members or to call their friends.

INTERVENTION ACTIVITIES

Two examples of how to embed this goal and the associated objectives within activities are presented next. For a list of intervention activities that address goals/objectives across areas, see Appendix A.

Me Books (see Books/Book Making in Appendix A)

Children make books about themselves by stapling paper together or by making more elaborate creations with fancy covers (e.g., wallpaper sample books) and bindings made with yarn tied through punched holes. Children are asked to bring pictures of themselves, pictures of their families, and pictures of their homes. If pictures are not available, then children can draw pictures with crayons or markers. Opportunities can be provided for children to relate identifying information by giving their names, ages, birthdays, siblings' names, addresses, and telephone numbers. The books might follow a format such as "My name is _____. I am _____ years old," and so forth. The interventionist should provide the least level of assistance necessary for children to complete their books. Children will have opportunities to practice relating information as they "read" their books.

Social

Example: Eric, who has a visual impairment, uses thin cardboard shapes (e.g., an outline of a child to represent himself, a number 4 for his age) in addition to written words to make his Me book. Eric reads his book by touching the outlined shapes and explaining what they represent. (Soc D:3.6)

Post Office

Children write a letter, put it in an envelope with a "stamp," and "mail" it in a mailbox (e.g., a shoebox with a slit cut in the lid). The interventionist can provide a variety of art materials, such as rubber stamps and stamp pads, stickers, markers, crayons, and pencils for children who cannot yet write letters but like to make pictures. Throughout this activity, the interventionist provides opportunities for children to relate identifying information about themselves and others. As children decide to whom they will write their letters, the interventionist might suggest their siblings and ask the siblings' names. The interventionist prompts children to "write" their names, ages, and telephone numbers. When children address the envelopes, the interventionist asks them their own addresses.

Example: As the interventionist writes down a child's return address, she says, "And this letter is from . . ." pausing to allow the child a chance to say, "Alice Morris." (Soc D:3.4)

Bibliography

Barrett, J., & Barrett, R. (1978). *Cloudy with a chance of meatballs.* New York: Atheneum.

Bloom, L., & Lahey, M. (1978). *Language development and language disorders.* New York: John Wiley & Sons.

Bourgeois, P. (1995). *Franklin wants a pet.* New York: Scholastic Trade.

Bricker, D., Pretti-Frontczak, K., & McComas, N. (1998). *An activity-based approach to early intervention* (2nd ed.). Baltimore: Paul H. Brookes Publishing Co.

Bridwell, N. (1997). *Clifford, the big red dog.* New York: Cartwheel Books.

Burmingham, J. (1971). *Mr. Grumpy's outing.* New York: Holt, Rinehart, & Winstin.

Carle, E. (2001). *The tiny seed.* New York: Aladdin Paperbacks.

Dodge, D.T., & Colker, L.J. (1992). *The creative curriculum for early childhood* (3rd ed.). Washington, DC: Teaching Strategies.

Ehlert, L. (1992). *Planting a rainbow.* San Diego: Harcourt.

Flavell, J.H., Miller, P.H., & Miller, S.A. (1993). *Cognitive development* (3rd ed.). Upper Saddle River, NJ: Prentice Hall.

Harper, W. (1967). *The gunniwolf.* New York: E. P. Dutton.

Hill, E. (2000). *Where's Spot?* New York: Putnam Juvenile.

Hoff, S. (1985). *Danny and the dinosaur.* New York: HarperCollins.

Kraus, R. (1989). *The carrot seed.* New York: HarperCollins.

Marshall, J. (1988). *Goldilocks and the three bears.* New York: Puffin.

McCormick, L. (1990). Bases for language and communication development. In L. McCormick & R. Schiefelbusch (Eds.), *Early language intervention* (pp. 37–70). Columbus, OH: Charles E. Merrill.

Pfister, M. (1992). *The rainbow fish.* New York: North South Books.

Piaget, J. (1970). Piaget's theory. In P. Mussen (Ed.), *Carmichael's manual of child psychology* (Vol. 1, pp. 703–732). New York: John Wiley & Sons.

Scheer, J. (1964). *Rain makes applesauce.* New York: Holiday House.

Sendak, M. (1963). *Where the wild things are.* New York: HarperCollins.

Slobodkina, E. (1947). *Caps for sale.* Reading, MA: W.R. Scott.

Stewig, J. (1991). *Stone soup.* New York: Holiday House.

Williams, L. (1986). *The little old lady who was not afraid of anything.* New York: HarperTrophy.

Zion, G. (1976). *Harry the dirty dog.* New York: HarperTrophy.

APPENDIX

A

Intervention Activity Ideas

CONTENTS

Art Activities

Dramatic Play Activities

Construction/Manipulation Activities

Exploratory Activities

Games

Literacy/Communication Activities

Make-it-Change Activities

Make-it-Move Activities

Nature Activities

INTRODUCTION

When working with teachers, interventionists, and support staff, we are often asked to suggest intervention activities that meet two important criteria: 1) they provide appropriate and frequent opportunities for embedding children's IFSP/IEP goals/objectives, and 2) they are interesting and fun for children. Throughout the years that we have used activity-based intervention, we have tried hundreds of activities with infants and young children who are at risk for or who have disabilities. The activities described in this section of the curriculum are those we have found to be generally useful for children whose development ranges from 3 to 6 years.

We selected the planned activities that follow because they can generally be introduced throughout the child's day. Some of the suggested activities target specific skill areas (e.g., gross motor area), whereas others may permit the embedding of children's goals from several areas; for example, a dress-up activity involves children developing peer relationships, manipulating objects, talking and listening, and engaging in pretend behaviors.

In addition to choosing appropriate activities for children, materials for the activity should be carefully chosen. Both activity and materials should be selected to help children practice their targeted goals/objectives. Materials used for multiple purposes are generally preferable to those with only one specific use. Commercial toys are often designed for one purpose, whereas materials such as sand, water, blocks, or paints invite involvement and use in a variety of ways. Materials should be selected that stimulate child initiations and actions; therefore, materials requiring constant adult intervention and guidance should be used sparingly. Finally, materials should be selected that are relevant and meaningful to children as they participate in daily and routine events at home and in the community.

When planning intervention activities, it is important to remember that most children thrive when offered a consistent daily routine, either at home or at a center. The interventionist or caregiver should first devise a daily schedule. An example of a daily schedule for a center-based program is contained in Figure 11 (see page 39). It may be useful to plan activities for specific times of the day, with the understanding that child-initiated activities may supercede the activity the interventionist has planned.

A variety of activities within and across areas can be planned, as shown next, and children should be permitted to choose between activities or make choices within activities (e.g., "What color of paint would you like?") when appropriate. Activities and the interventionist's responses should focus on encouraging process rather than product. The focus should be on the learning that occurs during the activity, rather than the final product of the activity; for example, during an art activity, the interventionist supplies children with paper, scissors, glue, and crayons and asks how they might be used to create a butterfly. The goal is to stimulate child initiations, problem solving, and manipulation of objects, all process-oriented activities that possess a myriad of teaching and learning possibilities.

ACTIVITIES HELPFUL FOR
ELICITING SKILLS WITHIN A CERTAIN AREA

Fine Motor
Construction: Stringing, Weaving
Literacy/Communication: The Writing Center
Dramatic Play: Post Office
Art: Group Fingerpainting

Gross Motor
Games: Obstacle Course; Follow the Leader; Duck, Duck, Goose
Dramatic Play: Police Officers
Make-it-Move: Targets

Adaptive
Dramatic Play: Washing Babies, Restaurant
Make-it-Change: Cooking
Construction/Manipulation: Dressing Babies

Cognitive
Literacy/Communication: Group Story
Construction/Manipulation: Paper Chains
Blocks: Unit and Large
Dramatic Play: Hospital or Doctor's Office
Games: What's Missing?, Teddy Bear Counting Game

Social-Communication
Literacy/Communication: Audiotape Recorder, Puppets, Acting Out Stories,
    Books/Book Making
Art: Fall Colors

Social
Dramatic Play: Birthday Party, Hospital or Doctor's Office, Restaurant, Train
Exploratory: Bubbles
Art: Body Tracing, Group Murals

When guiding activities, the interventionist or caregiver should follow the child's lead whenever possible and expand on child initiations. The interventionist should observe and wait until a child responds before offering help and should provide the least support necessary for the child's successful completion of an activity. On occasion, unsuccessful completion of a task offers rich training opportunities. Interventionists should ask questions sparingly and use open-ended questions that generally require children to use more language. Typically, open-ended questions begin with *what, how,* or *why* (e.g., "What will happen if you mix yellow with green?" "How do you do that?"). It is helpful for the caregiver or interventionist to describe actions, objects, and events while a child is participating in an activity. A running verbal account may enhance the child's learning during activities.

The descriptions of intervention activities that follow have been organized into the following categories: Art, Dramatic Play, Construction/Manipulation, Exploratory, Games, Literacy/Communication, Make-it-Change, Make-it-Move, and Nature Activities. Although most of the activities listed in this appendix incorporate skills across areas, some activities may be particularly helpful for eliciting skills within a specific area.

ART ACTIVITIES

Art activities provide children opportunities for self-expression. Creative activities involve all aspects of the child—cognitive, motor, and social/emotional. Interventionists should encourage children's imagination, and art is a useful vehicle. The interventionist should try not to make models for children but instead encourage children's ideas through self-expression; for example, if a child painting at the easel experiments with fingerprints or gets a leaf and paints it, both may be meaningful learning experiences. Children should be encouraged to write their names on completed art work (children can make a mark for their names if they are unable to print letters). The first word most children learn to write is their name.

Art centers can be set up with materials that provide a multitude of opportunities for children to engage in creative projects and develop fine motor skills. Available materials can be rotated within the art center to maintain the child's interest and enhance learning opportunities. Materials should be nontoxic and safe for children to use independently. Materials that might be included in the art center include

- *Surfaces for drawing and writing:* easels, tabletops, walls covered with paper, chalkboards, sidewalks

- *Paper materials for writing:* note pads, recycled paper, computer paper, butcher paper, origami paper, tissue paper, scraps from a local print shop, junk mail

- *Drawing/writing tools:* pencils, pens, crayons, chalk, magic markers, felt pens, colored pencils, fingerpaints, watercolors, tempera paints

- *Adhesive materials:* paste, glue, tape, sticky dots, Scotch tape (in a desktop dispenser), hole punches, staplers, stamps with stamp pads, templates

- *Scissors:* safety scissors, right- and left-handed scissors, training scissors, loop-handed scissors

- *Collage/construction items:* pine cones, leaves, seeds, buttons, yarn, fabrics, paper bags, paper plates, building materials (e.g., wood scraps, bores, tiles, cardboard tubes, wallpaper, newspaper)

Body Tracing

Children lie down on pieces of butcher paper while a peer or the interventionist outlines their bodies. The outlines are taped to the wall or floor and children are encouraged to paint or draw in their faces and clothes. A mirror should be close by so children can look at themselves. The interventionist asks questions about such things as color of eyes and hair and points out body parts. This activity encourages cooperation, self-concept development, and creativity.

Collages

Children create collages out of scrap materials available in the home or classroom. Items that the children gather in nature make beautiful collages, as do paper scraps, material scraps, buttons, wood, macaroni, and pictures from magazines. Plastic or paper plates work well for dividing collage materials so children can see all available materials. Collage material collections, small containers of glue, and 8- by 10-inch pieces of cardboard or heavy paper are placed around the table. The interventionist might put buttons and sequins in one tray; construction paper scraps and tissue paper in another; and yarn, string, wallpaper, and stick-on stars in another. Children walk around the table with a plastic plate or piece of cardboard to collect materials to glue on wallpaper, a plastic or paper plate, or heavy cardboard.

Dinosaur Eggs

Children make dinosaur eggs by cutting out oval shapes from paper and decorating them with crayons, markers, and glitter. Children have the opportunity to cut the eggs, cut out shapes with straight or curved lines as decorations for the eggs, and cut in half a piece of colored paper on which to glue their egg. Children may have many other ideas.

Fall Colors

This activity has many variations, all of which include painting with fall colors such as red, orange, and yellow. The children paint on any type of paper and may enjoy cutting out paper in the shapes of leaves to paint. The interventionist can cut out a large tree trunk to put on the wall of the classroom. After the leaves dry, the children can hang them on the tree. Children pick up leaves on a fall walk and paint them, make prints using the leaves, or spatter paint around the leaves by placing them on a piece of paper and using a toothbrush to spatter paint over them.

Feet Painting

Children take off their shoes and paint with their feet on a big piece of paper. This is a very messy and slippery project, and it helps to have tubs of warm water, soap, and towels to clean up. Children should be allowed to do as much for themselves as possible.

Group Fingerpainting

Children fingerpaint as a group on a large sheet of paper on the floor or table. Powdered tempera is placed in shaker bottles or small bowls, and children sprinkle paint and starch on paper and use their hands to mix and change colors. Fingerpainting can be done to music, as the interventionist models drawing shapes, letters, and names. The activity promotes cooperation, motor abilities, and practice in color concepts.

Group Murals

Group painting presents opportunities for cooperation and creativity because it encourages children to interact with peers, cooperate, and share. Children can discuss what they want to draw and how to arrange the elements on the paper, wall, or chalkboard. Children can choose what part they want to paint and can choose to work together.

Group Painting Projects

Children participate in creating the environmental theme in the dramatic play center or create other projects such as a river made of paper on the floor. Examples of group projects are painting large constructions such as a bus or fire engine made of a refrigerator box or painting the "river" in the "woods" dramatic play center.

Marble Painting

The class gathers shoeboxes or deep cooking tins, white paper cut to fit inside the boxes or tins, marbles of various sizes, several colors of tempera paint in shallow cups, spoons, smocks, tarps, and cleanup materials. Children first place a piece of paper in a box or tin. They then choose a marble, drop it in the paint, spoon it out, and drop it in the box or cooking tin. When the box is moved in different directions, the paint-covered marble will make a design. Two or more children can move a box together.

Painting

Children enjoy fingerpainting, painting with their feet, easel painting, painting with watercolors, and painting large objects (e.g., making a playhouse by painting a refrigerator box and cutting out windows and doors, painting outdoor play structures or walls with paint or colored water). A variety of materials are used for painting activities, including hair brushes, toothbrushes, sponges, assorted shapes to print with, watercolors, and tempera paints and paintbrushes.

Paper Bag Animals

Children make animal puppets out of small lunch sacks and glue on construction paper, fabric, buttons, and yarn. They make their puppets "talk" by putting one hand in the sack and moving the "mouth" up and down. Children can operate their puppets for a puppet show or play, stimulating creativity as well as motor and communication skills. This activity should be presented in a flexible manner, and children should be prompted to develop their own ideas.

Potato Prints

This activity requires a large potato for every two children, a cookie cutter, a sharp knife, a pie pan, liquid tempera paint, paper towels or flat sponges, and suitable paper. The interventionist cuts the potato in half, presses the cookie cutter into the potato, and cuts around it with a knife to make a shape. The children pour tempera on a pad of paper towels or sponge in the pie pan, dip the potato in, and print. This activity is useful for developing creativity, motor, and math skills.

Printing

Printing activities include 1) using objects dipped in paint to form a repeating pattern on paper and 2) pressing a blank piece of paper on a prepared surface, then removing the paper to lift the print from the surface. Materials needed for these activities include liquid tempera paint in a shallow pan; a variety of papers; and objects such as corks, cookie cutters, plastic blocks, thread spools, pieces of styrofoam, sponges, leaves, or flowers.

DRAMATIC PLAY ACTIVITIES

The dramatic play center, whether a hospital or a dollhouse, provides children with the opportunity to use cognitive, social, social-communication, and motor skills. Children pretend to be various characters, and dramatic play centers provide excellent contexts for them to experiment with forms of communication that they have been exposed to at home and in their community. Dramatic play facilitates cooperation with peers as children make plans, assign roles, exchange play ideas, and negotiate conflicts.

The most common role-play theme for promoting cooperation is house or family play, which can be extended to include baby washing and care, food identification and preparation, and literacy activities. The house play area may include a telephone, books, pads and pencils, newspapers, blackboards, and calculators. Children practice preparing food, conducting personal hygiene, and dressing and undressing as they act out dramatic play scenarios. Children also work on gross motor goals in a naturally occurring context while engaging in dramatic play.

Ideas for dramatic play are endless, and children should be encouraged to provide suggestions for themes of interest to them. Theme areas and props will vary according to the different cultural and experiential backgrounds of children. Changing materials in the dramatic play area renews children's interest and creates new communication opportunities. Dramatic play is an excellent context for children to practice cognitive skills, and props should be selected that will provide opportunities for children to practice targeted goals; for example, if a child has a goal to sort objects on the basis of physical attributes, then include materials such as socks, utensils, and coins that can be sorted by color, shape, or size.

In developing themes for the dramatic play center, the interventionist should use his or her imagination and follow children's initiation. One interventionist developed "Max's room" from the story, *Where the Wild Things Are* (Sendak, 1963), and later the "forest" of the wild things was developed. Another interventionist created the scene from *Mr. Gumpy's Outing* (Burningham, 1970) by helping children make animal costumes and construct a pretend boat. Children listened to the story and then acted it out over and over.

When developing a dramatic play center theme, start with a skeleton setup and add props as appropriate. Examples of theme areas with suggestions for props follow.

House Theme

- Books to read to dolls or stuffed animals

- Dolls, doll clothes, dishes

- Storage containers for food, toiletry, cleaning items

- Telephone books with children's names, addresses, and telephone numbers; cookbooks; newspapers

- Telephone, message pad, pencils

- Blankets and pillows

- Dishes, pans, plastic food, kitchen utensils

- Dress-up clothes with different kinds of fasteners, such as buttons, string-type fasteners, zippers, and Velcro fasteners; hats; mirrors

- Games and other props that children want to add

Store Theme

- Carts, wagons
- Food, cans, boxes
- Pretend money
- Paper, pencil
- Dress-up clothing
- Purse, billfold

Farm Theme

- Small tools
- Dress-up clothing
- Stuffed animals
- Large boxes for barns
- Dishes to feed animals
- Plants, seeds
- Plastic fruit, vegetables

Airplane

Props for this activity include paper and pencils for tickets, assortment of coins and play money, maps or an atlas, cash register, travel magazines, small trays with plastic food and utensils, suitcases with luggage tags, travel brochures, pilot and flight attendant uniforms, several chairs in rows, and headphones. Children make an airplane out of a large box or blocks. Other props might include a control panel, tape deck, microphone, and old computer keyboard.

Beach

Props for this activity include sand in plastic pools placed on tarps, towels, sunglasses, toy radios, magazines, stationery for writing letters, buckets, shovels, funnels, and animal figures. Other materials to include are fish shapes, fishing poles or nets, and posters of sea creatures.

Birthday Party

The class has a pretend birthday party at school. Children decorate a cake (whipped cream is fun), make birthday cards, sing "Happy Birthday," and wear party hats. When the children finish making their cards, the interventionist reminds them to write their names. Each child takes a turn saying his or her name, age, and birth date.

Boat

In a variation on the other transportation themes, a boat is made of a box, blocks, or carpet squares. Inventive props include paddles made of cardboard and binoculars made of empty toilet paper rolls; life jackets, picnic lunches, backpacks, books, and toy cameras can be included.

Bus

The class makes a bus from a large refrigerator box, including a steering wheel, money box, play money, telephone, bus schedules, and newspaper. This activity encourages cooperative play as well as language and math skills. Children use their imaginations to decide where to go on the bus. The interventionist facilitates this play by having the group go on the bus during circle time. Children act out riding on the bus, getting off of the bus, and pretending to see people and animals on the street. Extensions include children painting the bus or painting a mural on the bus.

Camping

The interventionist can introduce camping by asking, "What do we need for our camping trip?" A campground drama corner includes props such as a tent (sheets make good tents), a campfire (stones in a ring with blocks), cooking pots, backpack, water bottles, old blankets or bed rolls, and pictures of the forest and animals. Other props include flannel shirts, raincoats, boots, binoculars, maps, fishing rods, and a pretend stream.

Firefighter Play

A large refrigerator box can be transformed into a wonderful make-believe fire truck; props include tricycles, hats, and hoses. Opportunities can be provided for children to solve problems by asking them questions such as, "Can anybody think of how we can make a fire truck out of this box?" The "truck" may be created by an adult cutting the long side of the box with scissors or a knife and the children painting it with red paint. The interventionist can use strategies to elicit children's imaginative skills and engage in pretend play. Extensions of this activity are a discussion of fire safety at home and a fire drill.

Forest

The interventionist provides a big piece of paper on the floor for the creek, lake, or river. Children can help make magnetic fish in different colors and sizes and fishing rods, animal masks, and a bridge or trail made of blocks or carpet squares. Other props include backpacks, rocks, lifejackets, and a boat (real or pretend). The children can draw or paint big trees and add birds and other forest animals to the panorama. Extensions include hiking to a forest, feeding the birds at school, looking at real fish, and eating fish crackers for snack.

Grocery Store

A grocery store includes props such as a cash register, shopping carts, bags of different sizes, pretend food on shelves, and cardboard food containers. This activity encourages classification, object labeling, and cooperative play.

Hospital or Doctor's Office

A medical dramatic play center uses dolls and children as patients. The office has a telephone, note pads, pencils, typewriter, and waiting area with books and magazines. The interventionist provides bandages, plastic gloves, blankets, medical kits, and books about hospitals and doctors. This activity encourages cooperative play and language (e.g., "You be the doctor, and I will be the mom"). Signs such as "Quiet, Please" or "No Smoking" can be incorporated into the play.

Let's Go Fishing!

The class makes poles of strong, short sticks and string with a magnet attached to the end. Fish are made of different sizes, shapes, and colors, with a paper clip attached. A big piece of butcher paper on the floor serves as the stream. This activity can address motor and cognitive skills.

Post Office

Props for the post office include paper, writing tools such as pencils and crayons, scissors to cut out "stamps," envelopes, blue or white shirts with buttons or zippers for postal workers, play money, caps for mail carriers, a mailbag, a mailbox, and boxes and tape for packages. Children each make their own mailbox as a planned activity and then children and the interventionist can write and deliver mail to each other. This activity is useful for enhancing social, prereading, and prewriting skills.

Restaurant

For the restaurant, include menus, magnetic board and letters to post specials, placemats (make by writing the name of the restaurant on construction paper), notepads and pencils for taking orders, play money, cash register, chef hat, and pretend and real food. As an extension, the interventionist can take children out to a real restaurant.

Shoe Store

Props for this activity include old shoes of different sizes and with different closures, pencil and paper to record sales, shoeboxes, chairs, mirror, play money, cash register, and shoe ruler. This activity encourages social skills and classification and number concepts.

Spaceship

Props include an old computer keyboard for the control panel, headphones, flashlights, and large foam pieces or pillows under a large sheet that is taped down as the planet on which children walk. This activity enhances gross motor and sensory skills. Photos of planets and art activities to create a sun and moon can be incorporated.

Teddy Bear Picnic

Children bring their teddy bears to a picnic or tea party. The interventionist provides a special picnic basket with a blanket to spread out on the ground; napkins; pretend or real food items; and a tea set with plastic cups, saucers, and a teapot. Fine motor and adaptive skills are addressed as children dress themselves and their bears for the event, help prepare food and drinks, use social mealtime skills, and clean up after the activity.

Theater

A large curtain can be hung from a frame such as a swing set for the stage. Children use dress-up clothes and construct props such as animal ears, tails, and masks for the play. Props include water-soluble face makeup, scarves, a ticket office, a telephone, and small platforms. The interventionist begins with a play that uses stories familiar to children, or children create new scenarios. An extension includes shadow puppets that use light and shapes on a large screen covered with white paper or a sheet.

Train

The children place chairs, boxes, or large blocks in a long line to make a pretend train. This can be a group activity at circle or incorporated into the dramatic play center. Props include ticket-making supplies, hats for conductors, and objects to be carried on the train. An extension to this activity is singing train songs as children and adults hold onto a long scarf and weave around the room, in the hallway, or outdoors. Children take turns being the engine and the caboose.

Veterinary Office

The veterinary office includes stuffed animals, medical tools, notepads and pencils, charts of animals, examining table, telephone, leashes, and kennels. Children can bring their pets to the office and use communication skills to ask for help and explain their problems. Cooperative play can be encouraged also.

Washing Babies

Children wash their baby dolls in tubs of water with soap and washcloths, dry their babies with towels, and dress them in doll clothes with different fasteners. Children enjoy expanding on the activity by shampooing and brushing the baby's hair or pretending to brush the baby's teeth. To keep dry, children can wear smocks that fasten with zippers, buttons, ties, or Velcro fasteners and can learn body parts as they bathe their babies. The interventionist models reading baby a book, tucking baby in, or rocking baby to sleep. This activity can be incorporated into house play as well as doctor's office or hospital dramatic play.

CONSTRUCTION/MANIPULATION ACTIVITIES

Block play and construction activities enhance cognitive, motor, and social skills. As children play with blocks, they learn balance and construction skills. Cooperation is encouraged as they build with a friend and pretend by adding props such as animals, cars, or people. Encourage construction activities during free play or use as a planned intervention activity.

Blocks: Unit and Large

Unit blocks facilitate cognitive skills as children compare size, shape, weight, and balance. Children can also use their imaginations as they "build" their ideas. They experiment with gravity as they build and knock down towers. Large blocks are used to build ramps, bridges, and boats that children can actually walk and sit on. Cardboard blocks allow children to experiment with a lightweight block that does not hurt anyone if it falls down. Blocks can be used to construct roads and paths as well as upright structures.

Box Town

The children make a pretend city, town, or neighborhood with boxes of many sizes and shapes. They will need tape, boxes, and paper. The class can take a walk or bus ride around town to look at houses, buildings, schools, parks, and roads. Boxes can be used to build replicas of what children observe.

Dressing Babies

Children practice tying and fastening as they dress their dolls in different outfits. The interventionist should provide dolls of many ethnic origins, dolls with disabilities, and clothes with various fasteners.

Feely Bag

Children gather small objects from a nature walk, such as leaves, flowers, pebbles, pine cones, and seeds and put them in a bag or a large sock. Each child takes a turn putting a hand in the bag. The child feels the object without looking, describes the object, and tries to guess what it is.

Group Block Building for Circle

Children cooperate at circle time and build a block structure together that is photographed or saved for a time. Extensions include writing a story about the structure and adding people and other props.

Lacing Cards

Children cut out simple pictures of familiar objects from magazines, glue the pictures onto sturdy cardboard, and cover them with clear contact paper. The interventionist punches several holes around the outside of the picture with a hole punch and ties a shoestring or heavy piece of yarn through one of the holes. The other end of the string should have tape wrapped around it to make a firm tip. The child sews in and out around the card.

Large Constructions

Large or medium-size boxes taped together are used to facilitate dramatic play. Children help develop props such as a city bus by planning what is needed and then helping to find or create the necessary objects. One box can be used for different purposes (e.g., building, train, telephone booth, bus).

Manipulatives

Provide materials that can be manipulated, such as Legos, Duplos, Tinkertoys, puzzles, pegs and pegboards, geoboards, vinyl picture stick-ons, 1-inch cube blocks, wind-up toys, playdough with rolling pins or cylindrical blocks, cookie cutters, plastic knives, and objects that make impressions.

Paper Chains

The children cut construction paper into approximately 1- by 5-inch strips and make a link by gluing or taping the two ends of a strip together. A chain is created by inserting the next strip through the link.

Paper Strip Constructions

Children cut construction paper into strips of various lengths and widths. A base is provided for each child to construct a sculpture using strips and tape. In an extension of this activity, several children can construct one sculpture working cooperatively together.

Stringing Activities

The interventionist ties a large knot in the end of a piece of heavy yarn or string and wraps a short piece of tape around the other end to make a firm tip. Children string items such as round cereal, macaroni, cut-up pieces of drinking straws, and beads. This is an activity children can do repeatedly, or they can make a product by tying the string ends and painting the "beads."

Weaving

Children weave items such as pipe cleaners, straws, yarn, ribbons, or twine onto materials such as green plastic berry baskets, styrofoam trays with holes punched in them, or a weaving mesh. A variation of this activity is to hang large weaving mesh between two structures or trees and have several children weave various materials onto the mesh as a cooperative activity.

EXPLORATORY ACTIVITIES

Children learn many useful skills and concepts as they explore materials such as water, sand, cornmeal, bird seed, rice, and beans, as well as combinations of these materials, such as water and dirt (mud play), water and soap (bubbles), and water and cornstarch (oobleck). Classrooms often have a designated table for these activities indoors or a wading pool for them outdoors. Additional materials include cups and pitchers of various sizes, scoops and spoons, buckets, funnels, egg beaters, waterwheels, and water pumps. Children practice adaptive skills as they get ready for activities and clean up afterward (e.g., dressing and undressing, washing and drying hands).

Activities that explore materials such as shaving cream, lotions, pudding, and whipped cream facilitate many cognitive skills and can be designed to practice prereading skills by encouraging children to sound out letters and words written in the material. These activities can be conducted on any surface that is easy to clean (with pudding, it is helpful to have individual plates or cookie sheets for each child). Expansions of these activities include adding food coloring or tempera paints, sand or cornmeal (to explore tactilely), or popsicle sticks to draw or write.

Bubbles

This activity is fun to do outside! The recipe for bubbles is a capful of dishwashing liquid and water, which children mix until bubbles begin to form. Children hold about one third cup of this mixture in small paper cups and blow bubbles through straws. Bubble wands of all sizes can be used to blow larger bubbles. It is important that children blow through the straws in order to prevent the consumption of this mixture. Children should practice blowing through straws because some children suck through the straw by mistake.

Bubble Prints

Food coloring is added to soapy water in a margarine tub. When children have produced a froth of bubbles, they lay a piece of white paper over the top. When the paper is lifted off, a "print" of the bubbles will remain.

Mud Play

A place is selected to set an empty wading pool to make mud. Large shovels and buckets for children to dig and carry dirt and large pitchers for water are provided. Cooperation will occur as children work together digging, carrying dirt, and mixing water, as well as during cleanup time. The interventionist should have children wear old clothing and have a change of clothing for them afterward.

Playdough

Playdough is an excellent material for activities that embed cognitive, motor, and social goals. The interventionist can include a variety of materials and arrange the environment to provide children many opportunities to practice targeted goals. Materials such as cookie cutters of various colors, shapes, and sizes; rolling pins of different sizes; plastic utensils; and miniature figures can be provided. The interventionist should present the materials in creative ways;

for example, half of the playdough can be put in the refrigerator and half in the microwave to vary the temperature of the material and facilitate understanding of qualitative concepts.

Pudding Painting

The interventionist makes instant pudding (food coloring can be added), puts it on individual paper plates, and invites children to fingerpaint with it. Children will be surprised when they realize that they can lick their fingers and might discuss how the pudding feels, tastes, and smells. Children can be encouraged to draw letters and names in the pudding.

Shaving Cream Fun

This activity provides opportunities for children to experiment with their sense of touch while fingerpainting on a surface with shaving cream. The interventionist prompts children to copy shapes in the shaving cream and provides props such as sticks, animals, and sponges.

Tasting Party

This activity is particularly interesting when a classroom is composed of children from diverse cultural backgrounds. The interventionist asks children about different foods that they enjoy and asks caregivers what foods the children eat at home. A variety of foods can be provided for children to try, such as salsa, curry, sweet rice, sticky rice, and sushi.

Washing Objects

Children select many items to wash, such as dolls, clothes, tricycles, and trucks. One interventionist brought his car for the children to wash, with sponges, soap, hoses, and towels for drying. Children like to wash walls and need only sponges, spray bottles, soapy water, and towels.

Water/Sand Play

Materials other than water and sand (e.g., cornmeal, flour, beans, macaroni) can be substituted. The interventionist can provide materials such as cups of different sizes, pitchers, spoons, scoops, funnels, waterwheels, and plastic animals. The children are allowed to fill and empty the water/sand table with big buckets that require two children to carry. A wading pool makes an excellent water container in the summer, and water activities include washing rocks, pouring with different containers, dribbling (poke holes in the bottom of a margarine tub), basting, mixing colors in ice cube trays with eye droppers, making coffee filter blotches, and transferring water with an eye dropper to a dry sponge ("Where did it go?"). Children also enjoy filling small containers such as film canisters or jar lids, and squeeze-bottles invite children to experiment with water. Bubbles come out of squeeze-bottles under the water, and water dribbles as the bottles are held upside down. All of these activities enhance motor skills.

GAMES

Games promote thinking and memory skills as well as cooperation. In the early childhood setting, games should be noncompetitive. Board games are set up in an activity center, and large group games are played outside or at circle time.

A Polar Bear Is Sleeping

This game can be adapted to use any animal. One child is in the middle of a circle of children who tiptoe around him or her singing, "A polar bear, a polar bear is sleeping in her cave" (Repeat once). "Speak very, very quietly in a whisper, because if you wake her, if you shake her, she'll get very mad!" (Say the last part loudly.) Polar Bear wakes up and touches a child, who then becomes the next animal.

Board Games

Board games provide opportunities for children to participate in games with rules and provide practice in cognitive skills such as counting colors and shapes. Games such as Color or Shape Bingo, Candyland, and Chutes and Ladders and card games such as Go Fish and Old Maid can be included.

Duck, Duck, Goose

This is a favorite circle game of young children. Children sit in a circle as one child walks around the outside gently tapping heads and saying "Duck, duck, goose." When the child says, "Goose," the tapped child gets up and runs around the circle while being chased by the first child. The child who got up to run takes the next turn walking around the circle tapping heads.

Follow the Leader

One child or the interventionist is the leader, and the other children follow behind in a line, copying any movement that the leader makes.

Group Outdoor Games

Ball games such as basketball, soccer, kickball, and baseball can be modified so that young children can participate. Small basketball and soccer balls are available, as are minihoops and goals. Children enjoy practicing bouncing, catching, kicking, and throwing skills even though they may not be playing by the rules of the game.

Simon Says

Leader "Simon" gives directions to the other children. The leader calls out a command (e.g., "Simon says jump on one foot"), and the group follows Simon's direction and model. The instructions can be expanded to make this activity more cognitively challenging. If the leader does not precede a command with "Simon says," then the children should not follow the direction; for example, if the leader calls out, "Put your hands on your head," then the children do not follow the direction until the leader restates the command as, "Simon says put your hands on your head."

Teddy Bear Counting Game

This game requires two large wooden dice or homemade wooden dice. Teddy bear counters or other objects such as farm animals, plastic chips, or rocks are placed into a large basket. The dice are rolled and the numbers added up. Then, that number of bears (or other counters) is removed from the large container and placed in front of the children. Children also roll the dice to count the bears and put them back into the basket.

What Time Is It, Mrs. Monster?

Mrs. Monster is a game played outside with a group of children. One child (the monster) faces the larger group as the children ask, "What time is it, Mrs. Monster?" The monster answers with a time such as 3 o'clock. Children take three steps toward the monster. When the monster says, "Dinner time," the children scatter so they will not be eaten! Whoever is caught becomes the monster.

What's Missing?

This game can be played with any assortment of objects. It is best to start with a small number of objects and increase the number as children become more competent. Children look at and identify objects. One child hides his or her eyes while another child removes an object, and then the first child guesses which item is missing. If the child has difficulty guessing, then peers can provide clues (e.g., "This missing object is something you eat with;" "The missing object is blue.")

LITERACY/COMMUNICATION ACTIVITIES

Literacy/communication involves the child as listener, speaker, writer, and reader. Children need many opportunities to experience oral and written language. Most children are interested in communicating and enjoy printing when activities are available that encourage experimenting with writing tools. Literacy props can be added to dramatic play centers, signs posted at activity centers, names written on artwork, and lists made of what children saw on a walk.

Literacy/communication activities should be integrated into all aspects of the child's day. Activities especially designed to enhance the child's social-communication, motor, and cognitive skills follow.

Acting Out Stories

Children learn about the beginning, middle, and end of a story as they act out familiar stories such as *Caps for Sale, Mr. Gumpy's Outing* (Burmingham, 1979), and *The Gunniwolf* (Harper, 1967). You can change characters or endings to eliminate stereotypes and violence.

Audiotape Recorder

This activity promotes communication and fine motor skills as the child operates the machine and controls the tape. An audiotape recorder is used to record the group when they sing or talk, and later the group can play it back, listen, and discuss what they heard.

Book Time

Book time is an integral part of any home or classroom. Books can be integrated into daily activities and presented at special times. The interventionist can model reading for children and encourage them to read on their own or with peers or to read a story to a puppet or stuffed animal. The interventionist should create an atmosphere of love for books.

Books/Book Making

Children enjoy drawing and writing in their own books. Plan books around a theme or create them during unstructured play time. Ideas for books include forest book, leaf book, "anything" journal, animal book, group story book, photo album, and a book about an experience or field trip. Books are made of paper of any size or quality. Children use markers and crayons to create their own illustrations and practice drawing or writing. To make a book, the pages can be stapled, taped, or sewn together by punching holes and threading them with yarn.

Group Story

A story can be written about almost anything, from a shared experience to, "I feel frightened when . . ." When children see their words become print, magic happens. They become excited about writing and reading when they realize there is a message to be discovered and transmitted.

Group Time

This activity is successful when children's voices can be heard in both song and speaking. Questions are used to facilitate children's expression of their feelings, thoughts, and ideas. Children like to choose a song, story, or game for the group. Interventionists should monitor children's behavior as group time proceeds and, when children get restless, the form or pace should be changed.

Making Lists

Writing down children's thoughts and ideas helps in developing literacy/communication skills. The interventionist can make a list of the animals seen at the farm, what children saw on the bus ride, and names of fruits or favorite foods.

Music

Children experiment with instruments and listen to and sing songs, chant, and play circle games. Music and movement contribute to learning self-esteem, language, and cooperation. The interventionist and children can sing about cleaning up, who is here today, and moving to another activity. Children can sing to their "babies" as they rock them.

Photo Albums

Children form attachments with parents, caregivers, and peers. Children practice language skills as they look at and talk about pictures of themselves and their family and friends at home and school.

Puppets

Puppets are used to enhance language, concept, discussion about feelings, or problem solving. Puppets are "alive" for children, and they often talk to puppets about anything. Interventionists use puppets to facilitate social problem solving with children. Children can be allowed to operate the puppets, and access to puppets can be provided during any activity. Puppets can be created out of a variety of materials, such as paper bags, socks, sticks, construction paper, toilet paper rolls, or faces drawn on fingers.

Singing/Chants

Children's language skills are enhanced through repetition and rhythm. Chants and songs can be sung about anything at any time; for example, songs can be incorporated into routines such as transitions and group time. Chants and songs are found in many books and audiotapes, and instruments can be added to enhance the activity. Interventionists facilitate the children's exploration through modeling soft, loud, fast, and slow. Play instruments to tunes such as, "Play your instruments and make a pretty sound, play them fast, play them slow. Play the drums, stick, tone block . . ." Children play along with a chant or music on tape and will make up their own songs if encouraged.

Specific Theme Books

Theme books include The Me Book, My Animal Book, Our Trip to the Pumpkin Patch, I Feel, My Book of Fruit Prints, or others of interest to children.

The Writing Center

This activity invites children to regularly experiment with writing tools. They learn to hold a pencil correctly through practice and gain confidence when they can write or draw their own messages. This center can be located near the library or book area, integrated into the drama corner, or placed in a separate area.

Videotape

Most children are fascinated with seeing themselves on television. The interventionist can videotape the children giving a special presentation such as a puppet show or during regular play activities. The tape is shown to the group to stimulate language and discussion.

Water Music

Children experiment with tones by tapping jars filled with water. Glass jars provide the clearest tones, but safety should be considered when choosing containers. The interventionist should provide several sizes of containers for water and several items for tapping, such as blocks, spoons, or chopsticks. Children vary the amount of water in the jars and tap the jars to produce different sounds. Opportunities to demonstrate understanding of size concepts occur as the children use different sizes of containers, different levels of water, and different objects for tapping. This activity promotes listening, experimenting, and following directions.

MAKE-IT-CHANGE ACTIVITIES

Transformation of materials fascinates young children and helps them understand their world. Examples include flour when water is added or crayons when they are melted. Make-it-change activities enhance math, science, problem-solving, and language skills.

Applesauce

The interventionist reads the story *Rain Makes Applesauce* (Sheer, 1964). Children cut up apples to make applesauce and need only plastic knives, a cutting board, and a large bowl. Children add sugar and a small amount of cinnamon to the apples and transfer them to a cooking pot. The interventionist places the pot on the burner, adds a little water, and stirs occasionally, and the children watch the apples change!

Flour and Water Mixing

Children are given small bowls and spoons (tasting spoons from an ice cream shop work well). The interventionist places flour in small bowls or shaker bottles and provides water, eye droppers, and small pitchers. Children mix small amounts of water and flour and watch it change.

Fruit Salad

Children cut soft fruits such as bananas, watermelon, pears, and strawberries into chunks with plastic knives. They put the fruit in a bowl, stir in yogurt, sprinkle granola over the top, and eat their creations for snack. Children have opportunities to manipulate objects as they get ready, participate, and clean up.

Ivory Snow and Water

Ivory snow and water are mixed into a heap of lather. This activity can be done at a sensory table, on a flat table, or in containers.

Making Bread

The interventionist chooses a favorite quick bread recipe such as zucchini bread. The children gather all of the necessary ingredients and utensils and measure the ingredients, stir the batter, butter the pan, and help clean up.

Melted Crayon Art

This activity invites children to observe the properties of color mixing and solids turning to liquids. Materials needed are a warming tray, unquilted aluminum foil, crayon stubs, a variety of paper, paper towels, and a pencil with an eraser. The tray is covered with smooth, heavy-duty foil or two sheets of regular foil, folding over the edges and pressing so the foil does not slip off. When the tray is warm, the children draw on the foil with crayon stubs. The crayon markings will melt on the foil. When the children are satisfied with their designs, they place a piece of paper over the top of the foil and the drawing. The paper is pressed firmly using the eraser end of a pencil and then lifted to remove the design. The designs can be lovely. The excess wax should be wiped from the foil with a paper towel before using the tray again. Adults must supervise activity with the warming tray, but children can do the artwork independently.

Smoothies

Smoothies are a nutritious shake made by blending together different fruits (e.g., bananas, strawberries), juices, and anything else that tastes good and blends well (e.g., yogurt, milk, wheat germ). Children choose what they want in their smoothies and must be sure to include enough liquid to blend easily. Children count how many seconds it takes to blend their smoothies.

Super Soup/Stone Soup

After reading the story *Stone Soup* (Stewig, 1991), the interventionist invites the children to participate in making soup by washing and cutting vegetables and combining vegetables, broth, and spices. Opportunities can be provided for children to sample foods of different textures (e.g., cooked meat, raw and cooked vegetables).

Toilet Paper and Water

Toilet paper and water can be mixed together and then molded into interesting sculptures and dried. Large pans of water are used to allow children to wet the paper and watch it change.

MAKE-IT-MOVE ACTIVITIES

Children learn about their physical world in part through interacting with objects, such as when a toddler accidentally bats a ball and it rolls. Children need to understand the physical attributes of their world to advance cognitively. The following activities may enhance a child's knowledge of the physical world.

Fun with Straws

In this activity, children use straws to blow objects (e.g., ping-pong balls, feathers, blocks) across different surfaces such as tabletops and water. Children can be encouraged to experiment with blowing objects and to compare and contrast attributes of the objects that they are blowing (e.g., "Is the feather harder or easier to blow than the ping-pong ball?" "What do you think would happen if you used two straws?"). The interventionist should allow time for reflection (e.g., "What happened when you blew on the block?" "Why didn't it move?").

Make-it-Move Painting

This activity promotes cooperation, motor skills, and creativity. One child puts paper on a lazy Susan or old record player and draws as the wheel turns. The interventionist provides markers or paint and paper cut to the size and shape of a turntable on a record player, with a hole poked in the middle. Children work together by having one friend spin the turntable while the other draws. This activity requires adult supervision.

Ramps

Ramps are made from wooden planks or from cardboard or plexiglas tubes of varying lengths that are supported at an angle by a chair, crate, or block. The interventionist should offer materials such as balls of various sizes and weight, marbles, and cars or trucks of various sizes, as well as objects that slide rather than roll. Children experiment with how the height of the plank affects speed and the distance the objects move. Opportunities for children to participate in activities, learn new concepts, categorize, sequence, solve problems, and demonstrate premath skills can be embedded within this activity.

Targets

Children love to throw objects at a target, such as bags into movable containers. Children can also set up plastic bowling pins or roll balls at large, soft cardboard blocks. Minitargets can be developed using blocks and small rolling objects on a table with sides or a container. These activities promote problem solving and knowledge of the physical world.

NATURE ACTIVITIES

The natural world is a wonderful tool to help children understand themselves in relation to their environment. Children learn about animals through observation, touch, and experience. Children can learn much about nature and their environment through hands-on experiences; for example, during an outdoor walk in the fall, children collect leaves, find seeds, observe squirrels scurrying about, and feel the cooler temperature. Through learning respect for the natural world that includes bugs, birds, animals, and plants, children's curiosity is stimulated and they learn to appreciate beauty.

Bird Binoculars

Children make binoculars with toilet paper rolls and colored or clear cellophane. Children decorate the rolls with markers, tape or staple them together, cover the ends with colored cellophane, and attach a string. When the binoculars are completed, it is time to take a bird walk!

Bug Search

This activity can help alleviate children's fear of bugs. Children become involved in looking for insects on the playground or surrounding area and collecting them to observe for a short time. To prepare for this activity, children can look around the classroom for containers that might be usable. The interventionist can ask questions about what is needed (e.g., "Do we need a lid?" "Does it need holes?"). To find bugs, children theorize about where bugs live (e.g., in eggs, under rocks, in the ground).

Note: Make sure this activity is safe and that the bugs found are not poisonous. Children should treat the living creatures with respect and return them to their homes. Children can also observe the bugs in their natural habitats, such as a spider on its web.

Collections Walk

Children love collecting pieces of nature. The class can take a walk in any season and pick up items found on the ground. Fall is particularly interesting, with colorful leaves, nuts, seeds, and flowers. These objects can be placed on a sensory table to examine or be made into individual or group collages.

Exploratory Table

The interventionist fills a table with nuts, leaves, shells, moss, flower petals, sand, and shells and allows the children to examine or use the materials in a variety of ways.

Expressive Arts

The class can dramatize stories such as *Goldilocks and the Three Bears* (Marshall, 1988) or *The Gunniwolf* (Harper, 1967) or pantomime, "We're going on a lion hunt. We're not afraid. What's that up ahead? Big, tall grass (or a mountain or a river). We can't go over it, we can't go around it, we can't go under it. I guess we'll have to go through it." Children make movements (arms moving forward and back) and sounds (swish, swish) as if they are moving through tall grass, over a great big mountain, or across a river. The interventionist can elicit children's ideas about how they will get across the river or up the mountain. "When you find the lion, take a picture of it and run, run, run back the way you came." Many children love this activity and may ask for it daily. The interventionist should listen to the children for ideas and adapt and make up the story as they go along. Puppets can also be used.

Feed the Birds

The interventionist can instill respect for the world's living creatures in the children by inviting birds to the playground with sunflower seeds, suet, and water. This activity provides an opportunity for children to practice a variety of language skills.

Leaf Prints

Leaves of all shapes and sizes are placed on a table. Children dip leaves in paint and print with them on paper.

Leaf Rubbings

The children take a walk and gather leaves in small bags. Leaf rubbings are made by placing a piece of lightweight paper over a leaf and rubbing a crayon over the top of the paper.

Litter Walk

Children and the interventionist take a litter walk to identify litter that should be in garbage cans. Children wear plastic gloves to put litter in garbage bags.

Pine Cone Bird Feeders

In small groups, children spread peanut butter on large or medium-size pine cones and then roll the pine cones in birdseed to make bird feeders. The interventionist can enhance children's problem solving by posing questions such as, "I wonder how we can put the peanut butter on the cone?" "Where should we put the feeders so the birds can get them?" or " How can we put them on the high branches?" The interventionist should listen to and attempt to use the children's ideas even if they will not work.

Planting a Garden

Planting a garden can be a rewarding project for children. Because this activity involves several steps (e.g., hoeing the ground, planting the seeds, watering the ground, weeding), it provides opportunities for children to retell events in sequence. Reading a story about growing things (e.g., *The Carrot Seed* [Krauss, 1945]) gives children information about the sequence of events. Children and the interventionist keep a record of planting, sprouting, and so forth and retell the sequence of events.

Seedy Faces or Seedy Collage

A face is carved in a pumpkin or other vegetable. Later, children use dried pumpkin seeds or birdseed to make faces on paper (gluing the seeds down). The class can take a walk in the fall to collect seeds and grass to make a collage.

APPENDIX

B

Planned Intervention Activities

INTRODUCTION

The 12 planned intervention activities contained in this appendix can be used with individuals or with small or large groups of children. These planned intervention activities are particularly useful for developing activities in center-based and child care programs; however, interventionists may find this format helpful when assisting caregivers in the selection of activities for home and family settings.

The planned intervention activities in this appendix consist of a sequence of nine components that facilitate thoughtful preplanning to embed goals/objectives for individual and groups of children. The plans follow an activity from setup to closing in order to maximize the number of opportunities to practice target skills. The nine components and a brief description follow.

1. *Activity name*

2. *Materials*, lists materials that are needed for the activity

3. *Environmental arrangements*, includes suggestions for setting up the activity and materials in a way that enhances opportunities for children to acquire targeted goals/objectives within the activity

4. *Description of activity*

   • *Introduction*, includes set up of the activity and provides a brief preview of the activity before it begins

   • *Sequence of events*, suggests a sequence of actions that may facilitate the activity. Although the suggested *sequence of steps* may prove successful in most situations, variations should be expected. Following the child's lead within the activity is advisable, as long as IFSP/IEP goals/objectives continue to be addressed.

   • *Closing*, informs the child that the activity is about to end and provides an opportunity to recap the activity with the child. This can be helpful in reinforcing the learning experience and supporting a smooth transition to the next activity.

5. *Opportunities to embed children's goals/objectives*, includes a list of specific AEPS goals/objectives that are likely to be integrated within the activity. Goals/objectives can be included that are specific to an individual child, and/or general groups of items from particular strands within areas may be included for groups of children.

6. *Planned variations*, suggests additional materials, steps, or actions that are appropriate for the activity and that vary learning opportunities for children; for example, during story time, in addition to working on reads

---

The term *teacher* is used in these activities, but it is assumed that teacher is interchangeable with parent, caregiver, assistant teacher, or other adults in the classroom who are running activities.

words by sight, a variation could include having children exchange books with each other to facilitate peer interactions

7. *Vocabulary*, provides a list of specific words and/or categories of words that can easily be incorporated within the activity

8. *Peer interaction strategies*, provides suggestions that are specific to encouraging interaction among peers; for example, the circle time activity suggests selecting songs that require partners such as "Row, Row, Row Your Boat" as a strategy to encourage peer interaction

9. *Parent/caregiver input*, elicits feedback from caregivers that might make the activity more relevant for the child; for example, the caregiver might suggest some of the child's favorite songs that are sung at home for the circle time activity, or parents might be invited to attend the child's preschool when the Birthday Party activity takes place. In addition, interventionists can send home materials or information about activities that take place during the child care setting that may be useful at home; for example, a tape of songs that are sung during the circle time activity can be made and sent home with children.

The activities included in this appendix may be modified to meet the needs of individual children and families by incorporating specific child goals/ objectives or might serve as a model for developing a "bank" of activities to be used in your program setting. Utilizing planned intervention activities supports successful intervention efforts by ensuring that opportunities to practice targeted IFSP/IEP goals/objectives are arranged within activities that are fun and meaningful for children.

ACTING OUT A STORY

Materials

- *The Rainbow Fish* by Marcus Pfister (1992)
- Large paper grocery bags with holes cut out of the bottom (for child's head) and sides (for arms)
- Large "scales" of different colors made of stiff paper or fabric; some covered with blue cellophane or other shiny material
- Velcro
- Sheer blue and purple scarves or strips of fabric
- Containers for sorting materials

Environmental Arrangements

Prepare a defined area of the classroom to be a "stage." Attach several 1-inch squares of Velcro to paper bags. Attach the other side of Velcro to backs of scales. Place scales in a large container. Keep the shiny scales (which belong to the Rainbow Fish) separate from other scales. Place scarves to the side of the stage.

Description of Activity

Introduction

- Teacher reads *The Rainbow Fish* to children. Teacher asks children to look at the "stage" area and then tells children that they will be able to act out the story during choice time.

Sequence of Events

- Children choose roles to play (Rainbow Fish, other fish, water).
- Children who are playing fish put on grocery bags and attach scales to their costumes.
- Children in charge of scenery choose scarves and wave them while pretending to be water.
- Children act out story; Rainbow Fish shares scales with friends at end of play.

Closing

- At the end of play, teacher talks with children about the story; for example, teacher asks, "How did the Rainbow Fish feel when he had all of the beautiful scales but no friends? How did he feel when he shared his scales with the other fish? Do you like to share toys with your friends?"

Opportunities to Embed Goals/Objectives

Cognitive (B:1, C:3.1, F:1, 1.1, 1.2, G:1.1)	Children engage in imaginary play by acting out the Rainbow Fish story. During cleanup, children sort costume items (e.g., plain scales, shiny scales, scarves, paper bags) and place them in separate containers. After acting out the story, ask children to retell the story. Children count the number of scales on each "fish."
Social-Communication (A:1.1, 1.3)	While reading the story, ask children to tell you what they think will happen next. After acting out the story, ask children to talk about the feelings of the different characters in the story.
Social (A:2.1, 2.2)	Place scales on the back of the paper bag costumes so children must help each other remove the scales.

Examples of goals/objectives for individual children

Child	Goal/objective	Opportunities
Mia	Shares or exchanges objects (Soc A:2.3)	Encourage Mia to share her scales with the other "fish." When children reenact the story, encourage Mia to exchange her costume with another child so that they can play different roles.
	Uses words, phrases, or sentences to label own or others' affect/emotions (SC A:1.3)	During closing, ask children questions about how the Rainbow Fish felt before and after he gave away his scales. Ask Mia to tell about a time when she felt happy.
Brian	Holds object with one hand while the other hand manipulates (FM A:1.1)	Brian takes the fish scales off of his costume after the play. Ask Brian to help his friends take the scales off of the backs of their costumes.
	Uses imaginary props (Cog F:1.3)	When Brian is the Rainbow Fish, encourage him to share his scales with his friends. When Brian is not playing one of the fish, encourage him to wave the scarves like water.

Planned Variations

- Children act out other familiar childhood stories (e.g., *Goldilocks and the Three Bears* [Marshall, 1988]).
- Use a felt board to help retell a story during circle time.

Vocabulary/Signs

- Friend
- Happy, sad
- Share
- Fish, scales
- Off/on
- Colors of scales and scarves

Peer Interaction Strategies

- Encourage all children to take turns playing different roles including the Rainbow Fish.
- Encourage children to help each other put on and take off the costumes and decorate with scales.
- Discuss feelings expressed with the story in a group.

Parent/Caregiver Input

- Children can act out the Rainbow Fish story for parents.
- Children can attend a play at a local theater with their families.

DOING THE LAUNDRY

Materials

- Toy washer and dryer or cardboard boxes with doors cut in them to simulate washer and dryer
- Toy ironing board and iron
- Two laundry baskets
- Adult and child-size clothing
- Plastic clothes hangers
- Clothespins
- Clean, empty detergent bottles
- Measuring cups
- Cardboard set of drawers or boxes; label each drawer with pictures and words (e.g., one drawer for pants, one for shirts)
- Clothesline or rod to hang clothes on

Environmental Arrangements

Washer, dryer, ironing board, cardboard drawers, clothes hangers and clothes pins, detergent bottles, and clothesline or rod (hung at children's eye level) set up in a designated area of the room. Have laundry baskets and clothes set aside on counter in classroom.

Description of Activity

Introduction

Teacher announces that he or she has lots of clothes that need to be washed and asks, "Who would like to help me do the laundry?"

Sequence of Events

- Children help carry laundry basket and clothes to laundry area.
- Children sort clothes and put clothes in washer.
- Children "measure" detergent and put in washer and set controls on washer.
- Children transfer clothes from washer to dryer; some "delicate" clothes can be put on the line to "air dry."

- Children take clothes out of dryer and off of the clotheslines and put them in laundry baskets.

- Children fold or iron clothes and hang them on hangers or put them away in drawers.

Closing

- Teacher makes suggestions to each child about one final part of the laundry that each child can finish before cleaning up.

- Children help neaten up laundry area.

Opportunities to Embed Goals/Objectives

Cognitive (B:1.3, C:1.2)	Children sort clothing into dark and light piles before washing; sort clothes by type when putting them away (i.e., pants, shirts, socks). Encourage children to talk about the colors of the articles of clothing and count the number of each type of clothing.
Social-Communication (A1:7, 2.1, 2.4, 2.5)	Encourage a discussion about the sequence of events that occurs when doing laundry (e.g., sort clothes, put soap in washer, put clothes in washer).
Social (A:2.1, 2.2, B:1.1, 1.2)	Children show each other where clothes go in drawers.

Examples of goals/objectives for individual children

Child	Goal/objective	Opportunities
Sasha	Groups objects, people, or events on the basis of specified criteria (Cog B:1)	Encourage Sasha to put folded clothes in the appropriate drawers. Encourage Sasha to sort laundry by color/size.
	Claims and defends possessions (Soc A:3.3)	Provide a limited number of props. If conflicts arise, then encourage Sasha to use words to tell peers what she wants.
	Shares or exchanges objects (Soc A:2.3)	Encourage interested peers to join the laundry activity. Prompt Sasha to play near her peers and share the same materials. Encourage Sasha's peers to ask her for items that they want. Encourage Sasha to respond.

Planned Variations

- Wash towels and washcloths instead of clothes; practice folding the towels into rectangles and squares.

- Provide large nonclothing items such as blankets that would need to be folded by more than one child.

- Invite children to help with real laundry tasks when doing the classroom laundry.

Vocabulary/Signs

- Laundry, washer, dryer, laundry basket, detergent
- Measure, wash, dry, fold, put away, hang up
- Iron, ironing board
- Clothes hanger, clothespin, clothesline, drawer, label
- Names, sizes, colors of clothing

Peer Interaction Strategies

- Make sure children have plenty of room to perform tasks to prevent unnecessary conflict.
- Encourage social interaction by providing opportunities in which children need to help each other.
- Provide limited numbers of props and materials to encourage children to cooperate on tasks.

Parent/Caregiver Input

- Encourage families to have children help with laundry. This can include sorting before and after washing, helping hang up clothes on clothesline or transferring from washer to dryer, and putting clothes away.
- Talk about children's home laundry chores during circle.

MAKING A SANDWICH

Materials

- Bread
- Peanut butter and jelly
- Plastic knives (one for each child)
- Plates, napkins

Environmental Arrangements

Each child has a personal area at the snack/meal table to make his or her sandwich; on each plate, place two slices of bread, a dab of peanut butter, a dab of jelly, and a plastic knife. The children may choose to sit or stand. High adult-to-child ratio is helpful for this activity.

Description of Activity

Introduction

The teacher explains to children that they will be making their own sandwiches for snack/lunch. The children and adults wash their hands prior to going to the table area. Once everyone is at the table area, the teacher goes through the sequence of what to do first, second, third, and last, modeling the steps as she gives a verbal explanation.

Sequence of Events

- The teacher shows how to first put one slice of bread to the side of the plate. Second, she uses the knife to spread peanut butter on the other slice of bread. Third, she spreads jelly on the peanut butter. Last, she puts the top slice of bread on top of the jelly.
- Children make their own sandwiches after the model.

Closing

- Once children have completed their sandwiches, they can cut them in half with the knives. Adults or children can print their names on their plates. Children may eat the sandwiches for snack/lunch following the activity.
- When the children are finished making their sandwiches, the teacher asks who remembers what the steps are to make one. If children need assistance remembering, then the teacher can repeat the sequence and ask the children to repeat it.

Opportunities to Embed Goals/Objectives

Adaptive (A:2.1, 2.2)	Children spread sandwich ingredients.
Cognitive (D:1, 1.1)	Children watch steps of sandwich making and later talk about them. Ask children to tell their parents what they made for lunch when they go home.
Social-Communication (A:1.1, 1.4, 1.7, 2.1)	Encourage children to discuss sandwich making when they are at the table. Children can discuss what foods they like and dislike, ask questions about sandwich making, and anticipate what the sandwiches will taste like.
Social (B:1, 2, D:1.2)	Children listen to directions and watch adult before they make their own sandwiches.

Examples of goals/objectives for individual children

Child	Goal/objective	Opportunities
Jon	Recalls events immediately after they occur (Cog D:1.2)	After Jon has finished making his sandwich, offer to write out the recipe for him to take home so he can make a sandwich for someone in his family. Have Jon tell you each of the steps for making the sandwich.
	Responds to request to finish activity (Soc B:1.1)	Encourage Jon if he does not finish the activity on his own (e.g., "I see you've gotten peanut butter on your bread, what else do you need to do?"). When asking children to clean up and get ready for the next activity, prompt Jon with the next tasks he needs to do.
Rene	Holds object with one hand while the other hand manipulates (FM A:1.1)	Situate a peer next to Rene so she can watch. If needed, provide Rene with some physical assistance (e.g., support her hand that holds the bread while she uses the other hand to spread the peanut butter with her knife).
	Puts proper amount of food in mouth, chews with mouth closed, and swallows before taking another bite (Adap A:1.1)	Cut Rene's sandwich into smaller bite-size pieces. If needed, provide encouragement to swallow before getting another piece.

Planned Variations

- The teacher may choose to have only a small number of children doing the activity at one time in order to provide one-to-one assistance or as a whole group if there are additional adults to assist.

- Present a variety of ingredients so that children can select them (e.g., meats, cheeses, vegetables).

- Place spreadable ingredients in small cups.

- Make sandwiches for a picnic.

Vocabulary/Signs

- First, second, third, last
- Plate, knife
- Spread
- Bread, peanut butter, jelly
- Personal pronouns
- Possessive pronouns

Peer Interaction Strategies

- Children work independently because of cleanliness; however, they may carry on conversations with peers and imitate peers.
- Encourage peer interaction by having children work together at the table. Discuss what is needed to set the table. Children can share table-setting responsibilities.

Parent/Caregiver Input

- Parents can be involved in the activity by assisting their child and other children.
- Encourage parents to involve child in food preparation activities at home.

Materials

- Medium-size box with an opening large enough to place a medium-size object inside (a piece of fabric covers the opening)
- Variety of "mystery" objects (e.g., items that may be used during daily activities such as fruit, a paintbrush, a ball, a book, or a stuffed animal)

Environmental Arrangements

The teacher sits with the box (with mystery object inside) close beside her or on her lap at circle/group time. The children are seated in a semi-circle facing the teacher.

Description of Activity

Introduction

At circle time, teacher explains to children that she has a mystery box with something very special inside.

Sequence of Events

The teacher explains that the children need to guess what's inside the box by asking questions about it. The teacher gives examples of what kinds of questions the children can ask (e.g., What color is it? What shape? How big? Where did it come from? What is it used for?). As the teacher answers questions, the clues or characteristics are written on chart paper so that the children can talk about the object's qualities and guess what they think the "mystery" item might be. The teacher may need to give additional clues to ensure that the children guess the object.

Closing

After children have named what the object is, the teacher takes it out of the box and holds a discussion about any other information she wants the children to know about the object. She prints out the additional clues or characteristics of the object on the chart paper and later places the object in a play area for the children to use, or uses it again during story, snack, or another group activity.

Opportunities to Embed Goals/Objectives

Cognitive (E:2, 2.1, 2.2, F:2)	After the mystery object has been presented, the teacher encourages children to ask questions and guess what might be inside. Before beginning, the interventionist explains the rules of the game.
Social-Communication (A:2, 2.1, 2.3, 2.6)	Encourage the use of conversational rules when engaging in the activity; for example, encourage children to respond to others' topic initiations with a comment such as, "Reuben thinks it's something to eat. What type of food do you think would fit in that box?"

Examples of goals/objectives for individual children

Child	Goal/objective	Opportunities
Miko	Asks questions for clarification (SC A:2.3)	Before Miko takes a turn to ask questions about the mystery item, have one or two peers provide a model of appropriate questions.
	Looks at appropriate object, person, or event during large group activities (Soc B:3.3)	During circle activity, make sure the mystery box is clearly visible to all children. If Miko needs encouragement to focus on the box, then give her a turn to hold and shake the box to help motivate her to guess what is inside.
		To encourage Miko to turn her attention to other children as they ask questions, have Miko be a helper who knows what is inside the box and helps answer other children's questions.
Jack	Uses words, phrases, or sentences to obtain information (SC A:1.6)	Encourage Jack to ask questions about what is in the box. If necessary, provide an example (e.g., Is the object hard or soft? Is it something you can eat?).

Planned Variations

- Teacher has one child as assistant who helps answer the other children's questions.

- Children take turns being the leader.

- Children can take the box home and, with the help of parents, choose an object for the activity.

- Teacher can use concrete clues to answer children's questions, such as colors or shapes of paper or related objects.

- Teacher can have a variety of clues visible, one of which is identical to the object in the box.

Vocabulary/Signs

- Mystery box, clues, hidden
- Words that are used as clues or characteristics (e.g., shapes, colors, sizes)
- Inside/outside

Peer Interaction Strategies

- Children build on what their peers say.
- Some children may talk over clues with a friend to develop a question; a more assertive child may ask a question that a shy child is uncomfortable asking.

Parent/Caregiver Input

- A parent can assist by leading the activity or printing the words on the chart paper.
- If children take the box home, then provide some guidelines for parents to choose an item (e.g., pick an item familiar to most children, avoid items that are dangerous such as scissors or a balloon).

PAINTED FLOWER POTS

Materials

- Small clay pots
- Craft paints
- Paint containers (one for each color)
- Paintbrushes (one for each color)
- Smocks
- Flower or plant seeds (select two or more nonpoisonous varieties that will grow quickly)
- Potting soil
- Plastic drainage trays
- Large clear plastic bags (*Caution:* keep the plastic bags out of reach of children)
- Twist ties
- Large watering cans
- Water
- Permanent marker

Environmental Arrangements

Conduct this activity inside or outside on a child-size table. Place all materials on a counter.

Description of Activity

Introduction

This activity takes place over 2 days. On both days, read a book about gardening such as *Planting a Rainbow* by Lois Ehlert (1988) or *The Tiny Seed* by Eric Carle (1990). On the first day, tell the children, "Today we are going to paint our own flower pots. Tomorrow, when they are dry, we will plant seeds in them. Each day, we will look at our flower pots to see if our flowers are growing."

Sequence of Events

Day 1

- Children help the teacher take flower pots, paint, paintbrushes, smocks, and permanent marker to activity area.
- Children help each other put on smocks.

- Each child chooses a flower pot.
- Teacher or children label the bottom of each child's pot with the child's name.
- Children paint their flower pots.
- Flower pots are left to dry overnight.

Day 2

- Children help teacher carry seeds, potting soil, watering cans with water, and other supplies to activity area.
- Children plant several seeds in their pots.
- Children water their seeds.

Closing

- Teacher sets the plastic tray inside a clear plastic bag, and then children help her place each pot on the tray inside the bag. They seal the bag with a twist tie and put the tray in a sunny window. (If the sun is very hot, then seedlings may burn when they come up. Move tray to area with indirect light in this case.)
- Children help teacher clean up materials.
- Children wash their hands and remove smocks.
- Children and teacher watch each day to see if their flowers have grown.
- Keep the flower pots in the plastic bag until the plants are a few inches high.

Opportunities to Embed Goals/Objectives

Fine Motor (A:1.1, B:3)	Children hold pot with one hand while painting with the other. Children practice writing names on pots.
Adaptive (A:2.3, C:1.1, 1.2, 3.1, 3.2)	Children pour water from watering cans into flower pots. Children help each other fasten and unfasten smocks.
Cognitive (A:1.1, 2.1, G:1.1)	Talk about the colors of each child's flower pot. Count how many flower pots have been painted; when the flowers begin to grow, count how many flowers/plants are in each pot. Talk about qualitative concepts such as wet/dry and dirty/clean. During reading of introductory book, give children opportunities to tell about the pictures in the book. Provide opportunities for children to follow directions during activity.

Social-Communication (A:1.1, B:5)	Talk with children about the flower pots, seeds, and the planting process using a variety of descriptive words. Talk about how a seed becomes a plant to encourage children to ask questions. Have children talk about what will happen in the next few days (i.e., seeds will begin to grow).
Social (A:2.1, 2.3)	Provide only one container of each paint color and only one paintbrush per container to encourage sharing; children help each other fill pots with soil. Children compare each other's plants as they grow.

Examples of goals/objectives for individual children

Child	Goal/objective	Opportunities
Tyler	Uses adjectives to make comparisons (SC B:5.2)	When the plants begin to sprout, encourage Tyler to compare them by talking about which ones are bigger and smaller, shorter and taller, and so forth.
	Demonstrates understanding of seven different temporal relations concepts. (Cog A:3.2)	During the first day of the project, talk about how you will need to wait until *tomorrow* to plant the seeds; the next day, talk about how you painted the flower pots *yesterday*. Ask Tyler when he thinks the seeds will sprout.
	Responds to request to finish activity (Soc B:1.1)	Near the end of the activity, inform Tyler that the activity is about to end. Provide additional prompting if necessary.

Planned Variations

- Tape stencils to the children's pots during painting.
- Have a group of children paint a large pot together.
- Plant indoor plants in pots so children can care for them in the classroom.

Vocabulary/Signs

- Plant, grow, grown
- Seed, flower, sprout
- Paint, pot, brush
- Sun, water, soil
- Colors, numbers of pots and sprouts, size concepts
- Wet/dry, dirty/clean
- Possessive "s"
- Personal pronouns (I, he, she)
- Possessive pronouns (mine, his)

Peer Interaction Strategies

- Providing limited materials (bags of soil, watering cans, paints and paint-brushes) encourages sharing.

- Materials that are too heavy for one child to carry (watering cans, bags of soil) encourage cooperation among children.

- Encourage children to help each other with tasks (filling watering cans, distributing seeds).

Parent/Caregiver Input

- Families can help plant a vegetable garden on the playground.

- Have a gardening day on the weekend; invite parents and their children to work in the garden and tell about their gardens at home.

PAINTING ON AN EASEL

Materials

- Paint (four colors)
- Containers with lids to hold paints (eight of each, with lids to match paint colors)
- Eight paintbrushes
- Trays to carry materials
- Large roll of paper
- One easel
- Two smocks with fasteners
- One pair of child-size scissors
- One marker

Environmental Arrangements

Place the easel in a clear, level space outside or on a tarp inside. Hang smocks on the easel. Place the painting supplies (paint, containers, lids, paintbrushes, paper, child-size scissors, and marker) on a large, child-size table.

Description of Activity

Introduction

Teacher asks for volunteers to help set up the painting area.

Sequence of Events

Setup

- Children help pour paint into containers (each color in two containers).
- Children select lids that match the paint color in each container.
- Children carry containers to easel.
- Children count out eight brushes and place one in each container.
- Children help each other carry the roll of paper and other supplies to activity area.

Painting

- Children cut paper for painting from large roll.

- Children hang paper on both sides of easel.
- Children help each other put on smocks.
- Children paint pictures.
- Children write their names on paintings.
- Children help each other take down pictures and carry to drying area.
- Children help each other remove smocks.

Closing

- Children help carry supplies back to counter and help each other take off smocks.
- Children help each other carry paintings and hang them up to dry, and help teacher wash out paint containers and brushes.

Opportunities to Embed Goals/Objectives

Fine Motor (A:2.2)	Children help each other cut paper from large paper roll.
Adaptive (C:1.1, 1.2, 3.1, 3.2)	Children help each other fasten and unfasten smocks.
Cognitive (A:1.1, 2.1, C:1, 1.1)	Name colors during the activity, and ask children questions about the colors they are painting with. Talk about concepts of inside/outside, wet/dry, today/tomorrow (e.g., ask, "When will the paint dry?"). Ask children to follow directions during the activity.
Social-Communication (A:1.7, B:5)	Encourage children to tell each other about their paintings.
Social (A:2.1, B:1.1)	Children help each other carry paintings inside and hang them up to dry.

Examples of goals/objectives for individual children

Child	Goal/objective	Opportunities
Maria	Demonstrates understanding of eight different colors (Cog A:1.1)	Ask Maria what colors she is painting with. Ask Maria to name the paint colors as she puts a lid on each one.
	Initiates cooperative activity (Soc A:2)	Ask Maria to carry the large roll of paper; wait to see if she asks a friend for help; if not, then suggest that she ask another child to help her carry the paper. After Maria and her friend carry the paper to the activity area, encourage them to begin cutting sheets of paper together. Rather than helping Maria put on her smock, wait for her to ask for help from a peer. If she asks the teacher for help, then encourage her to ask a favorite peer instead.

Examples of goals/objectives for individual children *(continued)*

Child	Goal/objective	Opportunities
Jake	Groups objects on the basis of function (Cog B:1.2)	When setting up the activity, ask Jake to hand you painting supplies (e.g., paint, paint containers, lids, brushes).
	Uses descriptive words (SC B:5)	When paintings are competed, talk about wet and dry paint. Ask Jake if his painting is dry yet. Hang paintings in the drying area and compare wet and dry ones.

Planned Variations

- Children create their own paint colors by mixing existing paints.
- Children paint a mural together.
- Invite a local artist to visit the classroom.

Vocabulary/Signs

- Paint, paintbrush, paper, scissors, smock, easel
- Artist
- Outside/inside, wet/dry, today/tomorrow
- Paint colors
- Action words (painting fast, slow)

Peer Interaction Strategies

- Children help each other with tasks (carrying paint and roll of paper, cutting paper, fastening paper on easel)
- Limited number of materials encourages sharing.
- Encourage children to look at and comment on each others' paintings.

Parent/Caregiver Input

- Encourage families to visit a local art museum with their children.
- Encourage families to hang up their children's artwork at home.

PAINTING WITH ICE CUBES

Materials

- Child-size tables and chairs
- Ice cube trays
- Small pitchers
- Water
- Food coloring
- Popsicle sticks
- Paper
- Markers
- Freezer
- Smocks
- Sponges

Environmental Arrangements

This activity is designed to be completed across 2 days. On the first day, place the ice cube trays, small pitchers, water, food coloring, and popsicle sticks on a child-size table. On the second day, when the ice cubes are ready for painting, place the ice cube trays and paper on a child-size table.

Note: There must be a freezer available to complete the first portion of the activity. If a freezer is not available, then the ice cubes can be made ahead of time.

Description of Activity

Introduction

Teacher says, "Remember when we used water, food coloring, and eye droppers to paint? We are going to use water and food coloring again, but this time we are going to freeze the water."

Sequence of Events

Day 1

- Children put on smocks.
- Children help fill ice cube trays using small pitchers of water.
- Children add food coloring to each section of the ice cube tray.

- Children help teacher place ice cube trays in freezer.

- Wait about 1 hour until ice cubes are partially frozen. Children look to see if ice cubes are beginning to freeze.

- Children add popsicle stick to each section and help teacher put trays back in freezer.

Day 2

- When ice cubes are completely frozen, trays are placed on table with large pieces of paper while children put on smocks.

- Holding ice cubes by the stick, children paint with colored ice cubes on paper.

Closing

Children write their names on their paintings, place them in the drying area, and help teacher carry painting supplies to sink. Children help wash out ice cube trays and clean up table with sponges. Children help each other remove smocks. Children discuss with teacher and other children what colors they painted with, what happened to the colored ice cubes, and what it was like to paint with them.

Opportunities to Embed Goals/Objectives

Adaptive (C:1.1, 1.2)	Children fasten snaps or tie string closures on smocks.
Cognitive (A:1.1, 2.1)	Children talk about the colors of ice cubes. Children talk about concepts of cold, wet/dry, frozen/melting, full/empty, and now/later.
Social (A:2.1, 2.3)	Children help each other put on smocks and share different colors of ice cubes. Provide a limited number of pitchers and ice cube trays to encourage children to share materials.

Examples of goals/objectives for individual children

Child	Goal/objective	Opportunities
Cassie	Prints first name (FM B:3)	Encourage Cassie to write her name on her paintings.
José	Demonstrates understanding of eight different colors (Cog A:1.1)	Talk about what colors children are using to make their ice cubes. If José doesn't talk about the color of his ice cubes, then ask him what color his ice cubes are. Ask José to hand you different food coloring containers (e.g., "Could I have the red one, please?").
	Responds to request to finish activity (Soc B:1.1)	Provide reminders to José about the next step in the activity to encourage him to complete the activity (e.g., "Next we're going to add food coloring to the ice cubes. Who's ready to add food coloring to their ice cubes?").

Planned Variations

- Have children paint cooperatively on a large piece of paper to create a mural.
- Use ice cubes to "paint" on the sidewalk on a hot day.
- Have children make their own popsicles for snack using different kinds of juice.

Vocabulary/Signs

- Water, wet, cold, frozen, freeze, melting, pour, push, add
- Popsicle stick, ice cube tray, food coloring
- Colors, qualities of colors (dark, light)
- Paint, paper
- Location words

Peer Interaction Strategies

- Teacher models and encourages children to observe and comment on each others' pictures.
- Children help each other carry ice cube trays to freezer.
- Teacher limits the number of materials to encourage sharing.

Parent/Caregiver Input

- Encourage parents to make ice cubes with their children at home. Ice cubes can be used in drinks or played with in the bath; parents can talk about the concepts of frozen/melting, cold/warm.

Materials

- Cash register
- Play money
- Pet food in cans or bags
- Pet accessories (cages, leashes, pet toys, small pet beds)
- Assortment of plastic and stuffed animals
- Toy shopping carts and/or shopping baskets
- Paper bags

Environmental Arrangements

Place pets, pet products and accessories on low shelves in one area of the classroom. Place the cash register, play money, and paper bags on a small child-size table in the same area with shopping carts and/or shopping baskets nearby. The teacher sets activity up independently or with children's help.

Description of Activity

Introduction

- Dramatic play area is set up ahead of time with props.
- Teacher reads a story such as *Clifford, the Big Red Dog* by Norman Bridwell (1997) or another story about a pet, such as *Franklin Wants a Pet* by Paulette Bourgeois (1995) or *Harry, the Dirty Dog* by Gene Zion (1976). The teacher holds a discussion about pets and encourages children to discuss how they care for them. Teacher tells children that they will be able to play in the classroom pet store during choice time.

Sequence of Events

- Children choose roles to play in the pet store (customers, shopkeepers, etc.).
- Children shop for pets and pet supplies by putting the items they want to buy in shopping carts and baskets.
- Children purchase pets and supplies at cash register.
- Shopkeepers put items in paper bags for customers to take home.

Closing

The teacher alerts children that the pet store will close soon. Children put pets and pet supplies away. The teacher talks with children about what animals they bought, what supplies they needed at the store, and how much they cost.

Opportunities to Embed Goals/Objectives

Cognitive (A:2.1, B:1)	During cleanup, have children help sort the pet store items into appropriate categories (e.g., pets, pet food, pet supplies). Talk about characteristics of pets (e.g., furry, slimy, rough, smooth, loud, quiet, big, little).
Social-Communication (A:1.2, 1.3, 1.4, B:5)	Children talk about the pets and supplies that they have purchased.
Social (D:2.2)	Talk about how pets make us feel (e.g., happy, silly, possibly scared if we don't know them); ask children to tell about a time when their pet or another person's pet made them feel happy.

Examples of goals/objectives for individual children

Child	Goal/objective	Opportunities
Daniel	Counts at least 10 objects (Cog G:1.1)	When Daniel is the cashier, encourage him to count the money he gives to customers. He can also count how many items each customer buys. When he is a customer, ask him how many items he is buying for his pet.
	Uses regular past tense verbs (SC B:1.5)	During closing, ask Daniel to tell about a pet that he bought at the pet store and what supplies he bought for his pet.
	Joins others in cooperative activity (Soc A:2.1)	Encourage Daniel to pay the shopkeeper for his pet and pet supplies. Provide a small number of some pet supplies to encourage Daniel to ask his peers for items he wants.

Planned Variations

- Children bring in a stuffed animal that could be found in a pet store.

- Forget to provide important items such as the money for the cash register to encourage children to request items.

- Children help decide if they want a pet for their classroom, what kind, and how the class would care for it. Class could then take a field trip to the pet store to buy the pet.

Vocabulary/Signs

- Animal names (dog, cat, etc.)
- Animal sounds (bark, meow, etc.)
- Store, buy, money names (penny, dollar, etc.)
- Bed, food, water, cage, leash
- Alive, pretend
- Counting
- Descriptive words about animals (size, color, qualities)

Peer Interaction Strategies

- Children interact with each other in their roles in store.
- Children share shopping carts and baskets.
- Children tell each other how they take care of their pets.

Parent/Caregiver Input

- Encourage families to bring their pets to school.
- When family pet needs to visit the vet, encourage parents to take their child along.

Materials

- Pine cones (one for each child)
- Shoelaces (one for each child)
- Peanut butter
- Large mixing bowl
- Large spoons
- Plastic knives
- Birdseed in small pitchers
- Paper plates
- Self-sticking labels
- Markers

Environmental Arrangements

Conduct this activity outside or inside on a child-size table. Have all materials present and accessible to children.

Description of Activity

Introduction

Teacher announces, "Today we are going to make our own bird feeders. Have you watched a bird eat at a bird feeder before? When we put out food for the birds, they come up close and we can see them better. Birds especially like peanut butter and birdseed. We are going to put these on pine cones so they can eat it."

Sequence of Events

- Children choose pine cones.
- Teacher helps children attach shoelaces to pine cone as a hanger.
- Children write their names on labels; teacher attaches label by folding the label in half over the shoelace.
- Children help teacher scoop peanut butter into a mixing bowl.
- Children take turns stirring to soften peanut butter.
- Children use plastic knives to spread peanut butter over their pine cones.

- Children pour birdseed onto paper plates from the pitchers.

- Children roll pine cones in birdseed.

Closing

- Teacher takes children outside, where they tie their pine cones to trees or fences.

- Group returns to classroom, and children help teacher clean up materials.

- Children wash their hands.

Opportunities to Embed Goals/Objectives

Fine Motor (B:3)	Each child can print his or her first name on his or her label.
Adaptive (A:2.1, 2.2 2.4)	Children transfer peanut butter from its container into the mixing bowl, stir to soften, and spread the peanut butter on their pine cones by using plastic knives.
Cognitive (A:2.1, 3.1, D:1, E:1)	Children follow directions during the activity. Encourage children to talk about the qualities of the materials being used (e.g., sticky, soft, tiny, bumpy). Encourage children to talk about the location of the bird feeders outside (e.g., high, in, above). Children problem-solve how to hang feeders from high locations (e.g., get a chair from classroom). When caregivers pick children up from school, ask children to tell about the activity. Have children identify their pine cone bird feeder by sounding out and reading their name on the labels.
Social (A:1.3, 2.1, 2.3)	Children help each other tie on hangers and hang bird feeders outside. Children take turns stirring the peanut butter and share plates of birdseed.

Examples of goals/objectives for individual children

Child	Goal/objective	Opportunities
Max	Ties string-type fastener (Adap C:3.1)	Max ties the shoelace on his pine cone hanger; Max can also assist other children in tying their shoelaces.
	Prints first name (FM B:3)	Max writes his name on the label.
	Uses knife to spread food (Adap A:2.2)	Encourage Max to spread the peanut butter mixture on his pine cone using the plastic knife.

Planned Variations

- Hang bird feeder with a clear back wall on classroom window and have children take responsibility for filling and cleaning it.

- Make bird feeders out of precut boards or large jar lids with holes drilled in each end for twine to be tied for hangers.

Vocabulary/Signs

- Bird, kinds of birds (e.g., robin, blue jay)
- Pine cone, bird feeder
- Peanut butter, birdseed
- Roll, stir
- Descriptive words
- Location words

Peer Interaction Strategies

- Children share utensils and ingredients.
- Children help each other tie shoelaces to pine cone and to objects outside.

Parent/Caregiver Input

- Families can hang bird houses and bird feeders at home.
- Families can make binoculars out of empty toilet paper rolls at home for "bird watching."

Materials

- *The Little Old Lady Who Was Not Afraid of Anything* by Linda Williams (1986)
- Toy blackbirds from a craft/hobby store or made out of construction paper (two big and two small)
- Binoculars
- Props for story (white gloves, tall black hat, shoes, plastic pumpkin head)
- Set of clothes for the scarecrow (pants, long sleeve shirt)
- Photos from a previous fall field trip (optional)
- Child-size rakes
- Plastic pumpkin bags for the raked leaves
- Variety of books with a Fall theme (e.g., books about scarecrows, pumpkins, birds, and leaves)

Environmental Arrangements

Put Fall books on bookshelf and several binoculars on the science shelf. Blackbirds are placed around the room for the children to discover and are moved to new perches at the end of each day. The number and size of the birds can vary. Photos from a previous field trip to a pumpkin farm (e.g., hayride, tractor, pumpkin field, scarecrows) are displayed around the classroom. Props are prepared and ready to be used with the story. Rakes, pumpkin bags, and scarecrow clothes are placed outside. Provide dry leaves to rake if none are available in the playground. The activity begins at circle area with the interventionist and children reading the book, *The Little Old Lady Who Was Not Afraid of Anything* (Williams, 1986). The rest of the activity occurs outside.

Description of Activity

Introduction

The teacher invites children to hear a story. After children are seated, the teacher begins by using binoculars to look for the birds in the room. The teacher asks children about the birds (e.g., What color are they? What do they like to eat?)

Sequence of Events

- Teacher reads the book with the props and actions, placing the props on the floor in order while going through the story.

- Children then stand in front of the props and take on the role of the "little old lady."

- The props are put together at the end of the story to make a scarecrow.

- Teacher tells children they are going outside to look for birds, rake leaves, and make a scarecrow.

- Class goes outside, and children take turns using binoculars to look for birds and talk about the birds they see.

- Children pick up and examine leaves, take turns raking leaves and stuffing the scarecrow clothes and the pumpkin bags.

Closing

- Children and teacher tie the pumpkin bags and place them at the doors. Children help bring in the binoculars, rakes, and scarecrow pants and shirt into the classroom. They put the pants and shirt together with the other props to make a scarecrow.

Opportunities to Embed Goals/Objectives

Adaptive (C:1, C:3)	Children fasten/unfasten buttons or snaps on scarecrow shirt, unzip/zip zipper on scarecrow pants.
Social-Communication (A:1.1, 2.1, F:1.2)	Children describe the birds they see. Using props, children plan and act out a story about birds.
Social (A:1.3, 2.1, 2.3)	Children take turns using binoculars and rakes. Children work together to fill up pumpkin bags and scarecrow clothes and build a scarecrow together.

Examples of goals/objectives for individual children

Child	Goal/objective	Opportunities
Maya	Enacts roles or identities (Cog F:1.1)	Maya takes on the role of the little old lady when acting out the story. Encourage Maya to walk through the dark woods. Provide prompts from the story, "Oh, here comes the tall black hat." "What does the little old lady do when she meets pumpkin head?"
	Uses adjectives to make comparisons (SC B:5.2)	Encourage Maya to talk about the leaves she gathers outside. "Tell us about this one. Look how different these two are." If Maya doesn't talk about the different characteristics, then give her verbal prompts such as, "What is different about this one?" or "How are these the same?" During circle time, have Maya pick out a favorite bird in the classroom and talk about it. Ask questions about the different birds. "What do you notice about their feathers?" "What color is that one?"

Examples of goals/objectives for individual children *(continued)*

Child	Goal/objective	Opportunities
Guillermo	Completes sequence of familiar story or event (Cog C:3.1)	When children are acting out the story, ask Guillermo to tell what comes next.
	Shares or exchanges objects (Soc A:2.3)	When children are raking leaves, let them know that they can take turns using the rakes. It Guillermo doesn't voluntarily offer his rake to another child, then have a peer ask Guillermo for a turn.

Planned Variations

- Children collect leaves for the science table.

- Have a second set of clothes for children to dress up like a scarecrow.

- Print the action words (or provide pictures of the actions) on cards and place them with each prop as it is presented in the story.

Vocabulary/Signs

- Birds

- Colors, numbers

- Clap, clomp, wiggle, shake, fly

- Big/little

- Types of clothing

- Body parts

Peer Interaction Strategies

- Children work together raking and filling bags and making scarecrows.

- Children share materials (binoculars, rakes).

- Children act out story with peers.

Parent/Caregiver Input

- Invite parents for a family day to act out the story together with their children.

- Plan a field trip with families to a pumpkin patch.

- Send home pictures illustrating the story so children can retell story with parents.

TRANSPORTATION NUMBER BOOKS

Materials

- Round child-size table and chairs
- Rubber stamps with pictures of vehicles
- Stamp pads
- Stickers of vehicles (several for each mode of transportation)
- Small cut-out magazine pictures of kinds of transportation (several for each mode of transportation)
- Glue
- Baskets or containers to hold materials
- Small books made of white paper folded in half with colored construction paper covers; the pages are numbered 1–10 in large numerals
- A completed transportation number book to use as a model. The book is made by placing the numbers of vehicles on each page that correspond with the page number (e.g., page 8 has eight boat stamps on it)
- Markers or crayons

Environmental Arrangements

Place containers in the center of the table with books, stamps, stickers, pictures, stamp pads, and markers or crayons.

Description of Activity

Introduction

Teacher announces, "Today we are going to make books with pictures of different kinds of transportation. Remember, we call cars and buses and other things that "go" *transportation*. Who can think of another kind of transportation?" After the discussion, teacher asks, " Who would like to see the transportation book I made?"

Sequence of Events

- Teacher shows her book to children, reading through each page and explaining how the pages are numbered and have corresponding numbers of vehicles.
- Teacher passes out blank books to each child.

- Children choose transportation stamps, stickers, and magazines pictures.

- Children construct their books and decorate books using markers or crayons.

Closing

- Teacher alerts children when it is nearing time for cleanup.

- Teacher asks children to title their books and helps them write titles on cover.

- Children write their names on cover.

- Children return materials to baskets.

Opportunities to Embed Goals/Objectives

Fine Motor (A:1)	Children hold the books with one hand while writing/stamping with the other.
Cognitive (A:1, B:1, G:1.1, 1.2)	Children have many opportunities to count and also to talk about the colors, shapes, and sizes of the vehicles. Children group vehicles by type, function, or physical attribute.
Social (A:1.3, 2.3)	Children share materials and ask each other to pass materials.

Examples of goals/objectives for individual children

Child	Goal/objective	Opportunities
Angelo	Counts at least 10 objects (Cog G:1.1)	Angelo counts how many stamps/stickers/ pictures that he has on each page to make sure it matches the number on the page.
	Prints first name (FM B:3)	Angelo practices writing his name on the front cover of his book when he is finished with the activity.
	Demonstrates understanding of eight different colors (Cog A:1.1)	Make a book along with the children; ask Angelo to hand you different-colored materials (e.g., blue marker). Talk about the colors of the vehicles the children use in their books; ask Angelo about the colors of some of his pictures if he doesn't talk about them spontaneously.
	Uses possessive "s" (SC B:2.1)	During the activity, model use of possessive "s"; for example, "Angelo's book has five hot air balloons." At the end of the activity, play a memory game by asking questions about each child's book; for example, say "I saw someone making a book with three airplanes. Whose book has three airplanes?" Encourage Angelo to respond with a phrase such as, "Tyler's book." If not, then expand his phrase to include the possessive "s."

Planned Variations

- Provide toy cars, trucks, and other vehicles to assist children in counting during activity.

- Provide books that have objects on each page; have children fill in the number on each page with number stamps or by writing the numbers.

- Make number books with different objects (e.g., fruits and vegetables, clothing).

- Use vehicle stencils.

- For younger children, have the books go to the number 5 rather than 10.

Vocabulary/Signs

- Book, author, title, illustrations

- Front cover, back cover

- Numbers 1–10

- Transportation, types of transportation (car, bus, etc.)

- Possessive "s"

- Descriptive words (colors, shapes, sizes)

- Personal pronouns (I, he, she)

Peer Interaction Strategies

- Group children of different ability levels to help each other count.

- Encourage children to share materials

- Encourage children to compare and talk about their books (e.g., "Josh and Nathan both have three trucks in their books.")

Parent/Caregiver Input

- Encourage families to look for and count different kinds of transportation (cars, bicycles, trucks) when riding in the car or on a bus.

- Encourage families to take their child to the library where they can check out transportation and number books.

WHERE'S SPOT?

Materials

- *Where's Spot?* by Eric Hill (1980)

- Stuffed dog or other similar stuffed animal (could attach brown felt spots) to represent Spot

- Large basket with a blanket for a cover or a picnic-style basket with lid

- Two small bowls—one empty and one filled with dry dog food or some kind of play food

- Variety of Spot books and other dog books

Environmental Arrangements

Put a variety of Spot books and other dog books on the bookshelf. The activity begins in the story area with the teacher and children reading *Where's Spot?* The two bowls are placed in front of the teacher (one filled with dry dog food and the other empty). The basket with the dog hidden inside is out of sight.

Description of Activity

Introduction

The teacher shows the book and says, "I have a book about a dog named Spot and his mom named Sally." She engages the children in a conversation about their pets.

Sequence of Events

- The teacher begins reading the book and says, "That Spot! He hasn't eaten his supper. Where can he be?" The teacher asks if Spot's bowl is empty or full and refers to the bowls in front of her.

- As she reads, the teacher opens the flaps on each page, reads the word "No," and then spells the word, "No." She asks children to name the animal as each flap is opened and asks them to describe where the animal is, using the location word in each question.

- The teacher brings out the basket with the puppy when the turtle in the book says, "Try the basket." The teacher opens the basket to find Spot.

- The teacher then asks the children if they would like to play a game called "Where's Spot?"

- The teacher asks the children to close their eyes and put their heads down. She takes the first turn to hide Spot somewhere in the room. The interventionist asks children to open their eyes, and she chooses the first child to find Spot. The child returns to the group and tells everyone where he or she found Spot.

- The same child hides Spot again somewhere in the room, and comes back and tells the others to open their eyes. The child chooses someone else to find Spot.

- The game continues until everyone has had a turn.

Closing

- The teacher identifies the last child to play the game.

Opportunities to Embed Goals/Objectives

Social-Communication (A:2, G:1, 5)	Encourage children to use conversational rules during discussion about pets. The teacher can support by facilitating the conversation (e.g., "Micah just told us that his dog likes to play with tennis balls. What does your cat like to play with?"). Set up the conversation by going around the circle, giving each child a turn to talk. Focus on children's production of words, phrases, and sentences using verbs (e.g., ask questions about what different animals like to do), asking "why," "who," and "how" questions (e.g., have children ask a partner about his or her pet), and using descriptive words (e.g., ask questions about what pets look like, what color they are, if they are big or little).
Social (A:1.3, 2.2, B:2)	When playing the game, each child has a turn to find and hide Spot. If a child has difficulty waiting for his or her turn, plan the order of turns out loud so children can anticipate when their turn is coming. The teacher can provide encouragement by saying, "Whose turn is it next? Remember, Jim, your turn is right after Joseph." Encourage children to remain with the group during the activity. If a child has difficulty staying focused on the activity when looking for Spot, then pair the child with a peer. For a child who has difficulty staying with the group, provide him or her with a job such as being the keeper of Spot's food bowl.

Examples of goals/objectives for individual children

Child	Goal/objective	Opportunities
Paula	Reads words by sight (Cog H:3)	Read the story a second time, and have Paula help with the story by reading familiar words (e.g., *no*, *Spot*). Join Paula when she has selected another dog book at the reading area. Point out any words that may have been in *Where's Spot?* and other words that may be familiar to Paula (e.g., *dog*, *go*, *run*). Ask her to read them.
	Uses possessive "s" (SC B:2.1)	When engaging children in conversation about their pets, have Paula tell about her dog, using possessive "s" (e.g., My dog's name is ____. My dog's eyes are ____.).
Joseph	Engages in games with rules (Cog F:2)	Explain the rules of the game clearly to the children (e.g., You have to put your head down and close your eyes when it is someone else's turn to hide Spot. Everyone needs to stay and play the game until each person has had a turn). If Joseph has difficulty participating, then remind him of the rules.
	Maintains cooperative participation with others (Soc A:2.2)	When playing the game with a large group, pair children to find Spot. Encourage Joseph and a buddy to talk about where they will look for Spot and who will look where; help them persist in their search by saying, "I know you two can find Spot; where else can you look?"

Planned Variations

- After reading the story, the basket is opened and found to be empty (No Spot). The children work together to find Spot in the room.

- Spot's basket is empty when children arrive for school the next day. The children are encouraged to inform their peers about the missing Spot and look for him.

- Paw prints or dog bones are on the floor as clues to Spot's hiding places.

- Other stuffed animals are hidden around the room in addition to Spot.

Vocabulary/Signs

- Location (behind, inside, in, under)

- Quantities (empty, full)

- Sizes (big, small)

- No

- Open, close

- Eyes

- Animal names
- Peer names
- Names of toys and equipment in room

Peer Interaction Strategies

- Children tell each other about their own pets.
- Children respond to teacher's questions about the book as a group.
- Children interact with each other during the game.

Parent/Caregiver Input

- Schedule times for parents to bring family pets to school. Parents and their children can talk about the food their pets eat, who feeds them, where they sleep and hide.
- Parents can help their children choose a photograph of the family pet or cut one from a magazine to create a classroom bulletin board.

INDEX

Page references followed by *f, t,* or *n* indicate figures, tables, or notes, respectively.

making statements and answering
appropriately questions that
require, 148–150
Recalling events, 144–145
with contextual cues, 144
immediately after they occur, 144
test items, 118
without contextual cues, 144–145
Recognition of printed numerals, 157
Recognizable events, themes, or
storylines, planning and acting
out, 151
Representational figures, drawing with,
67
Requests
to begin activities, responding to, 219
to finish activities, responding to, 219
making with words, phrases, or
sentences, 180
Responding
to affective initiations from others, 210
to contingent questions, 183
to directions
during large group activities, 222
during small group activities, 220
to others in distress or need, 210
to requests to begin activities, 219
to requests to finish activities, 219
to topic changes initiated by others, 183
Restaurant activity, 255
Retelling events in sequence, 141–143
Rhyming skills, 161
Riding and steering two-wheel bicycles,
90–91
Roles
enacting, 151
social-communicative, establishing
and varying, 186–187
speaker/listener, alternating between,
183
Routine activity format, 29, 30*f*
Routines, daily, 15, 28–29
Rules
context-specific, 227–230
conversational, 183–186
engaging in games with, 153–154
following, 227
in games, 153
at home or in classroom, 227
outside home and classroom,
227–230
Running, 80
avoiding obstacles, 80–81

Sand Print Names activity, 74
Scarecrows activity, 304–306

Scheduling
activity schedules, 35–43
center/group activity schedules, 35–38,
40*f*
daily classroom schedules, 35, 39*f*
home/individual activity schedules,
39, 42*f*
picture schedules, 43, 44*f*
planning time for task completion, 26
weekly schedules for center-based
programs, 35, 38*f*
Seedy Faces or Seedy Collage activity,
271
Segmenting sentences and words, 161
Selecting activities and/or objects, 231
Selecting and eating variety of food
types, 100
Selecting appropriate clothing, 111–113
Selecting effective strategies, conflict
resolution by, 216–218
Self and others, knowledge of, 231–238
test items, 205
Self-talk, 26
Sensorimotor period, 120
Sentences
describing past events with, 180
describing pretend objects, events, or
people with, 180
to inform, direct, ask questions, and
express anticipation, imagination,
affect, and emotions, 180–183
labeling affect/emotions with, 180
making commands to and requests of
others with, 180
obtaining information with, 180
production of, 189–202
test items, 172–173
segmenting, 161
Sequencing, 138–143
according to length or size, 139–141
of familiar stories or events, 141
retelling events in sequence, 141–143
test items, 118
Serving food, 102–104
with utensils, 102
Shape(s), 127–130
complex, copying, 67
with curved lines, cutting out, 61–63
different, 127
simple, copying, 67
with straight lines, cutting out, 61
Shape Collage activity, 160
Shape Search activity, 129–130
Sharing or exchanging objects, 213
Sharing Time activity, 145
Shaving Cream Fun activity, 71, 260
Shoe Store activity, 255

Real Progress for Every Child

As an AEPS® user, you've seen first-hand how this assessment, intervention, and programming system helps children from birth to 6 years make meaningful, measurable progress. We've taken this highly regarded tool to the next level of convenience and functionality with the exciting **web-based management system, AEPSinteractive™ (AEPSi™)!**

AEPSi™ offers the powerful reporting functions and data management help you've been looking for. With this web-based system, you can report OSEP child outcomes with the click of a button; assess multiple children simultaneously; corroborate or determine eligibility with the new cutoff scores; track child progress more effectively; easily score, aggregate, and archive AEPS® Test results; and so much more.

To learn more about how AEPSi™ can help you improve child outcomes and save time, you can

- **Register for a FREE 30-day trial.** See how AEPSi™ can work for you! Get a month of hands-on practice with AEPSi™, and discover how easy it is to create child records, prepare OSEP data, generate reports in seconds, and conduct group assessments. Sign up today at www.aepsinteractive.com.

- **Discover the benefits of AEPSi™ with a free, one-on-one demo.** Sign up at www.aepsinteractive.com.

- **Bookmark www.aepsinteractive.com.** Keep visiting this always-expanding website for the latest AEPS® news, updates, and special features.

AEPSi™. . .Real Progress for *Every* Child!

ORDERING INFORMATION

Programs new to AEPS® should plan to purchase:

- annual subscriptions to AEPSinteractive™ (AEPSi™)
- copies of the Administration Guide, Test, and Curriculum for each professional who will use the system
- training on the AEPS® system

Place your order by:

PHONE 1-800-638-3775 (toll-free)
FAX 410-337-8539
ONLINE www.brookespublishing.com/ae
(secure server)

AEPSinteractive™

The subscription is billed annually at the following rate
(for more details, contact an AEPS® Sales Specialist at 1-800-638-3775):

1–100 children at US$19.95 per child record per year

101–250 children at US$18.95 per child record per year

251–500 children at US$16.95 per child record per year

501 or more children: call Brookes Publishing for a subscription model that meets your needs

Save on Print Volume Sets

4-Volume Set
(Administration Guide, Test, both Curricula)
US$239.00 | Stock Number: 65614 • ISBN 978-1-55766-561-4

Birth to Three Set
(Administration Guide, Test, Curriculum for Birth to Three Years)
US$179.00 | Stock Number: 66024 • ISBN 978-1-55766-602-4

Three to Six Set
(Administration Guide, Test, Curriculum for Three to Six Years)
US$179.00 | Stock Number: 66031 • ISBN 978-1-55766-603-1

> **SAVE 10% ON PRINT VOLUMES WHEN YOU BUY AN AEPSi™ SUBSCRIPTION!**
> See www.aepsinteractive.com for other subscribers' benefits, including free tech support, webcasts, and OSEP Child Outcomes reports.

Sold Separately

Print Volumes
Volume 1: Administration Guide
US$65.00 | Stock Number: 65621
2002 • 336 pages • 7 x 10 • spiral-bound • ISBN 978-1-55766-562-1

Volume 2: Test: Birth to Three Years and Three to Six Years
US$75.00 | Stock Number: 65638
2002 • 304 pages • 7 x 10 • spiral-bound • ISBN 978-1-55766-563-8

Volume 3: Curriculum for Birth to Three Years
US$65.00 | Stock Number: 65645
2002 • 512 pages • 7 x 10 • spiral-bound • ISBN 978-1-55766-564-5

Volume 4: Curriculum for Three to Six Years
US$65.00 | Stock Number: 65652
2002 • 352 pages • 7 x 10 • spiral-bound • ISBN 978-1-55766-565-2

Forms on CD-ROM (PC and Mac compatible; 8.5 x 11 pdfs)
English
US$249.95 | Stock Number: 66352 • ISBN 978-1-55766-635-2

Spanish
US$199.95 • Stock Number: 68127 • ISBN 978-1-55766-812-7

Forms also sold separately in paper format; see www.aepsinteractive.com.

> **SAVE 20%**
> on the CD-ROM when you buy any AEPS set!